THE PAPACY TODAY

THE PAPACY TODAY

FRANCIS X. MURPHY, C.SS.R.

MACMILLAN PUBLISHING CO., INC.

NEW YORK

Lucianae
qua non adujuvante
liber hic
editus non fuisset

Macmillan Publishing Co., Inc.
866 Third Avenue, New York, N.Y. 10022

Library of Congress Cataloging in Publication Data
Murphy, Francis Xavier, 1914-
The papacy today.
Bibliography: p.
Includes index.
1. Papacy—History—20th century. I. Title.
BX1389.M8 1981   262′.13′0904   81-869
ISBN 0-02-588240-6   AACR2

10   9   8   7   6   5   4   3   2   1
Printed in the United States of America

Contents

Preface

Seldom in the course of its turbulent history has the papacy experienced a more momentous series of events than in the present century. Many attempts have been made to record these happenings, giving them a benign or hostile, a hopeful or pessimistic, interpretation. This book represents an effort to chronicle the *magnalia Dei per Petrum,* 'the great things of God', accomplished by Peter's recent successors – by an observer who played a minor role on the outermost rim of Vatican affairs.

Though obviously in the nature of a journalistic analysis, this effort to put today's papacy in perspective also has deeper pretensions. Given a solid if old-fashioned theological education and trained to the exacting discipline of medieval history, I find myself constantly impelled *rerum cognoscere causas* – to seek out the meaning of events. In providing a running analysis of the papacy's achievements since the turn of the twentieth century I have attempted to examine both the theological presuppositions and the political convictions that have entered into these events.

Individuals who have the misfortune to appear in these pages by reason of their prominence in the world or the Church will, I hope, have the magnanimity to pardon a scribe for judgments possibly beyond his competence. It would be dishonest not to admit that I have indulged in value judgments, not infrequently of a negative nature. To victims, if such there be, I can only recommend the *parrhesia* of St Paul who, obviously nettled by criticism of his ecclesiastical policies, declared : 'I care not for the judgment of man, or man's day . . .'

It is impossible to give a brief, much less an exhaustive, account of the books, articles, interviews and conversations that have gone into this book. The most satisfactory account of the pontiffs down to the reign of Pope John is undoubtedly Carlo Falconi's *The Popes of the Twentieth Century* ; and a most extensive bibliographical listing can be found in Patrick Granfield's *The Papacy in Transition*. Suffice it to say that I have made considerable use of both these highly informative volumes.

Other than to thank George Weidenfeld for suggesting the topic and publishing the consequence, I will refrain from embarrassing the friends and acquaintances who have rendered invaluable assistance in the construction of this book.

Holy Redeemer College
Washington, D.C.

August 1980

THE PAPACY TODAY

1

Plus Ça Change...

Any attempt to write accurately about the Catholic Church in today's world is a bold undertaking. During most of its history, that bimillennial institution has been the object of intense scrutiny, angry criticism, violent persecution, and both intelligent and inane analysis. In the person of its popes and hierarchy the Church has challenged empires and civilizations, and has survived not merely to bury its opponents but to preserve their names for posterity. And under the hegemony of the papacy, the Catholic Church possesses a more accurate record of its own achievements and failures than any other contemporary institution. At each stage of its development, it has experienced controversy from within (wars of ideas that not infrequently ended in the banishment of books and the burning of their authors) and confrontation from without – a process that forced the Church to reformulate its tenets, and gradually absorb what was acceptable in the world about it.

While much that is now being written about the Catholic Church by its critics is neither true nor relevant, by the same token much of what is said by the Church's leaders and apologists lacks objectivity and, more to the point, candor. Thus the Church historian turned chronicler and analyst finds his task difficult. But the attempt to portray the Catholic Church through the prism of the papacy should prove fruitful in discovering just what is basically troubling the Church at this critical moment of history.

The Catholic Church sees itself as, essentially, the presence of Jesus Christ in the world. This is a pretentious self-image. Its Supreme Pastor feels he is the successor to St Peter not merely in an unbroken historical line, but as the re-embodiment of the Prince of the Apostles functioning as the Vicar of Christ. An awareness of this claim, however absurd it may appear, is necessary to a proper evaluation of the Church's activities.

Innumerable efforts have been made to describe the Church's terrestrial impact. In the New Testament record, the Acts of the Apostles represent a primitive essay in this direction. Though not claiming similar inspiration, a series of contemporary monographs devoted to the labors of the prelates, theologians, lay experts and observers at Vatican Council II (1962–65) have provided an instant history of that momentous event. Of these journalistic efforts, the first to catch the eye of the general public was a 'Letter from Vatican City' that appeared in the *New Yorker* at the time of the opening of the Council in October 1962. Subsequent letters, published in book form at the close of each annual session and eventually gathered into a single volume, provide great insight into both the Church and the papacy during those crucial years. Though possibly surpassed in anecdote or theological awareness, Xavier Rynne's *Letters from Vatican City* remain as relevant and authentic as ever.

An assiduous reading of the writings of Xavier Rynne led to the startling discovery that, while that perspicacious commentator of the papal involvement in Vatican Council II does not deal directly with the theoretical implications of his revelations, his analysis of ecclesiastical events projects a definite pattern of change discernible in the doctrinal, moral, disciplinary, and structural aspects of the Church. The recognition of this process adds up to a remarkable device for identifying the machinery and process of change in a Church the majority of whose elder statesmen have intransigently rejected the notion of a 'Development of Doctrine', in Cardinal Newman's phrase, and have repudiated Pope John's call for a modernization of the Church's structure with the puerile reaction of *'aggiornamento, si; cambiamento, no!'* ('Updating, yes; change, no!').

What Rynne illustrates is the fact that when faced with new or evolving social, economic, ethical, metaphysical, and political problems, the pope and bishops, functioning as the *magisterium*, or teaching authority, of the Church, tend to adopt a conservative stand based upon the reassertion of traditional doctrines and disciplinary decisions. Nevertheless, despite the continuity claimed for its teachings – Pope Paul VI was fond of asserting that 'the Church is consistent with itself' – the Church has frequently changed its explanation as well as its attitude in most of its theological and disciplinary beliefs. It would not be inappropriate to call this discovery about the evolutionary process in the Catholic Church *Rynne's Law*.

Succinctly stated, Rynne's Law maintains that actual change is accomplished by what can best be referred to as 'reverse English'. When, due to the reflection of its theologians or the attitude of its faithful who are confronted with evolving metaphysical, political, social or philosophical patterns, the Church is about to accept a mutation in doctrinal explanation or disciplinary directive, the whole edifice of tradition seems to draw itself up and refuses to acknowledge the *possibility* of change. With the publication of a papal or hierarchical document that expresses a refusal to budge on the issue, an unwitting acknowledgment has been made of the fact that the turnabout is already in process.

A corollary to this Law sees the papacy, down through the centuries, adapting itself to the political structure of the world about it. Originating in the synagogic atmosphere of the Jewish temple religion, the primitive Christian community, on rejection by the parent body, preserved the regulatory and liturgical aspects of the Judaic religion until forced by circumstances to acquire characteristics of the Roman imperial organization. With the legitimization of the Christian Church under Constantine in 313 A D, the papacy took on the clothes of authoritarian rule. In the early Middle Ages the Holy See became a feudal suzerainty. Then, with the rise of the nation states in the fourteenth and fifteenth centuries, the Church, as represented by the papacy, asserted a primacy in the political order, gradually adapting itself to the doctrine of the divine right of kings. Now, in the contemporary world, it is self-consciously attempting to acquire democratic characteristics. But at each stage of this politico-religious experience the papacy suffered the shock of challenge and response, using the mechanism which Rynne has unwittingly identified as the process of 'reverse English'.

A similar phenomenon of evolution is observable in the ideological sphere where, frequently, the papacy has adopted stances and attitudes whose acceptance would have filled a previous generation with horror. A classic instance of this procedure is the adoption of the term 'Supreme Pontiff' to designate the Bishop of Rome. To the early Christian, the Roman emperor in his function as Supreme Pontiff was the culmination of idolatry. A not dissimilar instance is the claim to infallibility of the Bishop of Rome. While final authority in doctrinal and disciplinary matters was gradually vindicated for the Roman pontiff, the notion of infallibility would have been identified with the pagan *hubris* or cognitive arrogance repudiated by the early Church.

In the past, the process of change required a considerable passage of time. The Church's jurisprudence spoke of 'immemorial custom' as capable of replacing positive laws; and it defined 'immemorial' in terms of sixty or eighty years. Doctrinal and disciplinary mutations were thus protected from premature discovery by communication difficulties and the simple passage of time. Before the age of instant communication, this passage of time usually enabled the Church's apologists to gloss over the fact of change with the aphorism that the Holy See viewed human events *sub specie aeternitatis* – under the shadow of eternity.

But the structure of the Roman Catholic Church is now undergoing a fundamental metamorphosis. As in every living organism, such growth is accompanied by internal difficulty. Peculiar to the Roman Church, however, is the fact that its current experience was occasioned by an ecumenical council called to reinforce its internal integrity and prepare it for union with the other Christian churches.

In the decade and a half since Vatican Council II the monolithic image of the Catholic Church has suffered severe damage. In trying to update the Church's awareness of its obligations to the contemporary world the Council revealed painful divergences in doctrinal and disciplinary understanding within the institution that considers itself the parent body of Christianity. The most notable difficulty now surfacing is the challenge to the position of the papacy, the dominating factor in the Church's institutional framework for close to two thousand years.

Rejection of papal decisions is not a new phenomenon in the Church's troubled history. *Roma locuta est, causa finita* (Rome has spoken, the case is finished) has been honored more in the breach than in the observance. Nevertheless, since at least the late second century the Bishop of Rome has been recognized as possessing a 'more important prominence', although the significance of this expression has been differently interpreted through the ages.

In the juridical concept of the Church's structure, since at least the middle of the fifth century with Pope Leo I, the notion of papal primacy has verged into that of papal supremacy. This was a characteristic of the political assertions of the great medieval pontiffs from Gregory VII in the eleventh century to Pius V in the sixteenth century; and it was the understanding confirmed by Vatican Council I which in 1870 declared both the primacy and the infallibility of the pope.

With Vatican II the Roman Church was propelled into the second half of the twentieth century. This involved a jettisoning of much of the sacral paraphernalia burdening the institution since the late Middle Ages. Pope John had no intention of doing away with the authoritarian structure of the Church. But he hoped to change the character of that authority.

The history of the papacy is a tangled skein that includes the gradual centralization of Roman jurisdiction in the West, the creation of papal self-consciousness that took responsibility for civilizing the barbarian nations from the North and East, and the emergence of a curia or administrative office that concerned itself with the political as well as the spiritual well-being of the Mediterranean and outside world. In all of this the papacy was deeply involved in the struggles accompanying the breakdown of the Holy Roman Empire and the rise of the national states.

As the conscience of Europe, the papacy attempted to preserve the universal character of the Christian involvement in worldly affairs, only itself to become a part of the political structure. The failure of the papacy to rid itself of temporal power following the harrowing experiences of the French Revolution blunted its vision of the fundamental mutations in human awareness that were set in motion by the noetic discoveries of the nineteenth and twentieth centuries. John's revolution was a hundred and fifty years late in coming. The chaotic experiences of this current decade are the penalty that is being paid for that monumental shortsightedness.

Through the ages popes have in fact been the architects of great social and political change as well as the engineers of myopic efforts to halt social progress. In the ninth century Nicholas I declared the use of torture inconscionably un-Christian; in the thirteenth Gregory XI justified the Spanish Inquisition. The papacy championed the rise of the medieval universities and supported the early stages of the Renaissance; but popes also sanctioned the burning of religious reformers as heretics and strenuously opposed the pursuit of human liberties promoted by the Enlightenment. At the close of the nineteenth century Leo XIII inaugurated a *ralliement* favoring democratic government and gave new impetus to the Church's social and political thought; but in the first decade of the twentieth century Pius X condemned as grave error the attempt to accommodate the Church's spiritual message to the consciousness of contemporary man.

It was only with the post World War II era, and the reign of Pope Pius XII, that the papacy addressed itself realistically to the changes that had long been affecting both the Church and the society about it. In a famous talk to the Tenth International Congress of Historians in Rome on 7 September 1955, Pius XII tried to bridge the gap between the Church's unchangeability 'in the constitution and structure given her by her founder himself', and its obvious need to adapt itself to the mutations affecting 'men and human institutions, philosophical and cultural inspirations, political forces, ideas, and social principles and activities'.

With Pope John XXIII, the full significance of these observations was given expression in an heroic attempt to bring the papacy along with the other ancient institutions of the Church into harmony with the religious requirements of a world on the move. The significance of Rynne's Law rests precisely in its penetration of the processes connecting John's call for an *aggiornamento,* or updating, to the radical achievement of the Johannine revolution.

With all its human faults and aspirations, the Church and its institutions confirm the ancient adage, *plus ça change, plus c'est la même chose. . . .*

2

The Papal Office

Twice in the late summer of 1978 the Roman Catholic Church experienced a traumatic shock the like of which is all but unique in its history.
Not only did the Church lose two popes within the course of two months
and gain two others, but the circumstances surrounding these events
appeared so obviously providential as to have occasioned concern in the
Kremlin and as far away as Peking. In the past, Roman pontiffs have
come and gone with the inevitability of human mortality. But the events
surrounding the sudden passing of the octogenarian Pope Paul vi, the
lightning-like election of the euphoric Patriarch of Venice, John Paul i,
and his swift demise, making way for the emergence of the 'man from
afar' – a Polish pope after 455 years of Italian dominance – all this has
given pause to the most cynical of Vatican observers.

The Church was not prepared for the immediacy of this triple turn-
over. While radical change had been in the air since the close of Vatican
Council ii in December 1965, the Church's 130 cardinals and well over
half a billion faithful had not the slightest intimation that fate – or the
Holy Spirit – was about to enter the historical continuum 'like a great
wind coming'.

In the short month of his pontificate – actually 33 days, from August
26 to September 28 – Albino Luciani caused considerable stir within
the Church and great concern to the Roman curia, the officials who
conduct Vatican business on a day-to-day basis. The very name he
adopted, John Paul i, re-embodying the person and the policies of his
immediate predecessors, John xxiii and Paul vi, was an innovation.
So was the intimate tone of his first public address to the multitudes
gathered in the piazza of St Peter's on Sunday, the day after his elec-

tion. 'Yesterday', he began, and immediately the crowd erupted into a roar of laughter. The new pope was about to entrust them with a confidence – to break with the obsessive secrecy that surrounded the conclave from which he had just emerged as pope.

'Yesterday!', he said again, after five or six futile attempts to calm his own as well as the crowd's laughter, 'I entered the Sistine Chapel to vote serene and unconcerned. . . .' Then suddenly, he confessed, he saw danger approaching. He had to be comforted by two of his cardinal colleagues who whispered that if God gave the burden, He would give the strength to bear it. Then he said decisively, 'When it came, I accepted it.'

Equally innovative was the fashion in which he handled his audiences with the diplomatic corps, the cardinals, the journalists, his family, and his former parishioners from Venice. Discarding a number of speeches prepared for him as too stiff and formal, he began speaking his own mind clearly, usually illustrating his points with a series of anecdotes. He reminded the journalists, for example, that the Belgian Cardinal Mercier, of World War I fame, had once suggested that if St Paul were spreading the gospel in today's world he would certainly have been a journalist. John Paul improved on the analogy. He assured his audience that the Apostle of the Gentiles would have been an insistent client of RAI, the Italian radio and television establishment.

Of greater import, of course, was the new Holy Father's decision to have himself installed as pope and Bishop of Rome not with the ancient coronation ceremonies – Pope Paul VI had reduced the flamboyant Byzantine ritual from six to three hours – but with a simple pontifical mass celebrated with the cardinals in the piazza of St Peter's. That rite would be preceded by a token ceremony in which the cardinal deacon, Pericle Felici, would place over his shoulders the sacred *pallium,* a small, square stole of white lamb's wool adorned with six black crosses, the sign of episcopal authority in the Church since at least the fourth century.

With that gesture, John Paul I abolished a thousand years of history during which popes were inducted into their office with the solemnities of an imperial coronation, adorned with the three-tiered crown known as the tiara, and enthroned in keeping with an oriental ceremonial to mark the papacy's involvement with the intricate business of civil rule since Carolingian times.

Papal political enmeshment had in fact ended, ideologically at least, with the French Revolution. Unfortunately for both the Church and Italy, the pope's civil rule over Rome and the papal states, which had been abolished by the French revolutionary armies of Napoleon in the early 1800s, was restored to the pope through the insistence of Cardinal Consalvi, the papal secretary of state, at the Congress of Vienna in 1815. The result was a rearguard action in both the political and ideological sphere fought by apprehensive Roman pontiffs who felt their religious independence was intrinsically bound up with their territorial sovereignty. Down to 1870 the popes not only helped to prevent the unification of Italy by a fiercely reactionary type of ecclesiastical rule, but employed a similar tactic in refusing to modernize the Church's thinking, despite the urgings of a host of great Catholic thinkers such as de Lamennais, Count Montalambert, Bishop Ketteler and Padre Antonio Rosmini. In a long series of utterances that were eventually synthesized in the Syllabus of Errors of 1864 under Pius ix, the papacy condemned liberalism, democracy, relativism, pluralism and the claim that the Church should pay attention to the signs of the times.

Ironically, the spiritual liberation of the papacy was achieved with the taking of Rome by the armies of the House of Savoy in September 1870, and the rescue of the Papal States from their hopelessly oppressive clerical government.

By an incredible lack of political *savoir faire,* Pope Pius ix refused to recognize this *fait accompli* and, retiring into the Vatican, denied the legitimacy of the new Italian government. He rejected a law passed by the Italian parliament in 1871 guaranteeing the political independence of the Holy See and offering to indemnify the papacy for the loss of its ecclesiastical holdings that were taken over by the Piedmontese government. What was worse, Pio Nono and the much more astute Leo xiii (both of whom proved to be incredibly long-lived pontiffs – Pius ix reigned from 1846 to 1878 and Leo xiii from 1878 to 1903) forbade Catholics to participate in the new Italian government, thus turning over control of the nation's destiny to the Church's enemies – the anti-clerical, freemason and agnostic politicians who used the opportunity to introduce legislation offensive to the Church's moral and educational stand.

In fact, however, the overthrow of the papacy as a civil government greatly benefitted the popes. As 'prisoners of the Vatican', they re-

ceived the sympathy and support of Catholics the world over. Nevertheless despite great heart-searchings by a minority of the Church's more
courageous thinkers who attempted to confront the revolutions in the
industrial, cultural, scientific and scholarly realms of human progress,
these popes continued to fulminate like Old Testament prophets against
any idea of accommodating the Church to the 'spirit of the world'.

Despite its lack of territorial control, the Holy See continued to operate in the international order, exchanging diplomatic representatives,
receiving heads of states, and adjudicating a dispute over the Caroline
Islands between Spain and Germany. Even after the settlement of the
so-called 'Roman Question' with the Lateran Treaty of 1929, Pope Pius
XI rejected attempts to have the Church stand on its own two feet in
total independence of the totalitarian governments that were taking control of the Western world. In a series of concordats with Germany,
Spain, Portugal, Austria and Italy, he tried to achieve a position of
advantage for the Catholic religion. He succeeded merely in playing
into the hands of the dictators. Not until the arrival of Pope John XXIII
in 1958 and his Council was the practice of accepting favors from civil
governments recognized as political folly. But while denying that the
Church needed special consideration from governments, the Council
did vindicate the Church's right to play a part in world affairs as an
organization involved with the consciences of millions of mankind.

The participation of Vatican representatives in international agreements
raised a number of political questions, not the least of which was the
fundamental problem of the nature of the papacy as a sovereign power.
No other religious institution in the modern world functions both as a
church and as a political organization that exchanges diplomatic representatives and claims total recognition as an independent member of the
community of nations.

The Church is unquestionably one institution in today's world with
an authentic tradition that reaches back through well over fifteen
hundred years of political activity. Few contemporary institutions have
been more intimately, and none more continuously, involved with the
political order of both Western, Near Eastern and oriental civilizations,
in its attempt to bring the whole world under its spiritual solicitude.

Jesus Christ, confronted with the colonial system of his day, made no attempt to present the Church with a readymade solution to the problems that arose in the relations between man's earthly existence and his eternal destiny. While he acknowledged that he was a king, he was quick to add that 'his kingdom was not of this world'. He did accept the final hegemony of the Roman empire, acknowledging the legitimacy of the tax system and bowing before his own unjust condemnation by the Roman procurator, Pontius Pilate. But in his political aphorisms, Christ created more problems than he solved. Both the injunction 'Seek you first the kingdom of God and his justice' and 'Render to Caesar what is Caesar's' gave rise to a dichotomy between the religious organization and the state that, during the Middle Ages and down to modern times, have been the source of continual strife between Church and state.

It was St Augustine in the fifth century who set himself the task of unraveling the relationship between the City of God and the Worldly City. But despite the magnificent sweep of his vision of human history, he merely succeeded in further clouding the issue. Denying categorically that justice could be discovered in earthly kingdoms ('What are great states but robber kingdoms?', he asked), Augustine set his sights on achieving the kingdom of God as the goal of man's earthly existence. He thus introduced into the Christian perspective a note of pessimism regarding earthly politics that dominated the relations between the priesthood and the Holy Roman Empire throughout the Middle Ages.

Even when the popes functioned as sovereign rulers, they maintained that their right to intervene in secular matters was also justified *ratione peccati* – by reason of sin. It was primarily to correct injustices that the hierarch had the right to interfere in the secular order. Although this principle was a grave simplification of the complicated relations between church and state that predominated in the Western world down to the French Revolution, it did represent a basic fact of medieval politics.

Vatican authorities are today careful not to base the Church's claim to international sovereignty on the independent status of the Vatican City state. Concordats and international agreements with other nations are signed by a representative of the pope as supreme pastor of the Catholic Church, the recognized leader of more than half a billion faithful scattered over the world.

The Lateran Treaty of 1929 – a unilateral declaration of the sovereignty of the Holy See – embodied the main financial and political provisions of the Law of Guarantees originally passed by the Italian parliament in 1871, and recognized the sovereignty of the pope as supreme pastor of the Holy See as well as his independence as ruler of the Vatican City state, the 108-acre walled territory in the midst of the Eternal City. Despite the ambiguity involved, a clear distinction was made between the pope's two positions. In international relations, the Roman pontiffs have insisted that their sovereignty is constituted by the Church's traditional and universal character. On this basis, popes exchange ambassadors with independent nations, participate in international affairs, and on occasion serve as mediators in disputes between states.

Juridical foundation for this concept is supplied by the theory that the Church forms a *societas perfecta* – a perfect society, defined as an institution capable of maintaining complete welfare in its own order and, by right, disposing of all the means to achieve that aim. It is therefore self-sufficient and autonomous. It is this status that is recognized by the Lateran Treaty and reinforced by the Holy See's declaration of intent to remain outside any territorial competition, characterizing itself as a neutral state. As a consequence of this declaration, the neutrality of the Vatican City state has been acknowledged in the international order, particularly during World War II, when Vatican diplomats and Church officials were accorded free access to the Holy See by both Axis and Allied governments.

The concept of the *societas perfecta* had been developed out of the natural-law theories popularized by Samuel von Puffendorf and the Protestant champions of civil rights in the sixteenth and seventeenth centuries, mainly in reaction to oppressive Catholic kings and princes. By an inevitable process, described above as an application of Rynne's Law, the Catholic Church absorbed the notion as applied in the international order and has become its champion in the contemporary world. This development was given classic expression in Cardinal Alfredo Ottaviani's *Institutiones juris publici ecclesiae* (Institutes of the Public Law of the Church), a new edition of which was published in 1960 on the eve of Vatican Council II. By a strange irony, characteristic of papal history down the ages, the Council removed a main tenet of the Ottaviani thesis. It rejected the notion that the Church should seek the special treatment in the political milieu that was claimed by the cardinal as a prerogative of the institution as the unique representative of the kingdom of God on earth.

While the papacy was excluded from the peace negotiations that followed World War II, the Holy See played an essential role in the turmoil that followed the armistice. Through its international relief sources, the pope helped to feed and rebuild much of war-torn Europe and resettle millions of refugees scattered over the globe. During the subsequent struggle between Communist and Christian for the control of Western Europe, the Vatican took a not-so-subtle part through the support its diplomatic representatives gave, for example, Adenauer in Germany, de Gaulle in France and de Gasperi in Italy. And in the formation of both the United Nations Organization and its offshoot, UNESCO, in Paris, the papal nuncio in France, Angelo Roncalli, insisted that the Holy See participate as a charter observer, despite heavy opposition within the papal household itself.

Shortly before his death in October 1958, Pope Pius XII confided to a European diplomat '*Après moi, le déluge!*' Pius had in mind the chaos he saw threatening the structure of the Church that, over the past four centuries at least, had become so centralized in the papacy as to have outgrown governance by any one individual. There was great irony in the observation. For during the later portion of his nineteen-year reign (1939–58) Pius had become so disenchanted with the cardinals and clerics who functioned as the Roman curia that he withdrew from the normal consultations with the prefects, or heads, of the Vatican offices. The pontiff's withdrawal gave the curial bureaucrats control over the conduct of the Church's everyday affairs – its dealings with problems of doctrine and discipline; the appointment of bishops and diplomats; its hard line with innovators among the priests involved in worker movements; its monitoring of the Church's vast seminary system and the direction of its worldwide missionary enterprises.

In the years immediately following World War II, Pius XII had devoted himself almost exclusively to his own political and intellectual interests. With his two personal assistants, the gentle, almost delicate, Mons. Gianbattista Montini and the hard-nosed Roman Mons. Domenico Tardini, the pontiff personally helped to feed and reconstruct

Western Europe. And while directing the battle between Communists and Christians for control of Italy, particularly in the elections of 1948, Pius XII appeared before the world as an ascetic figure reaching out for mystical experiences. Receiving diplomats and heads of state with great hieratic dignity, he also delivered learned disquisitions on every subject imaginable to international gatherings of scientists and businessmen, philosophers and philanthropists, sportsmen and statesmen, and the millions of tourists for whom a visit to the Eternal City was unthinkable without an audience with the Holy Father.

Filling the vacuum created by the pope's withdrawal from day-to-day administrative decisions, a group of tough-minded Italian cardinals known profanely as *Il Pentagono* (Clemente Micara, Nicolo Canali, Marcello Mimmi, Giuseppe Pizzardo and Alfredo Ottaviani) ruled the post-war Church with an iron hand. No major ecclesial decision, no minor ruling affecting the Catholic Church's policies in its universal extension, was beyond their scrutiny. Erecting a solid wall of intransigence – Cardinal Ottaviani called his book of speeches *Il Beluardo* (the Bastion) – against the spread of communism and the perils of post-war heresy, these churchmen confronted the world with an invincible façade. In their vocabulary the word *déluge* existed nowhere outside the Book of Genesis.

With the successor to Pius, the 77-year-old Angelo Roncalli, elected as a transitional pope in October 1958, the deluge occurred. John's Vatican Council turned the Church upside down. It unleashed a torrent of change in the Church's concept of itself, and in its relation to the political and religious world, that was truly revolutionary. Its consequences are still cascading through the Church and the contemporary society of which that institution is an integral part.

In calling Vatican Council II into being, despite the resistance of the curial cardinals and the opposition of his papal counsellors whom he stigmatized as 'prophets of doom' because 'they knew no history', John seems to have been aware of the Pacellian *bon mot* regarding the deluge. He felt the Church needed a totally new self-image ; and he knew that this re-evaluation could only be achieved by a thorough housecleaning by the Church's leaders.

In calling for a revitalization of the Church's presence in the world

Pope John disguised his full intent under the harmless-sounding word *aggiornamento,* an updating. But what he had in mind was to 'return the Church to the simple form it possessed when it left the hand of Jesus Christ, its founder'.

Under the guidance of John's successor, Paul VI, the Council achieved that goal, at least on paper. In sixteen constitutions and decrees it created a vision of the Church that mirrored the primitive Christian community in twentieth-century guise. But in the hesitant fashion in which Pope Paul and his advisers implemented the conciliar directives they lost control of the explosive developments to which the Council gave rise.

After a fifteen-year reign during which he strengthened the Church's political presence in the world and prevented schismatic offshoots on the right and the left, Paul VI bequeathed to his successors a church divided into three principal factions – the Pacellian division on the right, whose intransigence is best exemplified in the rebel French archbishop Marcel Lefebvre's Latin liturgy movement; the Johannine Church, at the other end of the spectrum, dedicated to an on-the-ground liberationist renewal of the Gospel commitment; and the Pauline church, holding onto the papal obsession with authority, sex and orthodoxy, but reaching out for a genuine updating of the Church's liturgy, discipline and doctrine.

With the sudden death of Paul VI in early August 1978 a series of lightning events hit the papacy, resulting in the election of the 'September Pope', John Paul I. His brief reign seemed intended as a prelude to the unprecedented elevation to the papacy of an outsider, John Paul II. From the start, the Polish pope's pontificate proved a momentous experience. In major voyages to Mexico, Poland, Ireland, the United States and Turkey, he amalgamated the intransigent elements of traditional papal teaching with a totally this-worldly commitment to human dignity. He emphasized the value of the human person, particularly in his address before the United Nations in New York. And he gave a fearless exposition on the spot of the evils in both the capitalist and the communist systems between which the Church and the papacy are inextricably poised.

Nevertheless his traditionalist stance on major problems confronting the Church's 700 million faithful – divorce, birth control, ecumenism, clerical celibacy, abortion, and the position of women within the Church – gave pause to the euphoria of many observers. At stake with the pontificate of this vigorous, comparatively youthful pontiff (he was 58 in 1978) was the turning point of the postconciliar period. In a precedent-breaking address immediately after his election to the multitude in the piazza of St Peter's and a world-wide audience glued to the T V and radio, John Paul II promised to open a new path in history. And in his contact with diplomats, journalists and the common people during the early weeks of his pontificate he exhibited an intense interest in the everyday problems of the world's political community as well as of the man, woman and child in the street. In his first encyclical, *The Redeemer of Man,* he outlined an ambitious program aimed at preparing the Church and the whole of mankind for the year 2000.

What the world wanted to know, however, was would the new Holy Father come to terms with the globe's most crucial problems: the billion or more people living in degradation, dying of starvation and never arriving at the possibility of enjoying the human rights and human dignity of which he seemed so great a champion? Would he put his finger on the Christians in the capitalist system who were guilty of manipulating world trade so that millions of human beings were reduced to a below-subsistence level of existence? Would he excoriate the Catholic rulers of states who were guilty of genocide, terrorism, and exploitation of their own people? And would he call to task the statesmen and entrepreneurs engaged in the unconscionable armaments race that was destroying the world's economy and threatening the survival of mankind?

Equally, would John Paul II be able to turn the tide within his own household, and then in the Church more generally, from a preoccupation with the niceties of dogmatic formulas and disciplinary regulations to the actuality of the Christian belief that one should love his neighbor – friend or foe – as himself? Could he make the objective of the Catholic religion orthopraxy – 'not everyone who says to me, Lord, Lord, but he who does the will of my Father . . .' – instead of an elitist preoccupation with a cerebral orthodoxy?

No one expected miracles of the new pontiff during the first year of his pontificate. And yet, with his powerful, charismatic presence, his devotion to youth, and his clear-headed knowledge of the world, could he not lead the Church towards a realization of Pope John's dream – to put the good news of the Christian message at the disposition of every human being throughout the globe by feeding the hungry, clothing the naked, comforting the depressed. This, after all, was the objective Christ placed before his disciples when he instructed them to 'preach his gospel to every nation!'

It was this question that John Paul II had to wrestle with as he meditated on the papal office down the centuries and the incredible circumstance that he, a Pole, should now be standing in the footsteps of Peter the Rock, functioning as the vicar or spokesman of Jesus Christ on the verge of the twenty-first century.

In its long, turbulent history, the papacy has survived every imaginable danger from the Neronian persecutions of the first century to the disruptions following the French Revolution in the nineteenth. In the course of this bimillenial experience, the papacy has been presided over by saints and sinners, idealists and rogues, men of the highest spiritual achievement and pious frauds, courageous pontiffs facing down emperors and pusillanimous prelates cowed by saints and demagogues. Nevertheless, despite occasional lapses – the Inquisition, the burning of heretics and witches, the condemnation of Galileo, and the more recent modernist heresy hunt – the papacy has served as the conscience of Western civilization.

During the barbarian invasions the popes took on the societal burdens that had proven too heavy for the declining Roman Empire. In the Middle Ages the papacy served as a catalyst in the political and intellectual order, condemning a dualist approach to material and spiritual reality, encouraging the rebirth of learning and the rise of the universities that led to the Renaissance and the Protestant Reformation. Amid the turmoil of intellectual, social, industrial and political revolutions following the advances of the nineteenth century, the papacy survived a temptation to withdraw from the world, only to display a miraculous rejuvenation in the second half of the twentieth century.

In dealing with the papacy two remarkable facts must be kept in mind. One is its incredible longevity. Despite its claim to absolute consistency in doctrine and discipline, the Church under the guidance of the papacy has exhibited an uncanny ability to renew itself in keeping with the social and political changes that have overwhelmed the universe during the past two thousand years.

The other remarkable fact is the Church's ability to mold history to its ideological needs. This is most noteworthy in the use it has made of the mystical facts surrounding its origins. In an age less sophisticated, but no less intelligent, than our own, the Gospel incidents relating to Christ's selecting Peter as the leader of the apostles were amalgated into the historical event of Christ founding the Church on Peter, the Rock, and assuring him and his companions that 'The gates of hell shall not prevail against it.' Fact or mythical symbol, that statement stands as the cornerstone of an institution that has played a principal part in the unfolding of Western civilization and that, despite the perils of today's global calamities, is still an important factor in world history. It gives substance to the claim that the Bishop of Rome in succession to the apostle Peter holds supreme authority in the Church, and thus is in possession of the keys to the kingdom of heaven.

Modern scriptural scholarship has cast doubt on the historicity of the incident and the idealistic ring of the statement. But it has not been able to dislodge the fact that, from the Church's beginnings, a certain leadership was exercised by Peter in the activities of the apostles and the conduct of the primitive Church's affairs. Nor can historical caution deny the fact that by the close of the second century AD, Church leadership in the Mediterranean was exercised by the Bishop of Rome. In the words of the late-second-century Bishop of Lyons in France, Irenaeus of Smyrna, Rome possessed a *principalior potestas* – a more imposing authority. This phrase has been interpreted by Catholic theologians as a jurisdictional predominance in the see of Peter. Modern scholarship believes that, more likely, it refers to the apostolic origin of the Roman Church's doctrinal tradition. Whatever the meaning of that historical phrase and the concomitant witness of similar early Church experiences, the fact is that from at least the pontificate of Damasus (366–84 AD) and incontestably with the papacy of Leo I (440–51) the Bishop of Rome has claimed a direct heritage as the vicar of Christ in governing the Church not as the successor to his predecessor as the Roman pontiff, but in immediate succession to Peter.

The significance of that conviction cannot be exaggerated if we are to understand the function of the pope in the governance of the Catholic

Church and in the Roman communion's relationship to other Christians. It supplies criteria for understanding many of the intransigent positions in doctrinal and moral matters assumed by a church that considers itself the direct and immutable custodian of divine revelation; and that believes itself to be the continuation of the mystical body of Jesus Christ in this world. Outrageous though that concept may appear, it is a conviction that enters into the papacy's involvement with the political, social, economic and cultural milieu in which the Church finds itself in each age.

In a talk to the tenth International Congress of Historians in Rome in October, 1955 Pope Pius xii declared that the word catholicism was not a proper term for the Christian religion. It represented an ideology, whereas Christianity was an experience that had straddled the backbone of history like a mountain range during the past two thousand years. It could be loved or despised; it could not be ignored.

While that highly competent pontiff was wedded to a fully conceptual view of the Church it was his struggle to refashion much of Catholic thinking during the middle decades of the twentieth century that prepared the way for Pope John's revolution. By encouraging a new Latin translation of the Psalms for use in the Church's liturgical prayer, he opened a path to both a rearrangement of the Church's sacramental life in its liturgical expression, and a total reassessment of the significance of the sacred scriptures. In a letter to the Dominican Father Jacques M. Voste in 1943, he had justified the use of modern methods of linguistic and cultural research as well as historical discoveries for interpreting the word of God in both the Old and the New Testaments. By attempting to solve problems dealing with particular cases of human freedom such as conscientious objection within the political sphere, he prepared the way for Pope John's insistence on human dignity as an absolute right before which both the civil and the ecclesiastical authority had to give way. And by his confrontation of the moral aspect of responsible parenthood he made possible the Council's thoroughgoing revision of the Church's definition of marriage. Finally, in a matter for which he has not been given credit nor followed consistently by his successors, in authorizing the ordination of married men under special circumstances in the Latin church, he initiated a reorientation of the priesthood that neither the Vatican Council nor the papacy has confronted with full honesty.

Pius XII thus raised most of the issues that had been fermenting within the Church's doctrinal storage-house since at least 1800. And while he tried without success to supply new directions for their solution on the strength of his own intellectual genius, he at least opened the way for a rethinking of most of these radical doctrinal and disciplinary difficulties.

Wittingly or not, John was a transitional pope, not only in the temporal sense of a brief pontificate, but in the metaphysical sense of confronting the Church with a totally new approach to its own self-comprehension. He forced the institutional Church to redefine its meaning for mankind in the twentieth century.

In a startling sentence in the midst of the discourse with which he inaugurated Vatican Council II, John laid the foundation for a fundamental change in the Church's theological thinking – a shift from an *a priori,* conceptual preoccupation with dogmas and moral principles to an existential commitment to the realities of human life in direct relation to the person of Christ operative in the contemporary world as 'the Way, the Truth, and the Life.'

'The salient point of this Council . . .', the pope asserted, is 'a step forward toward a doctrinal penetration and a formation of consciences in faithful conformity to authentic doctrine which, however, should be studied and expounded through the methods and research, and through the literary forms of modern thought. *The substance of the ancient doctrine is one thing, the way in which it is presented is another.*'

This last sentence was considered close to heretical in most Roman seminaries and clerical universities; and not a few cardinalatial eyebrows were lifted at its bold enunciation by the octogenarian pontiff. Nevertheless, it became the catalyst for the Council's main achievements.

It is not known just how much of the revolutionary mutations introduced into the Church's theological thinking by the Council was actually anticipated by Pope John. But his opening discourse at the Council will be recognized by historians of the future as the *magna carta* of Christianity in an age of worldwide transition.

John spoke of an updating as if he were interested merely in a sort of cosmetic retouching of the Church's façade; and many of his compan-

3

Leo XIII to Pius XII

e men have occupied the papal throne thus far in the twentieth cen-
. Each of these pontiffs has possessed great individual talents, and
haracter and a manner of rule decidedly different from that of his
decessors. Under the guidance of these popes, the Church has, on
whole, prospered, despite grave internal problems and a plethora of
secutions and disruptions from without.

t the turn of the century the Roman pontiff was a nonagenarian
tocrat, the frail Leo XIII, who had assumed the papal office in 1878
moment when most of the world felt the Church was slowly wind-
down to spiritual insignificance and cultural bankruptcy. His pre-
essor, Pio Nono, had reigned thirty-two years – a long, difficult
tificate that had begun in a blaze of hope and ended in a blanket of
om in 1878.

rom a worldly viewpoint, Pio Nono's reign was a series of disasters,
inning with his sudden and violent retreat from the liberal attitude
is first two years as pope. His experiment with a modified constitu-
al monarchy was brutally ended with the seizure of Rome by revo-
onaries in 1848 and the pontiff's forced flight to Gaeta. Restored in
9 to his rulership of the Papal States (some 40,000 square miles in
center of the Italian peninsula, roughly from Benevento in the south
Bologna in the north) by French troops under Napoleon III, Pius IX
pted the repressive political measures that he had so severely criti-
d in the dictatorial rule of his predecessor, Gregory XVI.

Vhat was worse, Pius transferred this retrogressive attitude to his
duct of the Church's interior affairs, condemning all attempts to
ralize Catholic doctrine and moral teaching, and ignoring the pleas

ions in the episcopate insisted that this was his intention. But what he
had in mind was a fundamental reorientation of the Church's thinking
and its way of life – a *balzo in avanti*, a leap ahead, as he repeated so
fondly when he insisted that the Council was to provide the Church with
a new Pentecost.

To bridge the gap between the first and the twentieth-first centuries,
John was conscious of the great cosmological revolution introduced by
Copernicus and Keppler in the sixteenth century by their discovery that
the earth was not the center of the universe; and confirmed by Einstein
in the twentieth by redimensioning the whole framework of man's image of himself in time and space. It was the vague perception of this
incredible reversal of humanity's relation to the universe that so disturbed the churchmen of the post-Renaissance and led to the agitated
condemnation of Galileo. For while these discoveries constituted a perception in the physical order, they had a metaphysical significance that
staggers the imagination. Man no longer saw himself as the center of
the universe and thus the prime object of creation. Nor was the tiny
globe of earth the pivotal point of the universe. It is a small speck of
materiality, on the edge of one of the minor constellations known as the
solar system, and unlocatable by co-ordinates of time and space within
the universe. Thus ancient and medieval man's concept of law and order
in the cosmos – based upon his observation of the sun, the moon and
the stars, his ability to chart the seasons, observe the tides, and cope
with the animal world, leading to man's concept of his own importance as the center of creation – has been thrown into frightening disar-
ray. The fact that the human race occupies an insignificant speck of dust
in an unimaginably immense and complex universe whose significance
and directional parameters are beyond current understanding has so dis-
concerted many Christians that they have had recourse to a biblical fun-
damentalism rejecting the evidence for evolution and taking refuge in a
simplistic reading of the Book of Genesis that would shock an early
father of the Church such as Basil or Ambrose despite their ignorance
of current concepts of the physical universe.

Despite the marvels of contemporary science that have broken
through the barriers of interstellar space, placing a man on the moon
and bringing the solar system's satellites under direct scrutiny, current

comprehension of the immensity of the macrocosm as well as the complexity of the microcosmic ion or the molecule is still at an infantile stage.

This realization, transferred to the religious sphere, has led to the questioning of the religious beliefs and practices that were based largely upon a biblical cosmology and a stoic vision of the universe that prevailed at the start and during the first eighteen centuries of the Christian explanation of reality.

It has entered intimately into the context of many of the Church's doctrines or explanations of its fundamental beliefs. The very concept of God, the Creation, the notion of man's redemption from sin through the incarnation, death and resurrection of Jesus Christ, and an eschatological restoration of all things in Christ, have been affected radically by these discoveries in the physical sciences. It is not the doctrines as such that are being challenged, for they represent mysteries that can only be believed. But, as Pope John indicated in opening the Council, it is how they are enunciated and fit into mankind's intellectual awareness that is in need of a fundamental reorientation. The Church's and the papacy's reluctance to rethink these dogmas in keeping with, for example, the apocalyptic vision of Teilhard de Chardin, without questioning their supernatural substance, has only encouraged the loss of faith of many of its educated adherents and the Church's own loss of credibility in the outside world.

Pope John's Council had not been called specifically to confront this new and unique challenge to human intelligence in reinterpreting the mysteries of creation and the questioning of the cosmological framework within which the Church's truth has been proclaimed. But it did deal with a reinforced sacramental concept of the nature of the Church, its liturgical practices, and mankind's moral, familial and political objectives – without, however, delving deeply enough into the spiritual significance of contemporary discoveries in the behavioral sciences as well as psychology and psychiatry.

It is within this quadrant of human questioning not so much about the nature of the supernatural and the cosmological parameters of human existence, as about the political and the sociological phenomenon of a world – in which at least one quarter of the human race are living close

to starvation and another half caught in an adva
two power-hungry inhuman political systems –
papacy must direct itself. Only thus will the new
redirect the Church's thinking and operations.

As the history of the papacy over the last hu
clearly, it will not be by allowing the bureaucrats
to distract him with their small-minded concern:
doctrinal expressions and their worries about suc
as the methods of contraception or the phenome
the Church that Pope John Paul will fulfill the p
very start of his pontificate 'to open a new path
will be by taking a courageous stand on the issu
issues that reach down to the prevention of starva
the degradation of billions of human beings, that
Church and the world to avoid the *déluge* predicte
of the omnipotent popes.

of its champions, particularly in the Germany of Bishop von Ketteler and the France of Count Montalambert, that it update its social and political thought. Instead, Pio Nono issued a Syllabus of Errors in 1864 that condemned out-of-hand the notion of progress and such movements as liberalism, socialism, democracy and pluralism, thus obviating the attempts of its forward-looking statesmen and prelates to bring Catholic teaching gradually in line with the demands of the 'signs of the times.'

In 1870, amid the fanfare of an intransigent triumphalism, Vatican Council I defined the primacy and infallibility of the Roman pontiff, giving rise to a strident secular reaction and serving as a disruptive element within the Church itself. Nevertheless, with few exceptions, the bishops and faithful who had opposed the definition on grounds that it was untimely accepted its basic teaching and decided to live with it. And the pope himself, once the doctrine was solemnly proclaimed, saw no need to use it in specific situations. When teased by a visitor as to what it felt like to be infallible, the weary pontiff replied: 'I do not know whether I am fallible or infallible. But one thing I am sure of, I'm *in fallimento* [bankrupt]!'

During the last years of his pontificate, Pio Nono seemed to be presiding over the final stages of the papacy's dissolution. Wed to the notion that the Church's independence was inseparable from its possession of worldly territory – a notion that explicitly contradicted Christ's statement, 'My kingdom is not of this world' – the aging pontiff took refuge in a quixotic refusal of the compromise offered by the Italian government with its financial indemnity and law of guarantees.

Paradoxically, this intransigent stand won him and the papacy the sentimental but powerful allegiance of the Catholic people throughout the world. While the Vatican policy that Catholics should not participate in the Italian government or even vote in national elections made certain that the country would be governed by the Church's enemies, Pius could comfort himself with the homage and support he received from the faithful and their leaders all over the world. In the political sphere nations engaged in diplomatic exchange with the Holy See continued that practice. And in the Church's missionary endeavors in the Americas, Asia, and Africa, the expansion and consolidation was heartwarming, even if punctuated by occasional martyrdom.

LEO XIII

The election of Gioacchino Pecci as Leo XIII in February 1878 promised to give the Catholic Church a new lease of life. His predecessor's pontificate was acknowledged even by his admirers as much too long. His successor was elected at the age of 68 after a three-day conclave, despite his protest to friends that 'if they elect me they will soon have to have another conclave.' The new pope seemed destined to a short pontificate, due to his apparently frail health. But twenty-five years later his longevity supplied Cardinal Oreglia di Santo Stefano with an overworked *bon mot:* 'In electing Pecci we sought a Holy Father, not an Eternal Father.'

A humanist, statesman, Latin poet and theologian in his own right, and well versed in the political aspects of Vatican governance – as a young cleric Mons. Pecci served as the political regent of both Benevento and Perugia; and he was papal nuncio in Brussels for three years – Gioacchino Pecci had been the cardinal archbishop of Perugia since 1853. There, in obvious exile from Rome, due, it is maintained, to the enmity of Cardinal Giacomo Antonelli, Pius IX's secretary of state, Pecci had established what amounted to a *Vaticano minore* – a court of intellectuals and scholars who kept abreast of the cultural movements and scientific achievements of the day. At odds with the obscurantist policies of Pio Nono, Cardinal Pecci issued pastoral letters that were in sharp contrast to the papal encyclicals. In dealing with the Syllabus of Errors of 1864, for example, he said that this document should not be a 'scarecrow to frighten the world'. He maintained that its condemnation of liberalism, socialism, positivism and democracy had to be understood in the terms of the documents whose ideology it was summarizing. Thus considered, he said, these condemnations did not anathematize the modern state nor contemporary civilization.

While Leo immediately repeated the protest of his predecessor against the usurpation of the Papal States by the Piedmontese regime and continued the *non expedit* policy of forbidding Catholics to participate in the national government, he worked feverishly to achieve a settlement of the so-called 'Roman Question', eliciting the aid of the Church's friends and opponents, from Otto von Bismarck to the German Catholic Center Party and the Austrian emperor. And in his first encyclical he announced as the aim of his pontificate the reconciliation of the Church and contemporary culture, an objective he had elucidated in pastoral letters while Archbishop of Perugia.

It was Leo's desire to have the Church and the papacy play a significant role in the affairs of contemporary society, thus removing the secular prejudices based on its obscurantism, that had burdened the Church all through the nineteenth century. This approach quickly won Leo a sympathetic hearing with the German Chancellor Bismarck, who was seeking a way out of the outmoded *Kulturkampf* against the German Catholics; with Italian statesmen such as Umberto Rattazzi and Francesco Crispi; with the Tsars Alexander II and III and Nicholas II, with whom he had cordial relations in his efforts to win back the Orthodox church into communion with Rome; with the Mikado of Japan who in 1898 allowed religious freedom and authorized the establishment of an archbishopric in Tokyo with three suffragan dioceses; and with the Sultan of Turkey, the Shah of Persia and the Emperor Menelik II of Abyssinia. In all these relationships Leo had the satisfaction of doing for the papacy what the Italian leader Cavour had achieved for the Kingdom of Savoy. He reaffirmed its international stance and strengthened its political recognition.

Leo had also won the admiration of scholars and humanists, including the Italian poet Gabriele d'Annunzio who admired his Latin verse, the French novelist Paul Bourget who utilized him in his novel *Cosmopolis,* and the historians for whom he opened the Vatican archives with the remark, 'The Church has no fear of history.' A shrewd judge of men, he selected as cardinals outstanding prelates and scholars, giving the red hat to the English convert and theologian, John Henry Newman; the American Archbishop of Baltimore, James Gibbons; the French missionary bishop, Charles Martial Lavigerie; the Italian littérateur, Alfonso Capecelatro; and the German historian Joseph Hergönroether. Of the 146 cardinals he created during his long regime few did not turn out to be men of significance in the Church, though not all of them were in agreement with his forward-looking policies.

In his personal bearing Leo was an aristocrat, but he lived a severely abstemious life, contenting himself with one large room at the entrance to the papal apartments. He had this foyer divided into a bedroom and a sitting-room where he took his meals alone. Outwardly he was somewhat careless in his dress, with almost always the trace of snuff stains on his white cassock. However, in public appearances and when meeting dignitaries or engaged in ceremonies he was immediately transformed, assuming an aristocratic pose and creating a hieratic atmosphere of inaccessibility.

In the sphere of public policy, Leo set out at once to make a radical change from the *dolce far niente* of his predecessor's last years. Only a few hours after his election he told an intimate collaborator: 'I intend to carry out a great policy!' and the use of 'I' instead of the papal 'We' was not lost on his shrewd observer.

Of Leo's sixty encyclical letters, ten were pious exhortations concerning devotions to the Blessed Virgin Mary and the recitation of the rosary. The rest were substantive documents dealing with social, political and theological matters of immediate interest to the Church and society. His attention to the problems confronting the Church with the development of biblical criticism among mainly Protestant scholars was revolutionary for his day. In his encyclical *Providentissimus Deus* (A Most Provident God) he called for a frequent reading of the scriptures by all the faithful and recognized the need for in-depth biblical scholarship using the methods of modern research. He also gave support to Father F. M. Lagrange and the Dominican school of biblical studies being organized in Jerusalem that was to prove a refuge for Catholic exegetes during the heresy-hunting days of the next pontificate. Acceding to the request of the German historian Ludwig von Pastor, Leo put the documents of the Vatican archives and library at the disposition of scholars of all persuasions, insisting that the Church had always welcomed serious historical study.

Early in his pontificate he recognized the need for a systematic philosophical background for the Church's theology to offset the diverse and confused thinking that had surrounded the Church ever since the discrediting of scholastic philosophy with the Enlightenment and the inroads of Cartesianism. He thus gave his support to the revival of the aristotelian-thomistic system and the inauguration of an Academy of St Thomas in Rome, one of whose first scholars was Achille Ratti, the future Pope Pius XI.

Leo had the satisfaction of welcoming into the Catholic communion early in his pontificate the patriarchate of Armenia and the Chaldaic church, but his attempt to achieve union with the Orthodox churches and particularly the Russian patriarchate of Moscow foundered on the Vatican's insistence that such a move would require a return of these communions to obedience to the Holy See, a demand they considered part of the inveterate attempt of the Roman curia to latinize the oriental churches. His hope of winning over the Anglican church foundered on the decision of a papal commission that sacerdotal ordination of Anglican priests and bishops was not valid in the sight of the Catholic Church.

Leo's primary interest lay in the political order, and in a series of encyclicals he clarified the Church's traditional stand on the relations between Church and state. Outlawing liberalism as essentially godless, he maintained the Church could live with any legitimate form of government since in its own right it was a sovereign entity with specific prerogatives in its freedom of access to the consciences of its faithful, whose independence had to be respected in the public domain and whose prerogatives extended to protecting the rights of Catholics all over the world.

Reacting favorably to the importunings of the English Cardinal Henry Manning and the American, James Gibbons, he recognized the legitimacy of the working man's right to unionize, and in his 1891 encyclical *Rerum Novarum* (Of New Things) he finally made the Church confront the social and economic plight of the poor and exploited, acknowledging that 'the Church had lost the laboring classes'.

Leo gave great impetus to missionary enterprises, particularly of the newer religious congregations spreading the word of God in Asia, Africa and Oceania and following the emigrants to the Americas. But in his dealings with France, Portugal and Spain, he suffered a series of diplomatic defeats that consolidated opposition within the Church to his politique of openness to democratic government and his call for a *ralliement* to the French Republic. He died at the age of 93 after flirting with death for more than a decade, but conscious almost to the end. Most Church leaders and other statesmen felt that his pontificate had achieved a note of greatness.

PIUS X

Leo's death on a sweltering day in July 1903 brought to the Vatican a number of cardinals desirous of a change in the Church's direction at the top (including James Gibbons of Baltimore who, to the surprise of the curia, arrived in a black clerical suit and straw hat perched above

his scarlet skull-cap). Among them were a curial coterie under the
French cardinal, Matthieu, strongly opposed to Leo's sympathy towards
democracy in France, and a group of Europeans who felt that his policy
of temporal engagement had been to the detriment of the Church's spir-
itual growth. Nevertheless an important number of electors favored
Leo's policies, and in the first balloting the contest was waged between
Leo's secretary of state, Cardinal Rampolla, and the curial champion,
Cardinal Gotti. Despite the fact that after the third ballot the cardinal of
Krakow, Jan Puzyna, invoked the veto of the Austrian emperor against
Rampolla, he rose to thirty-one votes on the fifth ballot. Meanwhile,
however, the cardinal of Venice, Guiseppi Sarto had arrived at twenty-
seven, and was in on the seventh ballot.

Approached by the dean of the Sacred College, Cardinal Oreglia,
Sarto answered his first 'Do you accept?' with a sigh. Then to the almost
truculent, 'Well, do you accept or not?' he replied with a decisive
'Yes', and quickly supplied the name of Pius, signifying that as pope
he would be 'a defender of the Church's doctrine and rights'. With that
decision about his name, Sarto had set the direction of his papacy.

A minor incident involving the Swiss guards quickly warned the papal household that, while their new Holy Father was a man of great
simplicity, he was not to be trifled with. Immediately after his election,
the guard asked for the equivalent of a bonus; and when it was not
forthcoming they threatened a strike. In a similar move at the election
of Pecci, twenty-five years earlier, they had simply been stared down
by that aristocratic pontiff. Now the new pope decided at once to dis-
band the corps ; and it took great persuasion by the commandant and
the Swiss ambassador to persuade him to change his mind.

Of medium stature with a full and handsome face, legend immediately stressed the poverty and humble origins of the new peasant pope,
exaggerating the latter, for his father had been a bailiff and his mother
a seamstress in the town of Riese where he was born. The family was
poor, however, and young Giuseppi's seminary education was paid for
by a benefactress. By no means untalented, he was a persistent student
and in the last three years of studies in the major seminary he served as
student prefect, having to render a fitness report on his fellow seminarians every six months. The task encouraged an insight into personality
and an ability to evaluate people and sum up situations that greatly
influenced his career. Without particular ecclesial ambition, his talents

were nevertheless recognized and he was brought into the chancery of the diocese of Treviso as a clerk dealing with problems of priests and ecclesiastical affairs. He stayed there for eighteen years until selected to be Bishop of Mantua.

Despite the fact that Sarto was unknown to the non-Italian cardinals and the press, he was well appreciated by the Italian prelates who were aware of his pastoral achievements in Mantua and as cardinal patriarch of Venice. In Mantua he had reopened the seminary and reformed the local clergy, while in the City of the Doges, where on his arrival the windows of the town hall were closed against him, he had told the faithful: 'Don't worry; we shall get them open'. A year later he helped turn out the Radical Democrats from the town council. He was also renowned as a preacher and an important figure in the Catholic Congresses, which were held mainly in the north of Italy and where he was associated with such lay leaders as Albano Medalago and Giuseppe Toniolo.

Turning aside from the intense political interests of his predecessor, the Sarto pope announced his intention of 'restoring all things in Christ'. He thus turned his attention to the Church's pastoral needs; and in short order issued decrees for the reform of liturgical music, abolishing the operatic and concert-hall extravaganzas that had overtaken the sacred ceremonies of the Mass, and called for a restoration of Gregorian chant and the polyphonic compositions of the Tridentine reform. Likewise he instituted the practice of frequent reception of the Eucharist for adults and first communion at the age of seven for children. Insisting on a vast renewal of catechetical practices, he himself gave these instructions to the people gathered in the Cortile of San Damaso in the Vatican on Sunday afternoons, a practice that would be imitated in public audiences by his successor – six removed – John Paul I, during his brief pontificate.

Conscious since his chancery days in the diocesan courts of Treviso of the chaotic state of the Church's laws, Pius x decided to find a way of codifying this vast conglomerate of canons, decrees and regulations that had accumulated over the centuries. In Mons. Pietro Gasparri, a Tuscan who like himself 'wore big shoes', he discovered his man. Gasparri had taught canon law at the Catholic Institute in Paris for twenty years, before returning to Rome to a position in the papal secretariat of state. Approached by the new pontiff to tackle this immense task, he promised to have it done within twenty years and at a minimal cost. True to his word, Gasparri delivered a perfectly integrated code of laws in 1917 – some 2,414 canons in all, that summed up the Church's discipline and practice in closely integrated legal style – after only thirteen years of assiduous labor. By then Pius was three years in his grave, but the code of canon law was promulgated by Benedict x v in 1918, giving its compiler and most of the Latin church the conviction that they were in possession of an instrument of supernatural guidance that would prove an enduring achievement. But such is the fate even of ecclesiastical foresight that within ten years some of the code's provisions had to be amended, and within half a century, with John's convocation of the Council, that pontiff had to call for a complete revision of this monument, so swiftly had the mores of modern civilization overtaken what had been considered an eternal vision of the Church and its functions.

Sarto's reputation as a saintly bishop whose sole interest was in people had followed him to Rome and he quickly gained the reputation of being a holy pope. There was no question of his great magnanimity in his pastoral care, and he had at once set up a series of visitations to the parishes of Rome and the dioceses of Italy, openly deploring his inability to conduct these pastoral experiences himself, prevented as he was by the policy of his predecessors who had made themselves 'prisoners of the Vatican'.

In the political sphere he followed the hard line of non-involvement, making only a few exceptions for outstanding Catholics to serve in the government. He extended this intransigence to the Church's dealing with the French government, which had laicized ecclesiastical property including churches and schools.

Here a side of his character that was well shrouded from the public came into play. One of the few cardinals who had remained for the final stage of the burial of Leo xiii, he had observed with a start that when the unwieldly triple coffin could not be lowered into its crypt, one of the *sanpietrini,* or Vatican workmen, gave it a stout kick, slamming it into place. The unimportant incident troubled him and he confided to a friend that popes like everyone else were of no consequence once they passed from this life. This trifling event had served to reveal a deeply pessimistic side of this pontiff and explained an attitude toward secular things closely reminiscent of Innocent iii's *De contemptu mundi* (On despising the world). It was to show itself most alarmingly in his return to the policy of Pius IX in condemning any notion of the Church's accommodating itself to the 'signs of the times'.

Under Leo's open if cautious attempt to bring the Church's teaching parallel with contemporary culture, a number of Catholic thinkers and theologians, particularly in France and Italy, sought to adopt the methodology of secular advances in science, history and sociology to the Church's approach to the sacred scriptures, its historical development and its disciplinary needs. Encouragement for these endeavors had been supplied by Cardinal Newman in England, the future Cardinal Mercier in Belgium and the aged Italian Cardinal Capecelatro, as well as the pace-making philosopher and priest Antonio Rosmini, whose tract *The Five Wounds of the Church* had made a great impression on the Italian scene before its condemnation by the Holy Office in 1849. Their interests ran to the primacy of the human conscience, a conciliation between liberty and authority, the autonomy of science, the liberation of the Church from superfluous ecclesiastical structures, the revival of the liturgy, the removal of the Church out of local politics, and a Catholicism relieved of outmoded fashions and devoted to a positive line of development in people's material as well as spiritual interests.

Within this atmosphere a spate of innovative champions appeared dedicated to modernizing the Church's outlook. Most prominent among them were the rapier-tongued historian of early Christianity, Mons. Louis Duchesne; the revolutionary scripture scholar, Alfred Loisy; the British Jesuit writer, George Tyrell; the mystical proponent, Baron von Hügel; the Italian political figure, Don Romolo Murri; and the historians George La Piana and Ernesto Buonaiutti.

Fiercely opposed to these innovators were a large group of ecclesiastics centered in the Roman seminaries, and a coterie of zealots in both the Holy Office and the Consistorial Congregation, who accused the innovators of a desire to destroy the absolute character of Catholic truth. These zealots felt that by accepting the fact that the Church's doctrine had developed over the centuries, the champions of modernity were supporting the Darwinian thesis of evolution and thus denying the biblical story of creation, reducing doctrine and discipline to a relativistic evaluation, and destroying the eternal quality of divine revelation, and thus the Church's unbending tradition.

One of the most adamant of these opponents of the new learning was Cardinal Francis Richard of Paris; others were the curial cardinal

Merry del Val, Pius' secretary of state, and his henchman, Mons. Umberto Benigni, a functionary in the Vatican. With the Cardinal's blessing, Benigni organized a spy system that made its way into every diocese in Italy and much of the outside world, as well as in the seminaries and chanceries, under the title *Sodalitium Pianum* – the sodality of Pius – in deference to the memory of Pope Pius IX. In France it was dubbed the *Sapinière*. This secret organization urged the reporting to the Holy See of the writings, sermons, speeches, and even the conversations of churchmen, from cardinals to seminarians, in which the slightest hint of divergence from true doctrine, or of nonconformity to papal policies, might be found.

A reign of terror throughout the Church in Europe ensued and reached its apex in 1907 with the publication of Pope Pius' decree *Lamentabili,* condemning the heresy of 'Modernism' outright. With that document, condemnation of individuals and their books took an extreme turn, and scholars such as Loisy, Tyrell, Buonaiutti, La Piana and Romolo Murri were relieved of their ecclesial positions, had their books placed on the Index and were hounded out of the Church.

Two churchmen escaped that purge, though not without being singed. One was the formidable French historian, Duchesne, whose three-volume *History of the Ancient Church* was placed on the Index only to be immediately translated into English and other languages, and which became a principal source for an authentic interpretation of early-Church history for all serious scholars. The other was the youthful Don Angelo Roncalli (later John XXIII), whose bishop, Giacomo Radini-Tedeschi, and friend, Cardinal Andrea Ferreri of Milan, had come under suspicion.

As pope, John made a point of clearing his good name by personally visiting the Consistorial congregation and examining his own file in that office. There he discovered letters accusing him of favoring the Modernist positions, when as secretary to Bishop Radini-Tedeschi he was teaching in the seminary of Bergamo. There were also copies of the letters sent him by the archconservative integrist Cardinal de Lai in 1914 after that over-zealous prelate, in a chance meeting with Roncalli in the Vatican, had warned him to be careful about his seminary teaching. The young priest had become upset and immediately wrote to the cardinal protesting that his loyalty to the faith and the Church was unimpeachable. John's reply to the cardinal had not been preserved. But he had his notes among his own papers and was able to reconstruct the original.

Actually Cardinal de Lai and his associates were more anxious to get at Bishop Radini than his secretary, as John admits in the biography he wrote of the bishop. It was this unfortunate experience that caused John to come down so hard at the start of Vatican Council II on the side of human liberty and to declare, 'There will be no condemnations!'

In the investigations preliminary to the canonization of Pius X, a goal sought feverishly by the curial successors to the opponents of Modernism, the problem of what to do about the pope's involvement in the heresy hunting, and the vindictive destruction of reputations of sincere and honest individuals, became an issue. Despite the fact that Pius and his cardinal advisors had been fully apprised and supportive of this dire business, the pontiff's virtues as priest, pastor and Church reformer were considered to be his essential characteristics, outweighing whatever faults his zealotry had led him into. He was canonized in 1954 by Pius XII, giving great satisfaction to the integrists in the Church's hierarchy as well as to millions of pious faithful consoled to have a Holy Father declared a saint who was so well beloved by ordinary people.

In the final years of Pius' pontificate, the more melancholy side of his personality prevailed in his talks and sermons, as he felt the heightening of world tensions and the almost inevitable signs of the outbreak of war. He died in May 1914, several weeks before the outbreak of the conflict, leaving the confrontation of that horrendous spectacle to his successor.

BENEDICT XV

The conclave of June 1914 resulted in the election of a small man but of great sagacity and definitely a mind of his own. Giacomo della Chiesa, the Archbishop of Bologna, was a man of the upper classes who had spent long years in the curia and suffered from his opposition to the repressive politics of the cardinal secretary of state, Merry del Val, and his minions. A diplomat of considerable experience and wide culture, he devoted his energies to attempts to prevent the spread of the conflict of World War I and in efforts to bring it to a swift close. For his pains he was mistrusted by both the belligerent parties, and upon the publication of his peace proposals in August 1917 he was accused of favoring one against the other, and caricatured as 'Maledetto' instead of 'Benedetto'. Nevertheless when President Wilson promulgated his '14 points for peace,' there was a considerable correspondence between the two proposals. And when the American president visited Rome, he was the first chief executive of the United States ever to be received by a Supreme Pontiff. In 1910 ex-president Theodore Roosevelt had been refused a papal audience because of his relations with the Methodist church in Rome; and immediately after his election, Benedict xv spoke of the incident to Cardinal Gibbons, deploring the mistaken intransigence that prompted the refusal.

Benedict had hoped the Holy See would be represented at the peace table, but the papacy's participation was prevented by the Italian and French delegations under Giolitti and Briand whose countries were not in agreement with Vatican policies. Nevertheless the pope turned his attention to an immense effort of charity, in an attempt to feed the starving and help rebuild their homes and cities. In his own personal life he was generous to a fault, almost throwing whatever money he had to the impoverished. Even as pope, anyone who approached or wrote to him for help was rewarded with whatever funds he happened to have at hand.

Benedict was a minor aristocrat whose father made him take a degree in law before allowing him to study for the priesthood. He did his seminary work under the Jesuits at the Gregorian University in Rome where he naturally took a special interest in canon law. After ordination he found his way into the College of Nobles to be prepared for the Vatican diplomatic service and on a chance meeting with Cardinal Rampolla he became his protégé. Under Rampolla as nuncio he spent six years in Spain, before returning to Rome, where, eventually, despite the opposition of Merry del Val, he worked his way up to under-secretary in the secretariat of state. His counterpart was Mons. Gasparri, the noted canonist. Both men were turned out of their positions in 1904 under Pius x when Merry del Val became the secretary, Gasparri as a cardinal and della Chiesa, though rumored as the next nuncio to Spain, being relegated to the archbishopric of Bologna. But he was not given the red hat until three months before the death of Pius x and his own elevation to the papacy.

At the close of World War I Benedict had turned his full attention to salvaging the Church's position in devastated areas. He sent Mons. Cerretti as his envoy to the Versailles Peace Conference to negotiate the transfer of the missions in the ex-German colonies. At Versailles Cerretti made friends with the French statesman Aristide Briand and began *pourparlers* for the resumption of diplomatic relations between France and the Holy See. To accelerate matters, Benedict decided to canonize Joan of Arc – burnt at the stake by her English captors as a witch – on 16 May 1920. The French government was officially represented at the ceremonies in St Peter's. And when, for the feast day of St Joan, Cardinal Granito Pignatelli de Belmonte presided as papal legate at the festivities in Orleans, negotiations were begun for an exchange of ambassadors. To round off good relations, Cardinal Gasparri in the Congregation for Extraordinary Affairs was instructed to accept the *'associations cultuelles'* – the French government's arrangement for the holding of ecclesiastical property that had been condemned by Pius x.

In Italy Benedict made a serious effort to solve the Roman Question. While he protested the usurpation of the Papal States, he authorized dependable Catholic politicians to serve in the government, allowing Giorgio Montini, for example, the father of the future pope, to stand for parliament. Asserting his desire not to embarrass the Italian government, he neither aided nor hindered Don Luigi Sturzo, the Sicilian politician priest, in his formation of the *Partito Popolare,* stipulating, however, that it was not to be known as a Catholic organization. When Cardinal Gasparri showed his unhappiness that a priest was at the head of a political party, the pope did not force Sturzo to resign and he showed his regard for the scholar and statesman by giving him a position of trust in the central body of Catholic Action.

In 1916 Benedict had published an Apostolic Letter calling for a *rapprochement* between the Catholic Church and the Christian peoples of the east. With the overthrow of the Tsarist government in October 1917, hope spread through the Vatican that an opening to the east might be possible. Under the Tsars there were some six million Catholics between the Baltic countries and the Ukraine, with seven bishops and 900 priests. But their contact with the Holy See had been strictly limited and their ability to expand or evangelize severely curtailed.

In anticipation of a possible Russian *détente,* Benedict had reconstituted the Congregation for the Eastern Churches in May 1917 and opened a Pontifical Institute for Oriental Studies later that year. When the new communist government took over in Russia and proclaimed its atheistic ideology and the separation of church and state, Benedict sent Mons. Achille Ratti first to Warsaw as Apostolic Visitor, then as nuncio to Poland and Lithuania, and Father Genocchi to the Ukraine. Ratti reached Warsaw and visited the Baltic states, but neither he nor Genocchi could set a foot in Russia. Nevertheless, the new government of Soviet Russia later allowed conversations between Mons. Pizzardo and the Russian envoy Voravsky, which led to a relief mission to Russia from the Holy See.

The pontiff showed himself anxious to establish relations with the new nations emerging from the break-up of the Russian and Austro-Hungarian empires; but he could not hide his dissatisfaction with the British settlement of the Jews in Palestine, fearing this would mean the exclusion of the Christian and Catholic presence in the Holy Land. On the other hand he worked hard to extract the missions in China and the Orient from the political control of the French and other colonial powers, anticipating the revulsion that would come when these peoples achieved their independence. He thus paved the way for the establishment of an indigenous clergy in China under his successor. Nearer home he encouraged the Malines Conference on church unity between Cardinal Mercier and the Anglican spokesman Lord Halifax.

Of greater significance for the Church's internal welfare, Benedict set about disbanding the anti-Modernist heresy hunt. Upon his election, Mons. Benigni had been astute enough to abolish his organization for informing, *Sodalitium Pianum,* at least formally. In his first encyclical Benedict had shrewdly renewed the condemnation of Modernism which he defined as 'a synthesis of all heresies'. He requested Catholics to divorce themselves not only from the errors of the Modernists, but from anything smacking of the spirit of Modernism. Then, asserting the right of the faithful to discuss matters of faith and morals not explicitly defined by the Holy See, he outlawed all recourse to detraction or vilification of persons because of their doctrinal viewpoint or social thinking. In professing the faith of a Catholic, he asserted, there was no need for more or less: 'Faith is either professed wholly or not at all.' He thus quashed the penchant of the integrists.

To the pope's surprise a series of documents seized by the German army in Belgium in 1914 and published in 1921 led to information that the *Sapinière* had been reactivated under Cardinal de Lai's protection in 1915 and had continued surreptitiously in spite of the pope's strictures.

In finally laying the anti-Modernist crusade to rest, Benedict fused the Holy Office and the Inquisition into one curial congregation, with the remark that one such bureau was enough for a whole Catholic Church.

Despite the pope's benevolence during his pontificate, a number of publications were banned by the Holy See and several individuals excommunicated. The most prominent was Ernesto Buonaiutti, excommunicated in 1921. When in 1916 he had queried Cardinal Pamphili regarding his latest anathema, that prelate, taking note of the antipathy between the Holy Office under Merry del Val and the secretary of state, Cardinal Gasparri, sent the ex-priest to the latter. Gasparri suggested an interpretation of the anti-Modernist oath imposed on all priests by Pius x that Buonaiutti could live with, and the two men became firm friends. Despite Buonaiutti's ambiguous position in the Church due to a series of subsequent condemnations, he had weekly meetings with the cardinal to discuss the Church's political problems. Gasparri actually had in mind making Buonaiutti the Vatican's press officer. But the notion died aborning when, after a two weeks' illness, Benedict suddenly found himself in January 1922 on the verge of eternity, his vast projects for the modernization of the Church hardly begun.

The irony of the pope's fate was that he had never been really sick in his whole life. Hence he could not understand how he could not get the better of this illness, the result of a cold he had caught when waiting to say mass for the nuns of St Marta outside St Anne's Chapel in the Vatican. Up to the evening before he died Benedict had refused to believe that God would take him at such short notice, with his work only half done.

PIUS XI

The election in 1922 of Achille Ratti as Pius xi came as a total surprise. He had been a cardinal only a few months; and was all but totally unknown to the non-curial world. The man had been buried in books for the better part of his life as librarian at the Ambrosian Library in Milan and in the Vatican. As information was ferreted out by the press, it was discovered that mountain-climbing was one of his pastimes and that he had spent three years as papal delegate and nuncio to Poland during the momentous months of the Bolshevik takeover in Russia.

His first action was promising. Immediately after his election he gave the blessing *Urbi et Orbi* – to the City and to the World – from the balcony of St Peter's Basilica, the first pope to have appeared openly before the outside world since the sequestration of the Papal States in 1870. The following Sunday, after his coronation, he again appeared on the balcony to bless the crowds, but saying nothing. It was a compromise in which he symbolized his desire to break out of the Vatican and at the same time protesting against the usurpation of papal territory.

Ratti's election had been engineered mainly by Cardinal Pietro Gasparri, Benedict's secretary of state, once Gasparri had realized that his own candidacy and that of his opponent, Cardinal Lafontaine of Florence, were not feasible. Lafontaine represented the intransigent wing of the Church, hearkening back to the rigid stand of Pius IX and Pius X, whereas Gasparri had inherited an opening to the world from Leo XIII and had helped to implement that policy as secretary of state under Benedict. His friendship with Ratti had started at the Ambrosian Library in Milan and was cemented when Ratti served under his tutelage as nuncio in Poland. In part at least, Ratti owed his service in Warsaw to a pleasantry he indulged when introducing the future cardinal, Eugene Tisserant, to Pope Benedict. Tisserant had been a scholar in the Vatican and was recalled to French military service in the intelligence corps, serving in the Near East during World War I. He was in uniform when he met the Holy Father and Ratti said, 'See, your Holiness, I have my own military attaché.' Benedict replied quickly, 'Well, if you have a military attaché you should be in the diplomatic service.'

Five months later Ratti was on his way to Warsaw as apostolic visitor to Poland and Lithuania, with instructions to make contact with the Russian situation, in line with the pope's great hope of bringing about a reconciliation of the Orthodox and Catholic churches once the Tsarist regime was at an end.

Until then, Ratti's career as priest and scholar had been almost without incident. He was the son of a cotton spinner from Desio near Lake Como; but his uncle was an influential parish priest at Pieve di Asso who frequently entertained the Archbishop of Milan, Mons. Nazzari di Calabiana, and other notables. Young Achille Ratti spent most of his youth in the midst of the magnificent hills and valleys of the lake regions of Northern Italy and there developed his penchant for mountain-climbing, a skill that contributed to his taciturn and inpenetrable personality. In the *liceo* one of his instructors was a noted geologist who inspired him with an interest in nature and the physical sciences, to go alongside his talents for mathematics and literature. Together with a vocation for the priesthood he received from his uncle a liberal outlook on life that included a belief in the harmony between true secular knowledge and his faith.

As a young seminarian, Ratti was fully aware of the frightening battle being waged between the two camps for control of the Church's thinking – the Leonine progressives inspired by the heritage of pàdre Antonio Rosmini and his philosophy of radical reform within the Church, and the anti-liberals, who combined the condemnations of the Syllabus of Errors with an intransigent defense of the papacy against the oppression of Italian politicians. They labelled as apostates anyone who favored the secular ideals of society or suggested a more liberal attitude toward the state. It was their belief that the higher the office of the individual tainted with Modernist tendencies, the more heinous his crime. Hence they did not hesitate to point a suspicious finger at, among others, the cardinal of Milan and the Bishop of Bergamo.

During the entirety of his pre-papal career Ratti kept himself severely clear of entanglement with either party. Sent by Archbishop Calabiana to Rome in 1880 to finish his theological studies with a fellow student and later cardinal of Palermo, Lualdi, Ratti and he attended the Academy of St Thomas Aquinas, recently opened by Pope Leo to promote a revival of scholastic philosophy and Thomistic theology. Its prefect was a Jesuit padre, Matteo Liberatore, regarded in Rome as a fierce opponent of the philosophy of Rosmini. He was delighted to have two young Milanese clerics whom he might indoctrinate against the Rosminian thinking prevalent in their diocese. But his influence on Ratti was minimal, for once the latter had returned home he had no intention of serving as spy or inquisitor among his Rosminian friends. After a short stint at teaching homiletics, apologetical theology and Hebrew at the diocesan seminary, Ratti buried himself in learned research into Milanese church history, and was eventually given charge of the famous Ambrosian Library.

Among the more important influences on Ratti as a student and young priest was his early mastery of German. In the final year of his teaching at the seminary, he translated a German study of sacred music and as a lecturer of oratory frequently referred to German books in the bibliographies he gave to his pupils. In the 1890s he served as chaplain to the

German colony in Milan, occasionally lecturing and preaching at the services he conducted. He had also founded an orphanage for girls that was staffed by the Grey Nuns from Breslau.

His ability to speak German led to a visit to Vienna in 1891 that helped to shape his political thinking. He was accompanying Mons. Giacomo Radini-Tedeschi, a former fellow student in Rome, who had been sent by Pope Leo to bring the cardinal's hat to the Viennese archbishop Gruscha and who had asked permission to have Ratti accompany him. In a conversation with the new cardinal about the status of the Church in the Austrian Empire, Ratti exclaimed: 'How fortunate your country is with no anticlerical liberalism and where the state doesn't bind the church with iron fetters.' To which the cardinal replied gravely, 'You are a young man so you have no notion of how much heavier are our chains of gold.'

While Ratti lived a comparatively inconspicuous life in Milan he was on familiar terms with the well-to-do families of the older aristocracy. In the homes of the Gallarati Scotti family, for whose son Duke Tommasso he served as tutor, and in the villas of his mountaineering companion, Count Guido Melzi d'Eril, he was exposed to the interminable conversations about the religious and political problems of the day. Actually he had no patience with the secular cast of mind of most Italian statesmen and politicians before the rise of fascism which prevented them giving priority to the solution of the Roman Question.

He had little sympathy, likewise, for the new Archbishop of Milan, Andrea Ferrari, who had replaced his patron, Archbishop Calabiana, in 1894. During the vacancy of the diocese, the conservative clergy had gained the upper hand and sought to pre-empt any attempt at bringing new blood into the diocesan offices. The new archbishop was only forty-four and sought to win over this group by, among other activities, shutting down the seminary in Villoresi because of the reputation of its professors as advocates of reconciliation with the Italian state. While always deferential to the prelate, Ratti could not conceal his personal dislike. And when the archbishop absented himself from the city during an outbreak of rioting among workers and laborers, to the fury of General Beva who was charged with restoring order, Ratti was persuaded by friends to contact the prelate and have him return to his duties as a pacifier. But the general was so angry at what he considered to be the archbishop's cowardice, that Ratti then had to use all his persuasion to convince the military commander to allow Ferrari to re-enter the city. During these years it was said that the archbishop feared two men – Ratti because of his reticence, and a minor prelate noted for his unrestrained tongue.

Ratti's posting to Warsaw was his first brush with politics in the raw, and it was one of the most difficult assignments imaginable. After more than a hundred years of domination by Germany, Austria and Russia, the three portions of Poland were suddenly thrown together by the Treaty of Versailles at the end of World War I to form a new state. But there were actually three separate cultural and devotional types of Catholicism with three episcopates, to be molded into a cohesive whole while attempting to deal with a newly formed government. Ratti set himself as his first task to master the topography and religious cultures of the new state – a job he accomplished meticulously, as his letters to Mons. Cerretti in the Vatican attest. He had hardly completed this assignment when Marshal Pilsudski's forces overthrew the provisional government and set up a socialist state. Mons. Ratti was appointed papal nuncio to the new government and charged with initiating formal relations between the Holy See and this benevolent dictator, whose primary intention was to institute a land reform that would include a reduction of the extensive Church ownership of properties. Ratti's first task was to persuade the tripartite episcopate, determined to retain its medieval ecclesiastic holdings and privileges, to moderate their claims. Next he had to induce the government to recognize Catholicism as the religion of the people and to agree to deal exclusively with the Holy See in questions relating to the Church. His purpose was twofold: to protect the majority status of the Catholic Church against possible future maneuverings of the Orthodox and Jewish minorities; then to stabilize relations between Poland and the Vatican via a concordat.

Ratti's Polish experiences were decisive in his formation as an ecclesiastical statesman. They were to determine the politique he pursued as pope. For in his contacts with Marshal Pilsudski he had to deal with a dictator who was at once a man of supreme genius (he once told a visitor that he had enough ideas for five Polands but had to be content with the only one he had), and an aristocrat of the old school, devoutly religious, benevolent in his human relations, but ruthless and iron willed. Without forming a party or political organization and living in semi-retirement some twenty miles from Warsaw, the Marshal still ruled the land almost uncontested. His aim was to insulate Poland from Russia by allying Poland with Lithuania, the Ruthenes of White Russia and the Ukraine, while stabilizing relations with Germany. His main opposition came from the Polish nationalist Roman Dmowski, who felt that the Germans were Poland's main potential enemy and demonstrated this contention by a scientific calculation showing that a *Drang nach Osten* would be a fatal mistake. The papal nuncio suddenly found himself caught between the two statesmen but leaning toward Pilsudski's ideas in the hope that the Polish influence would eventually lead to the conversion of Russia to the Catholic communion. He envisaged Pilsudski's armies controlling the three new states of Lithuania, Poland and the Ukraine, thus giving the nuncio an opportunity to create a slavic Catholic Church in each while reinforcing the majority rule of the Latin-rite Catholics in Lithuania.

This was the first time he had an opportunity to put into practice his conviction that the Catholic Church had a direct commission from Christ to predominate in the secular as well as in the religious sphere since it represented the kingdom of Christ on earth, a notion he would assert as pope in his encyclical *Ubi Arcano Dei* (1923) and again in *Quas Primas* (1925). It was a direct throwback to the absolutist claims of Gregory VII and Boniface VIII at the height of the Middle Ages.

Ratti's grandiose scheme for the revival of a slavic Church looked more of a possibility when the Ukraine set itself up as an independent republic in January 1918 with its capital at Kiev, and immediately sent a mission to Rome for recognition by the Holy See. The Ukrainian foreign minister, Livyckyi, even promised Ratti that there would be a return of the Orthodox people to the Catholic Church and that Mons. Szeptyckij could then be transferred from Lvov to Kiev as the new metropolitan archbishop. A similar arrangement was envisaged for White Russia. This politico-religious projection had been the dream of Rome for centuries. But it was to be short-lived. After patching up its internal difficulties, Bolshevik Russia confronted its rebellious western provinces and with a decisive victory at Kiev in the summer of 1920 the Red armies marched into the center of Poland. Ratti remained in Warsaw with the Italian and American ministers, facing the invaders with great courage. What he saw in the raw power of the Red Army was to give him an implacable opposition to communism as the re-embodiment of satanic powers. His intrepidity won him the homage of the Polish people. But it did not spare him from criticism when he served as an arbiter for the elections in Upper Silesia and was accused of showing favoritism to the Germans. On the completion of this assignment his mandate as nuncio was terminated and he was recalled to Rome. Both Pope Benedict and the secretary of state recognized the exceptional talent he had demonstrated in an all but impossible situation, and attributed his final failure to the unexpected victory of the Bolshevik revolution.

In March 1921 Ratti received a telegram appointing him Archbishop of Milan and in May he was called to Rome for the consistory (the official meeting of the cardinals with the pope) to receive the red hat of a cardinal. He took possession of his cathedral in Milan in September, only to discover fundamental changes in the atmosphere of this north Italian metropolis. Strikes and violence resulting from economic and political discontent were the order of the day. And the local authorities seemed incapable of dealing with the situation. Hence a new force was making its presence felt. It was called fascism, from the *fasces,* or bundle of sticks, carried by the Roman consuls as the sign of their authority, and it promised to guarantee order and social justice for all. Its exponent was a former socialist from the Romagna called Benito Mussolini, an orator with great personal appeal, who had set up his headquarters in the Piazza San Sepulcro in Milan, a stone's throw from the peaceful Ambrosian Library.

Cardinal Ratti was surprised to find many of his former friends, men of education, wealth and position, turning to this demagogue whose appeal to the old Roman virtues of courage and renunciation, austerity and patriotic fervor, seemed to have impressed the upper clergy. Though anti-clerical by conviction, Mussolini's call to the antique virtues had great attraction and there were voices of many intelligent people including clerics who felt that Italy was faced with a challenge it could not sidestep – the country would either decline into insignificance, or place its destiny in the hands of a strong man who would lead it to peace and justice. As the new cardinal of Milan weighed these possibilities with their religious ramifications, he was suddenly startled with the news that Pope Benedict was dead. Three weeks later, on February 6, shortly before midday, the world was told that the Catholic

Church had a new supreme pastor. It was the cardinal of Milan, Achille Ratti, and he would be known henceforth as Pope Pius XI.

Ratti's candidature had begun in earnest on the third day of balloting in the conclave after a futile battle between the followers of cardinals Lafontaine and Gasparri. The latter's assurance to the residential cardinals from Italy and the outside world that Ratti would continue Benedict's policies, concentrating his attention on solving the Roman Question, proved decisive.

In a conversation with Ernesto Buonaiutti in 1921 Cardinal Gasparri had stated that there was no longer any insuperable difficulty between the Vatican and the Italian state preventing the settlement of the Roman Question. What was needed was a statesman on the secular side who could carry the negotiations through to a successful end.

After the election of Pius XI a remarkable change of atmosphere was experienced among the black-shirt fascists. On the eve of their march on Rome they were instructed to show great respect for the Church and the clergy, particularly in the nation's capital. Conversely, two papal letters to the Italian bishops on 6 August and 28 October 1922 had urged the prelates to stress national concord in dealing with the faithful.

Fascist papers interpreted these homilies as a gesture towards themselves when Mussolini induced the king to accept his offer to form a new government. A few weeks later Pius XI told an Italian diplomat, 'I see that with Mussolini much can be done.' Between November 1922 and February 1923 the new government ordered the restoration of the crucifixes in the schools, law courts and hospitals, penalties for abuse of the Catholic religion, the clergy and religious, the return of military chaplains to the armed forces, and the resumption of catechetical instruction in the educational system. Meanwhile Mussolini had met Cardinal Gasparri in the home of Senator Santucci in a palace near the fascist headquarters in the Piazza Venezia. In their conversation about the path to a reconciliation, the fascist leader made it clear that for his party to obtain a majority of seats in the parliament, it would be necessary that the *Partito popolare* of the Sicilian priest, Don Luigi Sturzo, should vote with the new government. In turn the cardinal explained that the Holy See hoped to pull out of the political scene and would concentrate its efforts on Catholic Action – a movement strictly religious in its aims and totally under the direction of the hierarchy.

Neither the pope nor his secretary of state had great qualms about abandoning the *Partito popolare* despite the fact that in the elections of 1921 it had won a quarter of the deputies to the parliament. Neither prelate had much sympathy for democracy as a form of government because of the party strife that accompanied, and frequently destroyed, the ability of a democratic party to rule effectively.

The Vatican received its first setback when the Turin Congress of the *Partito popolare* refused the merger with the fascist movement and voted to continue the leadership of Don Sturzo. Mussolini's reaction was instantaneous. Ordering his black shirts to reinstate a mild harassment of the Church and its activities, he let the Vatican know that he was prepared to pass legislation against the Church if Don Sturzo could not be persuaded to step down and dissolve the opposition to fascist rule. On 10 July 1923 the Sicilian priest resigned as president of the *Partito,* and was persuaded to go into exile, first in England then in the United States. In September the leaders of Catholic Action were informed by the pontiff in an audience that they were to avoid politics, social and economic advocacy, and even cultural activities of a compromising nature. They were to cultivate their own personal religious formation.

With the final demise of the *Partito popolare* in 1926, the path was opened for the solution of the quarrel between the Italian state and the Vatican. In a letter to his secretary of state in February 1926 Pius said that negotiations for a concordat and a treaty were possible, and in August preparations were made by both sides for a series of preliminary conversations. Finally, in the Lateran Treaty of 1929, Italy recognized the sovereign status of the Holy See as an international entity and gave the Vatican the sum of 1,750 million lire (the equivalent of $70,000,000 at that time) – a substantial amount of money. Though little in comparison with the value of the property taken from the Church, it was sufficient to relieve the Holy See of financial worries for decades and allowed Pius to organize a vast construction program both in the Vatican itself and on its properties in the city of Rome.

In the concordat that followed, Catholicism was acknowledged as the religion of the land, and the privileges of clergy and churches were restored. Marriage was entrusted to the Church and Catholic education became a normal ecclesiastical right, with the continuation of catechetical instruction in the schools. While these agreements settled the 'Roman Question', giving the pope his sovereign independence, they reduced the Church to dependence on the state for much of its operations – a minimum government stipend for the clergy and the upkeep of the parish churches and, what was worse, political influence in the appointment of bishops – while the church in turn was involved with governmental policies. Pius XI seemed to have completely forgotten the lesson taught him by Cardinal Gruscha in Vienna when he spoke of the weight of 'golden chains'.

The ink was hardly dry on the treaty documents when the fascist dictator challenged the pope with a remark in one of his popular addresses that the Christian religion had been but a poor tribal affair until it was implanted on Roman soil and thus expanded into a universal creed. Two days later, Pius answered him publicly with the assurance that Christ's church was a catholic or universal religion long before it was associated with the Italian peninsula.

Very conscious of his divine prerogative as the Vicar of Christ, Pius had great difficulty in controlling a natural irascibility, particularly as he advanced in age. Early in his pontificate, he found himself depicted as *Pio undecimo sedente* – Pius XI sitting, i.e. in the papal cathedra or see. Rising indignantly, he shouted, *'Not sitting! Standing Upright!'*

In his memoirs the Rumanian minister to the Holy See, Nicola Commine, records an incident following a suggestion he had made to the pope that Pius might try arbitration of the difficulties leading to the violence Mussolini was indulging against Catholic Action. In the course of their conversation, the pope suddenly stood up and began to pound the table.

The rights and prerogatives of which I am the depository [he said] are of a divine nature. They have been entrusted to me as pope, and I cannot depart from them in any way. The essential problem in my disagreement with Mussolini concerns, primarily, the education of youth. On such a question no compromise is possible.

I have been threatened with reprisals and wrecking . . . I am ready for anything. I would even withdraw to a monastery if I am forced. But I will never abandon what I believe to be my mission, never, never, never!

As he spoke the pope grew more and more excited, frequently striking the table with his hand. Suddenly aware of the impression he was creating, he sat down and said, 'But you see, minister, I remain calm.' Then, having caught his breath, he concluded, 'Yes, I can understand if it were merely a question of secular or worldly matters, but not in the spiritual, indeed in the divine sphere.'

Again, in a note he sent to Mons. Eugenio Tosi appointing him his successor as Archbishop of Milan, the new pope had invited him to 'come and see Peter, your old teacher.' This Petrine consciousness prevailed throughout his pontificate. It was quickly realized in the curia that Pius was a tough task-master who brooked no opposition or, what was worse, delay or evasion in carrying out tasks entrusted to collaborators from cardinals to footmen. Having decided to condemn *L'Action Française,* the French political movement, he called for the document prepared under Pius x in 1914 but never promulgated. When told it could not be found, he threatened to sack all the members of the Holy Office. In short order the document was produced. And when the new condemnation was laid on the movement, Cardinal Louis Billot, the well-known theological writer and protector of the French colony in Rome, sent a note of condolence to the leaders. He was summoned to the papal presence a cardinal and left the papal apartments a simple Jesuit.

The key to Ratti's pontifical consciousness is supplied by two of his encyclicals, *Ubi Arcano Dei* of 1923 and *Quas Primas* of 1925. In both of these documents he denied the ability of secular society to bring about the peace and prosperity required for the well-being of the world after the devastation of the First World War. He declared bluntly that it was only the Church that could supply the principles and inspiration required for a just settlement of the social, political and economic problems besetting nations and peoples. In insisting that the Church was herself a 'perfect society' totally independent of all terrestrial considerations, he called for a recognition of Christ as the true sovereign over all peoples. Only if men and nations could be persuaded to accept Christ's laws could peace and justice be restored.

In the pope's mind was the concept of a theocratic society that would establish a true community of all peoples, in contrast to the politically entangled League of Nations from which the papacy had been excluded. In *Quas Primas* he revealed the full extent of his claim. Issued to commemorate the Holy Year of 1925* and to establish the feast of Christ the King, this document announced the theological foundations of papal predominance over the totality of mankind. Ignoring Christ's warning that his disciples should not lord it over their followers, Pius stated that as Christ, the Word incarnate, had redeemed all mankind, he, Pius, possessed a sovereign right to their obedience and loyalty. As the pope was Christ's vicar on earth, this predominance in all spheres of human activity belonged to him by right. Governments and rulers as well as individuals should be submissive to his injunctions.

Ratti's concept of the Church, not unlike that of the fifth-century pope Leo I, stemmed from his literal interpretation of Christ's 'All power is given to me on heaven and on earth. Therefore I say to you, whatever you bind . . . or loose on earth will be bound or loosed in heaven.' Applying this commission directly to his dealings with the secular world, the pope had no hesitation in making deals or using machiavellian tactics to obtain concessions and assure the Church's prerogatives.

It was in pursuit of this kingship of Christ given reality in the institutional Church that he entered into concordatory agreements, some eighteen in all, mainly with totalitarian governments such as Austria, Spain, Italy, Germany and Poland. His concern was directed much more to the privileges of the ecclesiastical institutions than to the personal rights of individuals. His aim was to safeguard the structure of the Church, the teaching of the Catholic religion, its marriage legislation and the security of its clergy, its organizations and finances.

In his dealing with France his adamant stance against *L'Action Française* brought both the hierarchy with its monarchic predilections and the integrist laity to bay. In March 1927 a decree of the Sacred Penitentiary struck priests, seminarians, and laity who continued to read or support *L'Action Française* with severe penalties. This action was prompted by a vilification program in that movement's journal that described the pope's condemnation as an abuse of papal power and por-

---

*The custom of celebrating a Holy Year was started by Boniface VIII in 1300, in imitation of the Jewish year of jubilee every half century. Later popes reduced the interval to twenty-five years.

trayed the Holy Father as the victim of a plot concocted by the papal nuncio Mons. Cerretti, in conjunction with the republican statesman Aristide Briand, the Locarno Treaty and the police, all of whom were intent upon resurrecting the Holy Roman Empire under Franco-Germanic dominance.

One victim of the papal condemnation was the rector of the French seminary in Rome, Père LaFloche of the Holy Spirit fathers. A famous conferencier and spiritual director of, among others, the youthful Marcel Lefebvre – now in rebellion against Vatican Council II – LaFloche opposed the pope's policies in this matter almost openly. Pius sent for his Superior General, a benevolent, bearded, ancient missionary. The pope told him to relieve LaFloche of his position as rector of the college. And when the old man said, 'Yes, Holy Father, I'll see what I can do,' the pontiff grabbed his beard and shouted, 'I did not say, see what you can do. I said fire him.'

In his reaction to the resistance in France to the condemnation of *L'Action Française,* Pius forced the French archbishops and cardinals to abandon their rigid doctrinal and anti-republican policies. The Archbishop of Paris, Cardinal Dubois, had to declare publicly that the Holy See had no prejudice against the French government, thus opening a path to more cordial relations with the political leaders.

Hundreds of incidents are recorded of the imperious ways of this strong-willed pontiff who had no hesitation in employing intimidation or whatever political ploy he deemed appropriate. In dealing with Lord Strickland, the British governor of Malta, who had accused the pontiff of trying to hand the island over to Mussolini while Italianizing the Church there, the pope got so incensed that he decided to destroy the governor despite the fact that Strickland was a devout, practicing Catholic. By having the Archbishop of Malta interdict Strickland's party, excommunicating Catholics who voted for it, the pope brought the governor to his knees. He only relented when Strickland wrote him and the archbishop public letters of apology.

When the Federation of Catholic University Students under the chaplaincy of Mons. Giovanni Battista Montini returned to Rome for a papal audience after suffering physically at the hands of Mussolini's ruffian squads during their annual convention in Macerata, Montini had to inform them that they would not be received by the pope. One of their number had sent a telegram of congratulations to the Italian King Umberto on his anniversary, which the pope considered an insult to his own person.*

Despite the papacy's experience with the total unreliability of the fascist party's promises, the tactic pursued in settling the Roman Question provided a precedent for the Holy See's dealing with the rise of Adolf Hitler's Nazi party. Unmindful of the Church's disastrous dealings with dictators in the course of its long and troubled history, confidence was placed in the rising Austrian demagogue's promise to bring economic and political stability to the German nation and a guarantee of freedom to the Church. Caught in his sacral concept of the papal prerogatives, and despite their personal experience of the perfidy of fascist totalitarian rulers, both the pope and his nuncio in Berlin, Mons. Pacelli, fell for the false promises of the new strong-armed national-socialist movement. As in Italy, they sacrificed a specifically Catholic political organ, the Center party, whose founder Ludwig Windthorst had bested the powerful Iron Chancellor, Otto von Bismarck, in the 1880s.

Windthorst had in fact predicted, however, that the moment a cleric took control of the party, its dissolution would be in sight. In the late 1920s the nuncio encouraged Mons. Ludwig Kaas to accept the Center Party's chairmanship. Then in 1933, in negotiations with Hitler for a German concordat, the Holy See had no hesitation in calling for Kaas's resignation and the disintegration of the party.

Completely taken in by the ease with which the German chancellor agreed to the Church's demands for freedom of worship, the religious education of its youth, ecclesiastical dominance in family and marriage legislation, and respect for Church property, the pope had no difficulty in signing the accord that gave the new government an outward semblance of legitimacy. As in the Italian situation, hardly was the ink dry on the treaty when the Nazi leaders turned their brown-shirt ruffians loose to harass the Church's youth and cultural organizations. During the mid-1930s a vilification program was instituted against convents and monasteries with structured trials of monks and nuns as perverts. A crescendo of protests from courageous bishops and the Holy See had

---

*Because the Piedmontese government had usurped the Papal States, rendering the king *persona non grata* to the Holy See.

lmost no understanding of the Protestant churches and evei
ny for their evangelical endeavors, particularly where the
npetition with Catholic missionary enterprises. He felt tha
conferences of 1921–5 between the Anglicans and Catho
ardinal Mercier were a complete failure. And when effort
o enlist Catholic interest in the inchoate endeavors towarc
cal movement inaugurated by Bishop Soderblum of the
church, Pius forbade Catholics to have anything to do with
nt. In his encyclical *Mortalium animos* of 1928 he poured
he conversations and meetings aimed at Christian reunion,
only by returning to obedience to the Roman pontiff could
sincere effort to restore true Christian unity. In his final
asserted: 'the unity of Christians can be achieved only
turn to the one true Church of Christ of those who are
m it.'

ntion to the internal needs of the Church Pius proved mag-
his material accomplishments, enlarging the Vatican Li-
oviding for its acquisition of invaluable collections of man-
initiating a papal Academy of Sciences to which the
tanding scholars were given membership whatever their re-
fs. He addressed himself to the education of priests and
with his encyclical *Deus scientiarum Dominus* (God, the
ices), demanding an updating of curricula and a careful
the scientific approach to biblical studies, philosophy and
is did not mean, however, a liberalization of theological
during his pontificate Catholic scholars and thinkers of a
received warnings or had their books placed on the Index,
oted secularists such as Giovanni Gentile and Benedetto

ire to promote excellence and efficiency in the Church's
Pius imported a number of his Milanese friends and assis-
a verve to Vatican activities, and he made full use of the
rking out his policies. Despite his tough exterior there was
side to the pontiff's spirituality, and it was exhibited in
to the young nun Thérèse Martin, who had died of con-
a convent in Lisieux at the age of twenty-four, but had so
mpress her zeal on the Church's missionary effort that she
d by the pope as the patroness of missionaries. Pius was

little effect on the powerful totalitarian government, with its racist, anti-semitic policies and its pagan, world-conquering aspirations.

In late 1936 Pius came down with a lingering illness and during his convalescence he seemed to have reconsidered the precarious position in which the Church was placed by a series of disastrous events in the political field. The Italian episcopate had been caught in a compromising situation with the outbreak of Mussolini's Abyssinian war, and the Holy See became involved at its close when it was forced to send Archbishop Castellani, an ex-military chaplain, to that country to supervise religious interests there. A ranking member of the fascist party, the archbishop had used his position to set up an intelligence system for the Italian command – and, later, during the early part of World War II, he was to act as an agent for the fascist government.

With the outbreak of the civil war in Spain, the Church there was ripped in two, with the powerful Cardinal Segura of Toledo defying both the papal policy of support for Franco and the falangist politics of the new government. But what truly troubled the ailing pontiff was the threat posed by the Soviet encirclement of Europe, with the encouragement this offered the republican elements. France already had a Popular Front government oriented toward Moscow out of fear of the expanding German militarism, and although Mussolini and Hitler were giving assistance to Franco's uprising in Spain, there was no guarantee that a falangist victory would not mean another totalitarian power with which the Church would have to contend.

As early as 1931 Pius had denounced the crimes of the fascist state against the Church with his encyclical *Non abbiamo bisogno* (We have no need). Now in March 1937 he published the three most startling documents of his pontificate within a week of each other. On 14 March *Mit brennender Sorge* (With burning concern) condemned the Nazi atrocities against the Church ; on the 19th, *Divini Redemptoris* (Of the divine Redeemer) earned its subtitle 'On atheistic communism' by pronouncing both the political philosophy and the atheistic ideology behind the marxist doctrine as intrinsically evil. Finally, on the 28th, *Nos es muy conocido* (It is well known to us) condemned the religious persecution of the Church in Mexico.

In early 1937 the German bishops under the leadership of Cardinal Faulhaber of Munich had requested the pope to intervene strongly in their perilous situation. Pius instructed that prelate to prepare the précis for an encyclical on the situation and shortly afterwards the pope's document made its appearance. A vehement protest against the violations of the concordat and a condemnation of the government's racist policies, the encyclical did not attack the evil of Nazism as such. Its aim was to assert the rights of the Church much more than to condemn the violation of human rights that was imbedded in the Hitlerian philosophy. The encyclical was brought to Germany clandestinely by an American cleric from the Vatican, Mons. Francis Spellman of Boston.

In contrast to the German document the encyclical on the Russian situation was an outright condemnation of soviet communism as an evil system whose godless policies and ruthless extermination of people could not be tolerated. The contrast between the two types of condemnation led critics to wonder whether it was the pro-German attitude of the pope and his secretary of state, or simply a machiavellian ploy, that had prompted the obvious failure to condemn the Nazi system along with its atrocities.

Earlier in the decade, Pius XI had turned his attention to the socio-political situation and for the fortieth anniversary of Leo's *Rerum novarum,* the encyclical on the working classes, Pius decided to publish a similar consideration but on a much wider scale. Father Oswald Nell-Bruening, the noted Jesuit economist, has recently revealed the details of the document's genesis, at the same time as describing the atmosphere surrounding the papal presence in those days. He had been suddenly summoned to Rome from Germany by the 'black pope',* Father Vladimir Ledochowski, the superior General of the Jesuits, who introduced him to Pius XI. He was instructed by the Holy Father to put together the elements of an encyclical that would be a fitting memorial to Leo XIII's thought, but to take into consideration the great developments in social, economic and political thinking since then. Under obedience to his Superior General and commissioned by the Pope, he set out to create an economic system far beyond his competence. But, as he later confessed, he had no doubts at the time about what he was

*In contrast to the Holy Father, or white pope, the Jesuit Superior General always wears a black cassock and is known as the black pope because of his powerful position in the Church.

doing since it was in obedience [...] When the pope offered him sev[...] pany his economic ideas, Fat[...] working them into the docume[...] harmony with his own ideas.

The papal concept of a corpo[...] of the medieval guilds than it w[...] developments, and the system v[...] cal experts. But it was used by t[...] to Hitler and Mussolini, as a co[...] social systems. It was only much[...] been made of it, that Nell-Bruer[...] document. While under the obed[...] pope and the Jesuit leader he cou[...]

In his imperious concept of hi[...] sympathy for the other Christiar[...] turnees' to the Catholic commun[...] missionary pope who would con[...] Far East, and somehow or othe[...] churches back into union with Ro[...] where he had contact with the o[...] that the enmity between Catholics[...] ter's political allegiances rather th[...] Latin Church, with its monolithic[...] turies to romanize the Orthodox t[...] mally separated by mutual excon[...] 1054, the Orthodox and Roman[...] when the crusaders sacked Consta[...] dom of Constantinople.

In 1922 Mons. Pizzardo had he[...] eign minister, Vorovsky, on a ship[...] which was a papal relief mission t[...] for the Vatican to establish several[...] prising of these endeavors was und[...] suit consecrated in Germany by th[...] to establish a Catholic hierarchy. [...] thorities he was tolerated for som[...] operation was terminated.

Pius ha[...] less symp[...] were in c[...] the Malin[...] lics unde[...] were mad[...] an ecum[...] evangelic[...] the move[...] ridicule [...] insisting [...] there be [...] judgmer[...] through [...] separate[...]

In his [...] nanimo[...] brary ar[...] uscripts[...] world's[...] ligious [...] semina[...] lord of[...] absorp[...] theolo[...] though[...] wide v[...] along [...] Croce[...]

In [...] enterp[...] tants [...] Jesuit[...] a sen[...] his d[...] sump[...] mana[...] was [...]

likewise assiduous in holding public audiences, giving special attention to newly-weds and making a great effort to share confidences with the innumerable people who greeted him in St Peter's.

During the summer of 1938 at Castelgondolfo, Pius began to show signs of weakness. Despite his eighty-one years, however, he would not be persuaded to curtail his schedule of audiences and papal business. On his mind were the obvious preparations of the German war machine and Hitler's encouragement to Mussolini to step up anti-semitism.

In December, the pope took to his bed, but continued to see visitors. Among them was Duke Tommasso Gallarati Scotti, who, in his memoirs, describes an afternoon he spent with the pontiff when Pius, obviously lost in his reveries, reviewed the whole of his life as a panorama of the rise and fall of the nations and governments that had been vainglorious forces in his youth and middle years. In early January 1939 he seemed to rally. Then suddenly, with the tenth anniversary of the signing of the Lateran Treaty and concordat on his mind, he summoned the whole Italian episcopate to assemble in Rome on February 11th, to be at his side as he launched a major address to the nation. Rumors immediately spread that the pontiff was about to break with the fascist state and condemn its leaders.

On the last day of January the pontiff began to prepare two speeches for the occasion. But on February 7th he had a grave set-back. Recognizing that his end was near, the feeble pontiff begged his doctors to keep him alive until the 12th. But fate, or divine providence, determined otherwise. At five in the morning on February 10th – and taking with him the content of those two discourses, which remain a mystery to this day – Pius XI went to meet his Maker, imperturbable to the end.

He received an immortal tribute from his great antagonist Mussolini, who, on hearing of the pope's death, remarked : 'At last that stiff-necked man is dead.' But at least the pontiff had died peacefully, working to the last, whereas the totalitarian dictator was to be executed and end up hanging head-downwards from a tree.

PIUS XII

Few men came to the papacy as well prepared as Eugenio Pacelli. He had been groomed for this office almost from the moment his predecessor was elected or, as some of his critics felt, from birth. In a one-day, three-ballot conclave, he emerged from the Sistine Chapel as Pius XII, obviously determined to carry out the policy of his predecessor amid the maelstrom of martial preparations that was ominously descending on Europe and the Church. Not unlike his predecessor, Pacelli was an enigmatic character, totally self-contained, it appeared, in an aristocratic devotion to his vocation as the ideal churchman. He was ascetic in his personal habits, omniscient in his intellectual aspirations, endowed with the gift of total recall, unswerving in his devotional activities, affable though reticent, thoughtful of subordinates, and eloquent and impenetrable as a personality.

A Roman of the Romans, Pacelli had been privately educated within the shadow of the Vatican. His grandfather Marcantonio had been a Vatican official who did special service for Pio Nono; his father Ernesto served as a counsellor to the Holy See, particularly in financial matters when he headed the Bank of Rome; and his brother Francesco was Cardinal Gasparri's right-hand man in the negotiations with Mussolini that led to the Lateran agreements. Co-opted into the Vatican diplomatic service in 1901 by Cardinal Serafino Vanutelli, despite his desire to serve as a parish priest, Pacelli rose quickly in the secretariat of state to become an invaluable collaborator with Cardinal Gasparri in the codification of the canon law, the preparation of a white paper on the Holy See's relations with France, and as a personal envoy from the pope to Franz Josef, the Austrian Emperor, in 1915.

In 1917 he was dispatched to Munich as papal nuncio to Bavaria. An accomplished linguist and a man of great erudition, the orderliness of the German intellectual atmosphere suited him perfectly and he developed a coterie of clerical advisers, mainly Jesuits, who were to be his closest collaborators in achieving a concordat first with the government of Bavaria (1924), then, five years after his move to Berlin, with Prussia (1929), and finally with Hitler's Nazi Germany in 1933.

The hieratic nature of Pius XI's concept of the papacy was communicated to Pacelli in a very specific fashion. In 1930 Cardinal Gasparri was suddenly relieved of his post as secretary of state and replaced by his protégé, Cardinal Pacelli. The latter was immediately enmeshed in the problems arising from Mussolini's truculent behavior and the harassment by his fascist bullies of Catholic college and university students, the Catholic press and units of Catholic Action.

Pacelli's imperturbability and his incredible capacity for unobtrusively handling detail and recalling precedents made his relations with the Holy Father a great satisfaction for the pontiff whose touchy irascibility struck fear into cardinals as well as statesmen and underlings who had to deal with him – even the Nazi leader Hermann Goering told a friend that in his audience with Pius XI in 1938, he had felt pangs of trepidation for the first time in his life.

On a number of occasions Pius XI had indicated to Mons. Domenico Tardini, his man of confidence, that Cardinal Pacelli would make an ideal pope, going so far as to say that if he were sure the conclave would elect Pacelli as his successor, he would retire. In keeping with these sentiments, in 1934 Pius dispatched the cardinal as his legate to the Eucharistic Congress in Buenos Aires, thus breaking a tradition that had kept the secretary of state close to home for well over a century. The following year Pacelli travelled to Lourdes for the close of a jubilee year celebrating the Redemption. In 1936 at the suggestion of Mons. Francis Spellman, the auxiliary bishop in Boston who had worked for Pacelli in the Vatican, the cardinal made a month's trip to the United States, the high point of which was lunch with President Franklin D. Roosevelt at the family residence in Hyde Park, New York. This meeting had a fruitful sequel for both men in their relations during the Second World War.

In 1937 Pacelli was back in France actually substituting for Pius XI who desired personally to visit Lisieux with its shrine of St Thérèse Martin, whom he had canonized in 1934 and for whom the pope had a special predilection. At the time, France had a Popular Front government supported by the communist party. Despite that fact, Leon Blum, the premier, extended a cordial invitation to the pontiff. But the pope's precarious state of health prevented the voyage and he sent Pacelli instead. The latter had already made a sensational impression in France by his visit to Lourdes where he had protested against 'superstitions of race and blood', obviously aimed at the horrors behind the Nazi pogroms.

The French government, now in grave difficulty with the Germans, made full use of this religious bonanza. They enlisted the country's Catholic intellectuals, such as Maurice Schuman, Mauriac, Bidault and Vladimir d'Ormesson, to cover the visit on radio, cinema and in the press, insisting that the distinguished churchman accept invitations to the Elysée and Quai d'Orsay in Paris. Not one to overlook an opportunity, Pacelli at Lisieux struck out against the 'iniquitous violence' and the 'vile criminal actions' being perpetrated by the leaders of a noble people across the Rhine. Later, at Notre-Dame Cathedral, he lauded the French nation in its ancient title of 'the church's eldest daughter'. His success was highly vaunted in the French press and measures were initiated to begin a *détente* in relations between the Holy See and the French nation. That same year saw him with his secretary, Mons. Gianbattista Montini, in Budapest, again as papal legate to the Eucharistic Congress.

A principal result of these voyages was, as the pope foresaw, Pacelli's contact with the cardinals and bishops not only of the countries he visited but of the whole Catholic world who attended these spectacular meetings. Most of the 57 European and 6 American princes of the church had had official contact with him in his office of secretary of state. Now they got to know him on a personal basis. Hence when they arrived in Rome for the conclave of 1939 there was little doubt in their minds that he was a highly viable candidate.

It was also known, of course, that Pius XI had practically designated him as his successor. But this was not the principal reason for choosing him. The Church needed, above all, a man who had proven himself in the political arena and who was known at the same time as intelligent and holy. Of all the competent diplomats in the cardinalate – Tedeschini, Marmaggi, Pizzardo and Maglione – Pacelli was by far the most accomplished. This estimate was confirmed in a 1946 critical biography by Ernesto Buonaiutti, the Italian Modernist leader, who had no reason to admire Pacelli's policies as curialist and statesman: 'He is undoubtedly one of the most eminent figures of the Roman clergy. His personal piety, his exemplary apostolic zeal, the religious sensibility of his temperament are all qualities that commend him to universal respect.'

Such was the man who emerged from that brief conclave as Pope Pius XII on the evening of 2 March 1939. With his coronation on March 12, the Church had another hieratic figure on the papal throne, who, crowned with the tiara and clothed in a spacious flowing cope with only head and hands exposed, looked the part of a royal oriental ascetic. Standing with his arms outstretched in prayer or petition, this frail, tall figure with an aquiline nose, pale skin and sharp surprised eyes peering out from his spectacles, became a prophetic figure, warning mankind of the catastrophe about to engulf the world.

At his coronation ceremony there were 36 monarchs or ambassadorial missions crowded into the diplomatic tribune facing the main altar in St Peter's. It was to be the last roll-call for the crowned heads of pre-war Europe. In his inaugural sermon the new pope referred to the 'immense evils afflicting their world,' and promised that 'though defenseless but trusting' he would give steadfast witness to the truth – 'not obscured by weakness nor ever departing from charity.'

And for the next nineteen years this was the policy he followed amid the catastrophic destruction of the war, and the immense battle for world hegemony that followed. The phrases he had used were oracular, an anticipation of the style he would employ for the next decade in his series of pre-Christmas sermons calling for peace and idealistic programs for world government, and in his intense diplomatic endeavors, particularly in Italy, Germany, Austria and Spain.

Soon after his election, the new pontiff appealed to Hitler for an international conference. Coming on the heels of a similar proposal by President Roosevelt, the papal suggestion was rebuffed as naive. Nevertheless he instructed his nuncios in Warsaw to suggest a softening of the Polish stand against German demands on Danzig and the Polish corridor, and requested his representative in Berlin, Mons. Orsenigo, to put pressure on Hitler for an easing of the situation.

Meanwhile he had been greatly disturbed by the Molotov-Ribbentrop pact of August 1939 that allowed Russia and Germany to carve up Poland, and he brought all the pressure he could muster to dissuade Mussolini from following the Hitlerian line. On August 24 he made his renewed appeal for peace with the cry: 'everything can be lost by war; nothing is lost by peace.' It was a final, prophetic flourish before the flood-gates came crashing down.

During the war the Vatican was organized like the command post of a general staff. Its intelligence sources were vast and intricate, playing off the regular diplomatic representatives, particularly in Berlin, Vienna, Lisbon, Madrid, Rome itself and Washington, against the clandestine agents of governments in exile, as well as the innumerable ecclesiastics on both sides of the developing conflict who reported to Rome via friends or acquaintances in ministries and nunciatures and through underground operatives in the various resistance movements.

Under the initiative of Mons. Gianbattista Montini, the Pope's man of confidence, a vast network of information regarding prisoners of war, refugees and missing persons was established between the Holy See and the warring nations, with a headquarters in the Vatican and relay stations in Lisbon, Madrid, Mombasa, Geneva, Istanbul, Bangkok, London, Tokyo, Ottawa and Munich. The Vatican in co-operation with the voluntary agencies provided medicine, food and clothing for refugees, deportees, the sick and wounded in Finland, Norway, Greece, France, Belgium, Holland, Ethiopia and Malaya.

Of greater significance was the pope's policy to shelter political refugees, particularly the Jews, within the precincts of monasteries, churches and ecclesiastical institutions, beginning with the Vatican itself, where not only diplomats of the countries inimical to Italy were quartered, but also anti-fascist Italians such as Alcide de Gasperi and Guido Gonella were given sanctuary and work in the Vatican Library. The pope countenanced the efforts of his nuncios and delegates who arranged escape routes for civilians and especially Jews fleeing from the Nazi and fascist pogroms.

While the pope had no illusions about the anti-religious nature of the German and Italian politique, he had developed an absolute phobia against atheistic communism, nourished not only by the repudiation of Soviet ideology in his predecessor's encyclical, but perhaps more so by his own experience in 1918 as nuncio in Munich where he had fearlessly confronted a group of armed communist guerrillas within the premises of the nunciature. By the dramatic force of his ecclesial presence, Pacelli had stared them down. All through his subsequent career he had nightmares that strengthened his conviction of the literally diabolical nature of the communist system, likening it to the dominations and powers of preternatural evil spoken of by St Paul.

In his wartime correspondence with President Roosevelt, Pius XII demonstrated his determination to have the Allied powers isolate Russia. Reacting to the Yalta conference, he censured in unmistakable terms the machiavellian partition of the world between the great powers, and pointed to the failure of settlements in the past based on the distinction between victor and vanquished, the strong and the weak, rather than true justice.

With the advance of the Red armies into the heart of Europe, the pontiff's fears grew stronger and he instructed the American bishops to inform the president and the nation of the incompatability of co-operation between democratic states and Soviet totalitarianism. Nevertheless in his Christmas address of 1947 he insisted that his position between the two opposing forces was exempt from prejudice, from any preference for this or that people, this or that bloc of nations, as it was from any purely temporal considerations.

Pius felt he had a special vocation to oppose the forces of atheism in all its manifestations. After the death of President Roosevelt the Vatican's attitude toward American co-operation with Russia stiffened. At the same time he launched an appeal for the security of Europe against the subversive forces of communism, going even so far in his Christmas message of 1948 as to recall the ancient axiom 'if you desire peace, prepare for war.' In 1956, with the Hungarian rising, he showed the extent of his commitment to a bastion mentality by the message of encouragement he sent to the rebels despite the futility of their situation. And in his attitude toward the cardinals victimized by the Soviet system he had much greater appreciation for the intransigent stand adopted by the Hungarian Cardinal Josef Mindszenty than he did for the Polish Stefan Wyszynski who stood his ground and learned how to negotiate with the communists.

During the war Pius was frequently reminded by the French cardinal Eugene Tisserant that all was not well with the Catholic elements in the conflict, particularly in such areas as Croatia where, under the control of Anton Pavelic at Hitler's behest, the Ustashi government was attempting to force rebaptism into the Catholic Church of well over two million Orthodox Serbs. Some half million of these eastern Orthodox Christians were massacred in this operation. During the trial of Cardinal Louis Stepinac, the Archbishop of Zagreb, whom Pius created a cardinal during his incarceration by the Tito government, charges of Vatican complicity with the Ustashi forces were strongly refuted by the pontiff who also exonerated the Croation episcopate.

The gradual engulfment of the Russian satellite countries in the Soviet empire and the suppression of the Church's activities, particularly in Poland, Hungary, and both the Baltic and the Balkan countries, greatly disturbed the pope and he determined to use every means at his disposal to oppose the communist advances in Western Europe, and, above all, in Italy.

In preparation for the 1948 Italian elections, Pius forced the premier Alcide de Gasperi to rid the government of its communist representatives and persuaded the labor leaders to separate the Christian from the communist trade unions. Utilizing the Institute of Pontifical Assistance, which reached down into every parish and ecclesiastical institution in Italy with food and clothing supplied mainly by US (Catholic) War Relief Services with the aid of the American government and the British Catholic Committee for Refugees Abroad (CCRA), the pope played a decisive part in swinging this crucial election in favor of the Christian Democratic Party.

Then in 1952, under the threat of a socialist-communist takeover of the city of Rome, the pope again entered directly into the fracas, encouraging the leader of Catholic Action, Luigi Gedda, to prepare a list of candidates for the municipal offices that would embrace the extreme rightist parties including the neo-fascists. Intransigently opposed to this strategy, Alcide de Gasperi was totally discomfited by the papal interference, particularly when the Jesuit demagogue, Father Ricardo Lombardi, attempted to recruit his wife as a supporter of the papal plan.

Saved from a political disaster by a technical rather than a political occurrence, de Gasperi became *persona non grata* to the pontiff. On the occasion of the anniversary of his wedding, and of his daughter's taking the veil as a nun, the pope refused to grant him a papal audience, even though he was still the prime minister.

Despite the Church's setback in eastern Europe, the end of the war saw Pius XI hailed as the inspired moral prophet of victory, and he became the object of visits from the great figures of the contemporary world. During the German occupation of Rome, he had frequently received hundreds of soldiers in his public audiences in St Peter's. Once the Allied forces took control, there was no end to the thousands upon thousands of first military and then civilian visitors who came to Rome explicitly to see the pope.

In his speech at the consistory of 1946, in which he created thirty-two cardinals, Pius called attention to the crucial part played by the

Church in salvaging the values of civilization so directly threatened by the war. Then with the millions of pilgrims who flocked to Rome for the Holy Year of 1950, he felt fully justified in the political policies he had followed as secretary of state, vindicating the concordats he signed with Austria and Germany in 1933, and then, as pope, with Salazar's Portugal in 1940, providing justification for the treaties he was to sign with Franco's Spain in 1953 and Trujillo's Dominican Republic in 1954.

The Holy See quickly became involved in the 'economic miracle' that characterized the Italian scene in the mid-1950s. The boom in land and building speculation of which Rome was the center was financed in part by Vatican capital through the papal bank – *Istituto per le opere de religione,* which Pius had established in 1942 to accommodate the needs of the religious congregations in their international operations – and through the ecclesiastical organizations and companies in which the Holy See had a large share. Inevitably a number of scandals and excesses involving prelates, priests and religious orders were exposed in the press. But their impact was minimal when compared to the triumphal experiences of the Holy Father in his contact with every type of enterprise from the sport world and circuses to political and scholarly organizations. He regularly received medical and juridical congresses, businesses and industrial associations who held their international meetings in Rome and who were treated to a dissertation on the ethical significance of their activities. At the same time, the great and notorious figures of the world of entertainment, films, the aristocracy, politics and religion had no trouble in being received in private by the Holy Father. To the pope's interior conviction of his spiritual primacy as heir to Peter was added a temporal exaltation as a dominating figure in the world's hegemony.

A primary result of this triumphalism was the pope's conviction that the Church was experiencing a period of incredible growth and spiritual development, the result of its deprivation and suffering during its struggles with totalitarianism and the ravages of war. In pursuit of its destiny to be the conscience of the world against the menace of communism, similar to the function of the papacy in the Middle Ages against the Moslem menace, and of the Catholic community of Europe against the ravages of secularism after the Reformation, the Holy See felt the need of presenting the Church as a bastion of truth, rectitude and spiritual consistency.

As we have seen, Pope Pius XI had been ruthless in suffocating movements for reform in the Church's social, liturgical and ecumenical practices during the pre-war period. With his encyclical *Quanta cura* in 1928, he had poured ridicule on the early stirrings of the non-Catholic efforts toward Christian unity, forbidding Catholics to participate in any of their activities. While he accepted a modest reordering of the Church's thinking about marital love, he condemned unmercifully the attempt to legitimize birth control as a solution for family and demographic problems. His encyclical *Casti conubii* of 1931 was a direct reply, instigated by the English Catholic hierarchy, to the mild pro-birth-control decisions of the Lambeth Conference of the Anglican church.

In the early days of his pontificate Pius XII had shown interest in the liturgical and theological stirrings of the inter-war years. In 1943, on the fiftieth anniversary of Leo XIII's encyclical on the Sacred Scriptures, Pius published his *Divino afflante Spirito* (Under the inspiration of the Spirit), a document that gave considerable encouragement to the biblical scholars intent upon using modern methods of research in their exegetical activities. The pope granted that the time and place of composition of the sacred texts, and the character and literary style of the inspired authors, had to be taken into consideration, using modern means of philosophical and historical research, to obtain an authentic understanding of the text. It was an idea repudiated by most of his curial subordinates who considered the word of God as anchored in the Vulgate Latin version of St Jerome as an absolute depository of divine truth, and that needed deep faith and constant meditation rather than the mechanisms of secular research to reveal its true meaning. The papal document was considered as giving the *coup de grâce* to the anti-Modernist repression and opened new hope for theologians intent on using biblical sources for their explorations of the word of God.

That same year the pontiff published his encyclical *Mystici corporis* (Mystical body), taking note of the advances in theological thinking about the nature of the Church particularly by German scholars intent on stressing the spiritual aspects of the institution as revealed in Christ's mysterious similes of the mustard seed and the light of the world, and

St Paul's insistence that it was the Body of Christ. The pope's encyclical accepted these notions. Eventually he followed them with his acknowledgement of the progress made in liturgical renewal, particularly in France and Germany, with his encyclical *Mediator Dei* of 1947. In consequence of this document, Pius gradually introduced modifications in the strict rules of fasting before receiving the Eucharist, legitimated evening masses for the convenience of the faithful, and revised the Easter liturgies. He also authorized the revision of the Latin translation of the psalter for use in the recitation of the monastic hours of the breviary. While comparatively minor, these modifications of century-old practices proved to be a signpost to his own theological thinking, and more significantly, to the determination of Pope John to call his Council into being. In the early 1950s Pius had played with the idea of a council and had had preliminary studies made; but he quailed before the complexity and the discouraging cautions of his immediate advisers.

While the pope had a coterie of scholars at his beck and call, particularly among the Jesuits, and used many of them to research his theological projects, he felt himself competent to make innovations on the Church's way of thinking. In one of his earliest addresses he had discussed the nature of man, stressing the spiritual quality of the soul but admitting that little was known about the anthropological aspects of human nature. Later, in his encyclical *Humani generis* of 1950, he returned to this topic and while acknowledging the validity of evolution as an hypothesis, cautioned against theories that would question the immediate creation by God of the human soul.

Confronted by the problems of human responsibility highlighted by the war, and the need to assert the absolute right of the human conscience, he investigated the problem of tolerance, particularly in the religious sphere, and maintained that authentic Catholic teaching required a respect for the beliefs of other religious convictions on the supposition that their proponents were in good faith.

And in his evaluation of political authority he showed an openness toward democratic forms of government that was far in advance of his predecessors. Considering the medieval theory of Gregory VII or Boniface VIII – that, as all authority came from God, it had to be given to the temporal ruler through the instrumentality of God's vicar, the pope – Pius said such a notion was a normal conclusion drawn from the political ideology of the times. Now it was obviously outmoded.

Pius addressed himself in a particular fashion to the problems of medical ethics, renewing Pius xi's prohibition of artificial means of birth control. But he legitimized rhythm or the use of the infertile period to control the size of one's family. And while he prohibited artificial insemination he made room for organ transplants, the search for new knowledge in the science of genetics, painless birth, and took a cautious but hopeful attitude toward psychoanalysis.

The post-war years, particularly in Germany and France, had produced a host of new theologians who sought to renew Catholic thinking by a return to the scriptures and the early fathers of the Church, and thus to confront the great problem of unbelief and the questioning of the criteria of human behavior infecting the contemporary generation. But the support these Catholic thinkers gave to the worker-priest movement, liturgical experimentation and an attempt to obtain a more effective approach to the notion of the supernatural as an answer to the secularization of society, were looked upon with great alarm by the men in the Vatican. Even before the war, solid scholars such as Jacques Maritain, Maurice Blondel and Emmanuel Mounier had been considered somewhat less than orthodox in their political and philosophical thinking. Now their disciples, particularly among the Jesuits and Dominicans in France – Henri de Lubac, Jean Danielou, Yves Congar and M. D. Chenu – were advocating a return to the theological notions of the early Church fathers and biblical sources, as they discussed 'true and false reform' of the Church and 'a theology of the laity'. De Lubac's treatise on the 'supernatural' caused particular concern in Rome.

With the publication of *Humani generis* in 1950 the rug was suddenly pulled out from under these new theologians. In France seminary professors lost their teaching assignments and provincial superiors were removed from their positions of authority. And a wave of warnings went out from the Holy Office cautioning bishops and the superiors of religious orders, to keep a strict eye on what was being taught in the seminaries and written for popular consumption of the faithful.

In fact the encyclical itself was a fairly well-balanced document with a paternal spirit. It contained no condemnation, though it warned against heretical tendencies and outlawed doctrinal explanations that would deny original sin, or give too great a consideration to modern positivism in theological research. At the same time it authorized Catholic scholars to utilize all the latest advances in scientific methods of research to deal with such difficult problems in theology as relativism

in the expression of revealed truths; the use of non-scholastic philosophies in the discussion of doctrinal principles; polygenism (or the plur-
alistic origin of men); evolution; the significance of the supernatural
order; the real presence of Christ in the Eucharist; existentialism; mysticism; and the objective value of religious teaching.

But it soon became evident that behind the encyclical was a deeper
substratum of papal thought. In one passage of the document an apparent leap ahead in doctrinal development was acknowledged. The pope
asserted: 'Theology, even when positive, cannot be equated with a
purely historical science, since God has given his church, together with
these sacred sources (scripture and tradition) a living teacher to illustrate
and develop these truths that are contained only obscurely and as it were
by implication in the store-house of the faith.'

While apparently innocuous in its obvious meaning that the pope,
and preachers more generally, had the right to search out the scriptures
for the application of Christ's teaching to particular circumstances in
the course of history, what Pius was after was a justification for his use
of the prerogative of infallibility that had been defined at Vatican Council I in 1870. He had in mind being the first pope to use that power
intentionally by defining the dogma of the Assumption of the Blessed
Virgin Mary into heaven – a doctrine without biblical roots that appeared only in the fifth century.

And this he did with his solemn declaration on 1 November 1950.
While there was no objection to the doctrine itself, there was a considerable disturbance among northern theologians. They saw this definition as a further usurpation of papal power in favor of teachings that
could only encourage the sentimental and exaggerated piety of Marian
and other devotions being used as a palliative for Catholics unwilling or
unable to face the sterner requirements of their religion.

This need on the pontiff's part to enmesh himself in the supernatural
aspects of the Catholic faith went hand-in-hand with claims he made of
mystical experiences, such as a vision of the miracle of Fatima while
walking in the Vatican gardens, and an experience of the agony of
Christ during one of his periods of sickness.

The nineteen-year pontificate of Pius XII proved to be a momentous
experience for the Church. It proved that the institution could survive a

worldwide war that had involved Catholics on both sides and, what was even more important, the frequent interference of the Holy See in the things that were properly Caesar's. Taking up his predecessor's program for heading off the outbreak of the world conflict, Pius had attempted almost frantically to bring the inimical powers together, and failing in his desire to be the preserver of peace, he stepped up his diplomatic contacts in order to bring strong pressures to bear on both sides of the contest. He welcomed emissaries of President Roosevelt bent on peace missions and, with the outbreak of war, received Mr Myron Taylor as the special envoy of the president to the Holy See.

Meanwhile Pius had alerted his nuncios and delegates in all the capitals of the world to keep in close contact with the diplomatic representatives of all sides and to use their position to aid refugees and care for the victims of the conflict. His man in Turkey was Angelo Roncalli, an old hand in the Vatican service who was on excellent terms with the German ambassador, Franz von Papen, and who used his position to extricate hundreds of Jewish families and persuaded the British to suspend their blockade of Greece to alleviate the starvation of that nation.

In his struggle to maintain the Church's neutrality, Pius was under unbearable pressure from all sides. His own counsellor, Cardinal Tisserant, disagreed with his failure to pronounce an outright condemnation of the outrages committed in the Nazi occupation of the Low Countries. And he had to discipline Cardinal Innitzer of Vienna who had to all practical purposes welcomed Hitler's *Anschluss* in Austria.

His policy in regard to the extermination of the Jews has been the object of bitter controversy since shortly after the war's end. All that can be said of the issue is that, faced with the circumstances in which his condemnation by name might have been a provocation to greater savagery, as he was advised by several Jewish leaders, he did the most prudent thing he could think of. *Ex post facto* criticism may be aimed at his judgment but not his lack of compassion or failure in courage. When Rome was bombed Pius rushed to the area to console the people whose homes were destroyed before complaining publicly of the violation of Rome's designation as an open city – a status it claimed not in virtue of the pope's person, but as the Eternal City, a symbol of Western civilization. In his cautions and appeals to the political leaders, particularly during the Nazi domination of Italy, he let it be known that he had no fear of being taken a prisoner or of having the Vatican invaded.

It would not be the first time that the Eternal City and St Peter's itself had been pillaged by barbarians.

In the final days of his pontificate Pius XII seemed to be incessantly in the public eye. He made innumerable speeches – prounouncements on every subject conceivable – and received thousands of pilgrims and visitors almost daily both in the Vatican and in the papal summer villa at Castelgondolfo. Despite his advanced age and several illnesses, the octogenarian pope continued to grapple with the world's problems and the troubles afflicting the Church. Caught in between the two great power blocs, he could not fully appreciate the growing significance of the new forces represented by the Third World, though he had encouraged new missionary methods in Africa and Asia, authorized the formation of a network of episcopal conferences in Latin America, and in 1946 created a native bishop, Thomas Tienchensin, as the first Chinese cardinal.

On 3 October 1958 the first news of the pope's illness was released from Castelgondolfo. Eight days later the pontiff was no more, having died peaceably in his sleep. There was a bizarre and undignified postscript to this pontificate. In the hands of an incompetent papal physician, actually an eye doctor of the pope's own choosing, a new and unsuccessful method of embalming was employed. The man whose hallmark had been majesty was reduced to a dishonored corpse. So ended a pontifical reign that had reached unprecedented heights of popular acclaim and political influence.

The Pacellian Church would be characterized at the Council to follow as an unfortunate display of 'Triumphalism, juridicism and clericalism'. Whatever its true evaluation, it marked the end of an epoch in which the Church had at least begun to literally fulfill its original commission to 'preach the gospel to every creature.'

The man who was next to pick up the reins of pontifical rule would be haunted by that command, and in his attempt to carry it out to the letter, he would bring about a revolution. However the pontificate of the Pacelli pope was to be evaluated, it has to be acknowledged that, without him, John's achievement would have been unthinkable.

4

John and the Johannine Revolution

Anyone with the good fortune to be standing in the piazza fronting St Peter's basilica in Rome, at eight a.m. on 11 October 1962 was treated to a pageant of dazzling splendor. Suddenly the bronze doors of the papal palace were thrown open. Out poured a torrent of light. Then, led by a phalanx of papal guards, row upon row of bishops in pontifical garb marched across the sun-bathed piazza, wheeled right, and disappeared into the great basilica.

Bringing up the rear of this august procession was a brace of ermine-caped courtiers and red-soutaned clerics, then the oriental patriarchs in their festooned finery, and finally the cardinals. Climaxing this splendor was Pope John, seated on the *sedia gestatoria* and looking small, uncomfortable, almost scared, until he suddenly reacted to the hurrahs of the immense crowd – perhaps fifty to sixty thousand people who filled the piazza and trailed down the Via Conciliazione. As Pope John wheeled to the right and was carried up the steps leading into the great basilica of St Peter's, an old man's tears trickled down his face. He had lived to fulfil his dream. Vatican Council II had begun.

In the decade and a half since that resounding event, the Catholic Church has been turned upside down. John had summoned the world's 2,500 bishops to Rome to modernize the Church. *Aggiornamento* – updating – was the innocuous-sounding word he used to camouflage the fact that he was calling for a revolution. In his great opening discourse, he set out a vast vision of ecclesial renewal that was meant not merely to reduce the Church to the simple form it had when it left the hands of

Christ, its founder (as John defined that *aggiornamento*). It was intended to be a challenge to the world that would reach the consciousness, and thence the consciences, of all mankind.

John had invited observers from the other Christian churches to attend this assembly in order to emphasize the fact that Christian unity was a primary objective of the Council. Committed Christians were sick and tired of the scandal caused by the bickerings and animosities indulged by the followers of Jesus Christ whose essential command had been: 'You shall love your neighbor as yourself.' By his neighbor John meant all of mankind, believer and unbeliever, friend and enemy alike.

The ground rules of preconciliar Catholicism called for total loyalty not only to the divinity in the person of Jesus Christ, but to the Church in the person of the pope. There were of course educated Catholics who were unhappy over papal policies; and within the Vatican there were prelates who condemned the pope's attitudes and decisions, and criticized his personal foibles. But for the vast majority of clergy and faithful the pope represented, unquestionably, a Holy Father. He was to be loved and venerated as the visible representative of Jesus Christ himself. The mystique that accomplished this almost universal admiration within the Church had not been manufactured purposefully. It had been greatly encouraged by the political situation in which the popes of the nineteenth century had been deprived of their possession of the Papal States and had made themselves 'prisoners' of the Vatican. This circumstance, along with the fact that in almost every part of the world Catholics felt themselves under attack, made the faithful look to Rome for a heroic figure under whose protective auspices they could rally. And Rome obliged – with the image of Pio Nono, living out his long pontificate deprived of his territorial heritage; Leo XIII, as an intellectual genius; Pius X, as a saintly, peasant pontiff; Benedict XV, as a princely mannered prelate, a voice crying out in the wilderness for peace; Pius XI, as an intrepid religious strongman; and Pius XII as an omniscient, spiritual aristocrat to whose audiences in St Peter's or at Castelgondolfo all the world flocked.

With the election of John XXIII this ecclesial image-making suddenly disintegrated. This pope was a extraordinary human being whose personality would tolerate no subterfuge. Quickly, the centuries-old panoply of Vatican pageantry began to come apart. In the context of John's spontaneous expansiveness, the cortège of brocaded nobles surrounding the papal presence at audiences and public ceremonies were recognized as faded if not comic hangovers from the Middle Ages. The ermine and the vermillion costumes were shabby; the antiquated swords and maces were useless; and the display of semi-oriental splendor was theatrical rather than religious. It certainly had nothing to do with the spiritual values of which the papacy was the protagonist.

Strangely enough Pope John actually liked this pageantry. Despite the fact that he seemed fearful each time he was raised on the *sedia gestatoria* he rather enjoyed the extravaganza represented by the papal cortège. Consequently he did nothing to abolish it. But he recognized it for exactly what it was; and knew that it had outlived its usefulness.

Journalists and historians question whether John knew that an ecumenical council held at a time of great social change would result in the chaotic situation that faces the Catholic Church and the papacy today. If he did not, he was certainly told in graphic terms by his shrewd, almost omniscient, secretary of state, Cardinal Domenico Tardini.

In the course of his opening discourse, John referred to the cardinals and other counsellors who saw him frequently as 'prophets of doom'. 'They pay no attention to history, the great teacher of mankind,' was the way he finally dismissed them. But he also laid down a crucial principle that in the Council the debate would be totally open and free. 'There will be no condemnations,' was his order. And despite the fact that many of the men serving him in the administrative offices of the Vatican openly opposed his policies and teamed up against him with conservative cardinals and bishops from outside, he pushed on with his plans for a thorough reformation of the Church 'in head and members'.

The genius of Pope John will only be fully appreciated when the Catholic Church accepts the fact that, in calling for an *aggiornamento,* he was really setting the stage for a total reorientation of the Church in keeping with the cosmological revolution between Copernicus and Einstein ; and the noetic revolution between Kant, Heidegger and Teilhard de Chardin. For in that transformation in human awareness, the Church's self-image was completely changed. From an institution, it became once more an 'assembly of the people of God'.

What John actually desired was a reformation of the Church, in the sense of bringing it back to its essential function as the presence of Jesus Christ in the world. This, he realized, was an all but impossible demand, given the complications that weighed down not merely the Holy See, but the worldwide Church – from the intricacies of canon law and the burdens of the Church's vast possessions to the rubrics for the sacraments. Yet inside the peasant priest, turned polished prelate and eventually beloved pontiff, there was a comprehension of the metaphysical changes separating his world of today from the remote age in which the Church had been founded, and a full consciousness of the many mutations, both good and bad, to which it had been subjected down the centuries.

Insisting that history is the great teacher John had opened Vatican Council II with the observation that the Church 'no longer needed to confront the world with severity'. Without repudiating the past, he said that the time had come for a re-evaluation of the Church's inner structure and a consequent updating in its dealings with mankind. This attitude of honest analysis prevailed during the subsequent four years of the conciliar discussions, despite the opposition of most of the Vatican officials attempting to curb the debates and dilute the Council's achievements.

John's knowledge of history was wide and embracive rather than technical and meticulous. He had authored a history of charity in the diocese of Bergamo as a young priest, and wrote a biography of his bishop, Giacomo Radini-Tedeschi, in justification of that innovative prelate's involvement in the Church's social problems at the turn of the twentieth century. He had likewise devoted his leisure time as apostolic delegate in Bulgaria, Greece and Turkey to editing a five-volume history of the results of the Council of Trent in Milan during the late sixteenth century. But fundamentally he was drawing on his own personal experiences when he insisted that history should be the great teacher.

Ordained a priest in 1905, John was appointed secretary to Bishop Radini-Tedeschi of Bergamo and became involved as more than an observer in the momentous events troubling the Church not merely in the north of Italy but all over Europe and the New World immediately before World War I.

In the early 1920s he supervised the revitalization of the Society for the Propagation of the Faith and thus obtained an inside view of the Church's great missionary enterprises in Africa and the Far East. Finally, as the papal nuncio in France immediately after World War II he built up an embracive understanding of world affairs as he held off the vengeful attempt of Catholic resistance leaders to expel thirty-three French bishops from their sees as collaborators with the Petain regime. In the end only three of the accused had to retire.

When elected pope in 1958, John XXIII appeared as a kindly, not very effective pontiff, selected as a stop-gap pope to allow the Church a cooling-off period after the whirlwind activities of his predecessor, Pius XII. To the world's surprise, he quickly revealed that he had an intimate knowledge of secular as well as ecclesial affairs, and that he meant to pursue a strictly pastoral approach to people in their difficulties while striving to renew inspiration in the Church's vast structures.

John had lived through the severe days of Roman repressive action in the early 1900s when a group of over-zealous curial prelates and theologians in Rome, with the concealed but positive approbation of Pope Pius X attempted to ferret out churchmen whom they suspected of the heresey of Modernism – the desire to have the Church adapt its teachings to the findings of modern knowledge and science. Several prelates as well as priests of his acquaintance had come under a cloud of suspicion along with many of his friends from his seminary years – and to his amazement he himself had been reported to Rome as a possible Modernist. This experience with a clique of narrow-minded clerics who had induced a reign of terror in the Church was one of John's reasons for insisting that the Council refrain totally from condemnations.

John had been on the wrong track as far as Vatican diplomatic advancement was concerned from 1925 to 1945, when he occupied posts in Turkey, Greece and Bulgaria. Here he had spent much of this time in absorbing Church history, and in feeding the starving and aiding refugees during the worst days of World War II.

While John, in keeping with his education, was essentially of a conservative bent of mind, and preferred to accept the essential truths of the faith in the traditional sense given them by the popes and councils of the past, he knew that their application to the world of today, and more particularly, tomorrow, required a total turning of the Church either upside-down or inside-out. This he called for with Vatican Council II. Those who say he had no notion of the mischief he was letting loose in the Church as well as the world have simply no notion of the depth of wisdom and understanding possessed by this octogenarian pontiff.

Those who search his *Journal of a Soul** for the paradigms of his

---

*This was Pope John's spiritual diary, in which he recorded his intimate thoughts throughout his life. It was published in 1965, after John's death, by his secretary Mons. Capovila, and became a bestseller even in English.

anarchic approach to much of the Church's tradition are looking in the wrong place. His whole program is outlined clearly and unmistakably in the short speech he gave upon accepting the burden of the papacy and announcing that he would be called John XXIII.

A minor but significant bit of evidence as to his ability to make far-reaching decisions was contained in that speech with his immediate settlement of the historical dilemma contained in the name John XXIII. There had been a fourteenth-century pope named John XXIII in the person of Baldassari Coussa; and historians were not certain that, even though he had been forced out of the papacy as an impostor, he might not have been an authentic pontiff. John settled the matter without blinking an eye: 'There have been twenty-two authentic popes called John', he announced, 'I will be the twenty-third.'

Behind that surety of judgment stood the genius of a peasant's mentality that had nothing to do with a lack of culture, finesse or nobility. What it recalls is the great humaneness harnessed in Virgil's *Georgics* in which, as a schoolboy, John recognized the genuineness of his family's status as peasant farmers. It was with this depth of wisdom that John was endowed as he trudged his way, several miles each day, to the local schoolmaster in Sotto il Monte, then to the parish priest for the elements of Latin and on to the nearby hamlet school, and eventually to Rome. What he received along with the elements of the Latin heritage and language was a touch of the Roman genius for poetry and humane letters that molded his inner consciousness and that one heard when listening to him as pope in St Peter's reading a sonorous Latin discourse at mass. There was something very human about the way he loved to roll those Ciceronian phrases with the full gusto of a resonant voice. Even more moving was hearing him booming out the *'Unam, sanctam, catholicam et apostolicam ecclesiam'* of the Creed, when one could feel him in his true glory.

It was in these apparently superficial adherences to the Church's Latin tradition that John betrayed a total at-homeness with the Church of the past. And in an incredible fashion, though he loved it so much that way, he also saw that its structures and even its theological expressions were completely inadequate to the task Christ had set before it – to preach the Gospel to every creature. This vision, turned into a conviction, was behind his calling of the Council – and also his neglect of all the other inadequacies in the Church, from the need for basic reform of the curia to his shortsighted appointment of the friends of his youth as cardinals, who immediately betrayed his trust by opposing his Council.

While John recognized this betrayal and regretted it, he was convinced that the only hope for the Church lay in a frank confrontation between the two principal forces operating within Catholicism – the traditionalists, verging on intransigency and desirous of preserving the Church's doctrines and prerogatives undisturbed by the maelstrom of change circulating about them, and the reformers clamoring for renewal. Hence he had decided on a council, allowing full freedom to all factions within the ecclesiastical continuum, convinced that, in the end, the will of God would manifest itself.

It must be recognized at once that the old guard among the cardinals, bishops and theologians were sincere and not lacking in clairvoyance in their resistance to the very idea of a council. In their efforts to block movements for radical reform, these ecclesiastics saw clearly that, once a change of any proportion was admitted in any major sector of the Church's teaching or government, there would be no way of controlling a break away from tradition in almost every sphere.

Men like Cardinal Spellman in New York, McIntyre in Los Angeles, Gilroy in Australia and Godfrey in London were astounded at the very idea of modernizing the Church. They felt it had reached a pinnacle of success. Their churches were flourishing ; their schools, from primary to college to university level, were inadequate for the numbers clamoring for entrance. Vocations to the priesthood and the convents never had been more plentiful; and the number of adult converts to Catholicism was astounding. In the mission fields their people were working wonders; and the aid and development programs sponsored by the US Catholic Relief Services, International Caritas, and the German Adveniat and Misereor programs, had the full support of their respective people and governments. While the Church behind the Iron and Bamboo Curtains was gravely persecuted, it was nevertheless giving witness to the strength of Christian principles. Hence the notion of a council with its threat of change to the Church's thinking or *modus operandi* struck them as exceedingly dangerous. Their fears were justified.

In the postconciliar world, there is hardly a teaching or law in the Church that has not been challenged. From a monolith, considered by the outside world as antiquated but powerful, clear-cut in its doctrinal and moral teachings and intolerably self-centered, the Roman Catholic

Church today gives the appearance of a monument cracking at the seams. It is manifesting many of the symptoms of an identity crisis. The authority of its pope and bishops is questioned from within. The relevance of its teachings regarding man in his relation to eternity is challenged on all sides. The very need for a Church at all is disputed by well-instructed Catholics who, a decade ago, would no more have thought of opposing a papal directive than they would have considered committing tyrannicide.

In calling for a council, John could rely upon the majority of cardinals and bishops from northern Europe – Frings and Doepfner among the Germans, Suenens and Alfrink from the Low Countries, Feltin and Liénart in France; but he had little support from the hierarchies of the English-speaking world. Nor could he trust the majority of the Italian and Spanish prelates. Within his own curia he was opposed by the friends of his youth, the men he had appointed cardinals, from Cento and Ciriaci to Giobbe and Confalonieri, only to have them turn against his policies. Under the iron-fisted control of his cardinal secretary of state, Domenico Tardini, together with the curial prefects of regulatory congregations or bureaus such as Alfredo Ottaviani in the Holy Office, Giuseppe Pizzardo in the Congregation for seminaries and universities, Clemente Micara as vicar for the diocese of Rome, they set out to prevent or at least emasculate the Council. They were able to control the so-called antipreparatory documents, overloading the agenda with some seventy-seven areas of discussion, and appointing their own theologians and canonists to the innumerable commissions set up to prepare and control the doings of the Council. They created an obstacle course, blocking all possibility of reform. Both the men and the documents associated with the Council's preparation represented the hard-line old school of ecclesiastical thinking.

John, of course, recognized the truth behind Tardini's original warning that a council would thoroughly upset the Church, and he appreciated the unwillingness of the older generation of cardinals and prelates to go along with anything as revolutionary as a full-scale assembly of the Church's bishops. They had been avoiding this suggestion for decades and in particular had headed off Pius XII's thoughts in that direction in the early 1950s.

John's selection of Cardinal Tardini as his secretary of state had been a shrewd political move, reassuring the conservative cardinals that he would follow a policy in keeping with their desires. Tardini was certainly the best qualified of the curialists, with a wide knowledge of the Church's political affairs and a hard-nosed judge of men and their motives. Short, stocky, with a quick Roman wit, he had been one of Pius XII's faithful retainers throughout his pontificate. In his previous relations with Pope John as Angelo Roncalli, though the latter was an archbishop and Tardini only a monsignor, John had come under his control in the diplomatic service. When John was called to Rome from Turkey in December 1944 he reported to Tardini's office with the remark: 'There must be some mistake, I'm supposed to go to Paris!' To which the Roman cleric replied, not without a touch of malice, 'Yes, there's been a mistake; but I did not make it. It's the man upstairs', meaning Pope Pius XII. It is reliably reported that when John became pope, he jostled Tardini with the remark, 'Well, monsignor, it's evident that another mistake has been made, and again not by you, but by somebody upstairs.'

As preparations for the Council progressed John had a series of run-ins with his secretary of state. Documents labored over by the pope with his private secretary, Mons. Loris Capovilla, would be severely criticized by the cardinal. John would change them, only to have Capovilla insist, each evening, that he restore the original text which the two men had worked and prayed over so assiduously. The next morning John would have to face Tardini with the original version of the document, and the cardinal would threaten to resign. 'There will be no resignations,' was John's invariable reply.

The cardinal's sudden death in late July 1960 was looked upon as providential. His removal from the scene allowed the preparations for the Council to bound ahead and John began to call to Rome prelates, eminent scholars and theologians who had been excluded by the curial clique preparing the agenda under Tardini's care. These *periti*, or experts, included the Jesuit theologians of Innsbruck, Karl and Hugo Rahner, the French Dominicans Yves Congar and Marie D. Chenu, the Jesuits Jean Daniélou and Henri du Lubac, and the American John Courtney Murray.

Shortly before John's election, a plan on the part of the cardinals and university professors in the curia had been proposed to get control of the teaching and staffs of the theological faculties in the Eternal City. Under the direction of the Lateran University and its exuberant rector, Mons. Antonio Piolanti, were to be brought the Jesuit-conducted Gregorian University, the Dominican Angelicum, the Appolinare and the Propaganda, together with the Biblical Institute and the Academy of Nobles. Unbeknownst to Pope John, an attack was launched against the Jesuit biblical scholars conducting the Biblical Institute in the December 1960 edition of *Divinitas,* a journal emanating from the Lateran University. This attack was to be followed at once by an intervention of the Holy Office that would condemn the writings of several professors at the Biblical Institute as well as a number of individual German and French theologians.

The plan misfired when an Italian bishop asked Pope John about the affair. When John read the article, he gave vent to one of his infrequent bursts of anger, and personally assured the rector of the Biblicum of his fullest confidence in the Institute's orthodoxy. This was followed by a public letter from Cardinal Pizzardo, as prefect of the Congregation of Seminaries and Universities, to the Jesuit Cardinal Bea assuring him that Pizzardo had no previous knowledge of the offending article – an outright and humiliating dissimulation, since such an attack could never have been launched by a member of the curia without his clearance.

Despite John's interference, agitation on the part of Mons. Piolanti, the Rector Magnificus of the Lateran University continued, in an attempt to have the Holy Office censor two Jesuit professors at the Biblicum, Max Zerwick and Stanislas Lyonnet, despite the assurance by the Jesuit Superior General that their teachings were orthodox. John seemed unable to get control of these machinations, nor did he take measures to penalize the curialists and professors who were openly opposing the idea of a Council. The matter was only settled the following year, when Pope Paul gave a severe public rebuke to Mons. Piolanti and his cohorts.

Another Jesuit who had the misfortune not to fare well under Pope John was Father Lombardi, whose global campaign, Better World, had had the full backing of Pope Pius XII. While cardinal of Venice John had been advised by that pontiff to make a retreat at Lombardi's center outside Rome. John obediently packed his bag and reported to the retreat master; but after listening to two conferences he quietly returned to Rome. When, in preparation for the Council, Lombardi published a

tract with mild suggestions for the reform of the papal household and
the restructuring of the curia, his book was censored on the first page of
L'Osservatore Romano and he was instructed to confine his activities to
his Better World.

By way of distracting John from the full prosecution of his plans for
the Council, Cardinal Tardini had suggested that the pope's first move
should be to hold a synod for the diocese of Rome whose spiritual and
pastoral situation was at a low ebb. Unconscious of the fact that John
had just completed a synod in Venice – he was actually correcting
proofs of its *acta,* or results, on the train that brought him to Rome for
the conclave that elected him pope – Tardini was surprised to find John
taking up his suggestion with glee. Quickly assembling large groups of
parish priests, pastorally oriented professors and experts in the social
sciences, John set them to a round of in-depth research and investigations regarding every aspect of Rome's parochial and diocesan life,
from care for the poor, immigrants and the homeless to census-taking
and the construction of new churches and parishes. The result of this
enterprise was a document of 755 articles, produced only a year later,
containing exhortatory regulations for living the Christian life in the
vast archdiocese of Rome. John's enthusiasm was expressed in a series
of sermons he delivered in the sessions of the Synod from 24 to 31
January 1960, in which he made it clear that he wanted the synodal *acta*
to serve as a vade-mecum for both clergy and laity.

The pope's pre-emptory ways in conducting the Synod were severely
criticized by both progressives and conservatives as constituting a 'rub-
ber stamp' assembly. And several professors of canon law made bold
to tell the pontiff outright that the synodal articles were exhortations and
not law. To which they received the reply: 'They may not be law in
your book, but they are in mine. And I'm the pope!' The pope was
highly pleased with the results of this exercise despite the fact that it
had little effect on the parochial life of the diocese, for it proved con-
clusively that, with good organization and determination, he would be
able to manage as unwieldly an organization as the Council. Besides,
in canon 35 of the Synod he corrected a long-standing, grave injustice.
Personally dictated by Pope John, article 35 changed the Church's attitude toward priests who had deserted their calling and refused to repent.
In the past, the pope admitted, these men were treated with total dis-

dain. Designated as *vitandi,* they were to be avoided by their former friends and, through provisions in the concordat with Italy, they were discriminated against in the civil law. Describing these individuals as *sacerdotes infelices* (unfortunate priests), the Holy Father decreed that henceforth they were to be treated with the greatest consideration. Even those who continued in their defection were worthy of the Church's great charity and should be given spiritual and even temporal assistance. According to Father Grosso in a semi-official commentary in *la Civilta cattolica,* the pope had to supervise the text on its way through the press in order to prevent its alteration.

What is unfathomable in John's decision to hold the Council is the depth of his knowledge about the inner life of the Church and his conviction that it was in need of a revolutionary shake-up from within. For his theology was of the traditional Italian stamp, with its precise definitions and reasoned elucidation of everything from the inner nature of the Trinity to the outer reaches of the sacramental system. His own spiritual formation was strictly conservative, as revealed by the jottings in his Diary or Journal and in his daily meditations, the way he said his prayers in private and public. He was devout in his celebration of the mass, recited the Divine Office faithfully, said his rosary, and spent an hour in spiritual meditation every day of his life – as a young priest, Vatican diplomat and as pope.

As pope, John saw innumerable people in private and public audiences, made countless decisions concerning the Church's daily life, from the appointment of bishops to the granting of indulgences, and sauntered out into the streets of Rome and the surrounding countryside to demonstrate the genuineness of his faith and his love for people. Nothing in his actions indicated that within him a turmoil was building up. Nevertheless anyone who paid close attention to the new pope's speech in accepting election to the papal office should have been forewarned.

Asked if he accepted the election, he said he did. Then asked what name he would take, he said, 'I will be called John!' That name itself was a shock, for no pope had taken that name for over four hundred years.

Reaching into his pocket, the newly elected pope took out his glasses and a crumpled piece of paper, and immediately gave a justification for the name, saying it was his father's, the name of the church of his baptism, and that he wanted to be for the Church a new John the Baptist, straightening out the path of the Lord.

John's action indicated clearly that he had recognized at least the night before the fact that the election would fall on him. He had evidently given deep thought to what his election at the age of seventy-seven would mean. And while the world immediately concluded that he was to be a transitional pope, allowing the Church to disengage from the high-powered political drive given it by Pius XII, John felt impelled to impress upon the Church a new imprint that would be at once more spiritual and more practical. Though by no means the intellectual equal of Pius XII, nor his peer in theological information or political experience, John had a competence all his own. And the new direction he gave the Church was precisely in the theological and political spheres. The great difference between the situations facing the two men lay in the fact that Pius had opened up most of the grave problems facing the Church midway through the twentieth century with his plan of supplying specific answers on his own. Thus Pius had made pronouncements about the use of scientific discoveries and philological methods in explaining the sacred scriptures; attempted to control, while also justifying, new methods in the pursuit of theological questions; and supplied precise answers for moral problems, from the use of the pill to control ovulation to the legitimacy of organ transplants and the employment of atomic weapons. John felt no such competence. And he believed it was not his function as pope to supply such information. It was the business of the Church; and it was his obligation as the supreme pastor to bring the Church's wisdom into play.

John recognized that the Church was one hundred and fifty years behind the times in confronting many of these problems. So that once he announced his determination to hold the Council he let nothing interfere with the time-scale he set for its opening. Numerous attempts were made by his collaborators, particularly Cardinals Tardini, Ottaviani and the Irish Dominican, Michael Browne, to slow him down. But it was said in Rome that each such suggestion that he put off the opening was met with a bringing forward of John's timetable.

One thing on the pope's mind was, of course, his age; the other was quite probably his inkling of the fatal disease that was to carry him off.

But his major concern seems to have been the long time-span since the Church universal had attempted to come to grips with the real world. In his opening discourse at the Council John made it clear that he felt history was on his side.

The theology that had become dominant with the sixteenth-century Council of Trent, its siege mentality and its legalistic solutions to the Church's problems, had lost its usefulness with the French Revolution. That political and spiritual explosion had thoroughly upset the Church in Europe. But with the destruction of the Napoleonic hegemony in 1814, the Church had the opportunity of totally reordering its structure and interior life. Its identity with the Papal States had been destroyed and its dependence on political support proven unnecessary by the clandestine election of Pope Pius VII on the island of St George in Venice at a moment when the world was convinced that the papacy was finished. These events were to affect one man's thinking, first as the nuncio in France immediately after World War II and again as the patriarch of Venice in the mid-1950s. Their impact came to fruition on the fatal morning when, as Pope John, Angelo Roncalli awoke with the words of Christ ringing in his ears: 'Go out into the whole world and preach my Gospel to every individual.' In his terrible concern over the fact that nineteen centuries later the Church was not achieving that goal, John suddenly heard the word 'Council' ringing in his ears. He took the experience as a sign from the Spirit.

In laying out his fundamental rules for the politique of the Council, John foresaw a rhythmical sequence of debates and maneuverings that characterize a political assembly such as a parliament; and the Council was nothing if not a conglomerate of parties and convictions, of persuasive speeches and artful manipulations, of power plays and dialectical joustings.

In setting out the parameters of this debate, John startled his immediate collaborators in the Vatican by announcing that the Roman curia was one thing, the Council another; that the former would continue their administrative functions while the Council would create its own structure. But this was a rule he broke immediately, to his own sorrow and the great hampering of the Council's liberty.

Fortunately, the curia's hold on the Council was overwhelmed at the very start of its first session when the German cardinal of Cologne Joseph Frings and the French cardinal of Lille, Achille Liénart rose and objected to the list of names presented by the curia to serve as members of the Council's committees and thus control the construction of the documents that would contain the Council's achievement. They objected that the curial candidates were for the most part handpicked conservatives who did not represent the mind of the majority of bishops. To the astonishment of the whole gathering, their objection was sustained by a majority vote. That unexpected rebellion served as a symbol against the Roman curia's control, enabling John's other directives to be introduced and sustained. For the working commissions, though numbering curial members, were now peopled and guided for the most part by the residential cardinals and bishops from outside Rome who accepted John's challenge for the *aggiornamento* of the Church.

John's final directive proved an almost fatal shock. Saying that the Council would not discuss the main tenets of the faith because 'They are well known and have been sufficiently explained down through the ages', he went on: 'The Truths of the faith are one thing. How they are explained is another.'

This statement was immediately challenged as heresy by cardinals and curial theologians. But it was accepted by the majority of the Council fathers and became the touchstone of the liberty that was to characterize the majority of the conciliar debates and decisions. Where John's successor, Pope Paul VI derogated from its application, allowing himself to be intimidated into withdrawing from the Council's consideration certain matters thought too delicate for open debate – for example, priestly celibacy and contraceptive methods – he lived to regret it. Meanwhile, John had set the Council to debate the liturgy, i.e. the way the Church said its prayers, under the mistaken impression that this would be the easiest of all the matters requiring updating. To his amazement, an ancient axiom, *'lex orandi, lex credendi'* (the law of prayer is the law of belief) suddenly took possession of the conciliar debate, and proved one of the toughest issues to resolve. But with that debate, the Council was on its way to confronting the Church's contemporary needs in a realistic fashion.

In his one major interference with the Council's activities, John rescued the discussion on divine revelation from being choked off by the conservative minority, confining the agenda for this debate to a joint commission under the arch-conservative curial cardinal Ottaviani and the liberated Jesuit cardinal Agostino Bea. John likewise backed the latter's herculean efforts to promote the ecumenical efforts for unity that was an important item on the Council's agenda.

Two months before his death, John had the satisfaction of receiving the Balsan Peace Prize, by the good grace of the Russian leader Krushchev who controlled a crucial vote. Of peasant origin despite the total difference of their religious convictions, the two men felt they had much in common in a down-to-earth approach to the problems of world peace. The formal ceremony of the Peace Prize reception brought John to the Quirinal, the old papal palace now the residence of Italy's president. It was to be the ailing pontiff's last public appearance. But it was a magnificent demonstration of his success in bringing to the Church a positive instance of worldly appreciation.

It is impossible at this date to do justice to the feeling of frustration suffered by the curial group – the cardinals and prelates who conducted the Church's business at the top, controlling the thinking on doctrinal and disciplinary matters, cautioning the Holy Father in his relations with statesmen and political movements, and keeping a tight hold on the Church's educational instructions and the world-wide appointments of bishops, papal representatives and nuncios – since the arrival of Pope John on the scene in late 1958; and more particularly, in the interval between the end of the first session of the Council in December 1962 and his passing, the following June.

For all practical purposes John had given his approval to an opening-to-the-left in the political order, compounding an open-handed approach to the communists in Italy, France and Eastern Europe by welcoming the hard-hitting editor of *Isvestia* to a private audience. John's enemies in the curia immediately blamed the gains of the Italian communist party in the April 1963 election on John's 'stupidity'. Cardinal Ottaviani in one of his speeches condemned those who had 'shaken hands with hands stained with blood', an unmistakable reference to the papal action.

With his spring 1963 encyclical *Pacem in Terris* (Peace on Earth), the pope had compounded this horror when he made a distinction between communism as an atheistic creed, and as a political, social and economic theory that one had to contend with in the historical order

– another blatant heresy in the minds of his opponents, not merely among the curia and in Italy, but all over the capitalist world.

Meanwhile, in the political order, John set in motion a new set of guidelines that greatly affected the Church's relations with contemporary states. With *Pacem in Terris,* published in the spring of 1963, the octogenarian pontiff cut through an argument about man's rights that had muddied the ecclesiastical approach to human liberty for close to a thousand years. John based man's inviolable worth on human dignity. In the Christian perspective, he maintained that as man was created in God's image and likeness, he was entrusted with an essential freedom that had to be respected by both Church and state. He found the same right justified in the purely secular order on severely philosophical or rational principles.

In each instance, John combined man's right to freedom with his entitlement to live in peace for the pursuit of truth, justice and love. The pope thus abolished the old presupposition, entertained by many Catholic theologians and philosophers, that the Church's primary objective was to safeguard the law of God.

On this latter premise the axiom 'error has no rights' had been pursued to the lengths of the Inquisition in the Middle Ages, and in outbreaks of heresy-hunting right down to modern times. In tossing out the axiom, John asserted that even though an individual was in error, he still retained the right to the inviolability of his person; and that while the error should be condemned, the person in error had to be respected.

In regard to the state, its main function was to acknowledge, protect, and facilitate the exercise of the rights of man. In turn, the Church was obliged to assert the fact that man's freedom signified his immunity from coercion by individuals, social groups or any human power. This was to be done in such a way that in political and religious matters no one could be forced to act in a manner contrary to his beliefs.

A corollary of this freedom was its extension to cases of conscientious objection, a matter on which many churchmen in the European tradition had been slow to move, because the right to refuse military service seemed to undercut the obligation to self-defense and to contradict the emphasis placed upon the virtue of patriotism. Of even more pertinence, of course, was the absolute condemnation of every type of discrimination based on race, color, nationality or religion, which proceeds from acknowledgment of the inviolable dignity of man's person.

This teaching arises from the principle that, in the final analysis, each individual must obey his conscience. And while he should form his conscience according to the rules of right reason and, for the Christian at least, the inspiration of the Gospel, he must not be coerced against his conscience so long as he is in good faith and does not injure the rights of others.

This teaching was not new in the church. But Pope John gave it a new relevance. In the political order he applied it to the solution of a problem gravely threatening the welfare of large groups of Christians as well as the peace of the world. Reaching out toward the communist nations whose ideology and political activities had been gravely condemned by the papacy (particularly in the 1937 encyclical letter of Pius XI 'On atheistic Communism,' and again in a decree of the Holy Office in 1949 which forbade all collaboration with communists), John sought a way of accommodating the fundamental Christian commandment, 'you shall love your neighbor – and this includes your enemy – as yourself' to the current political situation. He thus arrived at the distinction between a political ideology that had to be condemned because of its atheistic presuppositions, and a political system connected with that ideology which, in the historical order, was actually striving for peace and justice. John concluded that while the error had to be condemned, the government could be recognized and dealt with in the hope of arriving at a *modus vivendi* which allowed religious and eventually civic freedom for its citizens.

In preparation for the opening of the Council, John had engaged in direct dealings with the non-Catholic churches – Anglicans, Episcopalians, Methodists, Evangelicals, Calvinists, Baptists, Waldensians – using the octogenarian Cardinal Bea's Jesuit charm and wisdom as a *Bahnbrecker* in approaching the various churches and inviting them to send official observers to his Council. He had also dispatched secret emissaries to Moscow to discuss the possibility of having the Russian patriarch somehow represented at the Council. In all these moves he was knowingly and willingly contradicting the policy of Pope Pius XI who in his 1928 encyclical, *Mortalium Animos,* had condemned the then-inchoate ecumenical movement as exposing Catholics to the notion that these churches were acceptable depositories of the Christian faith. John had also inadvertently given the Moscow patriarch a political advantage over the pan-Orthodox patriarch, Athenagoras, in Istanbul, with whom the pope had established the closest personal ties. When Athenagoras out of delicacy hesitated to encourage the autocephalous Greek and Orthodox churches to send representatives to Rome, the Russians jumped in and made the first move. Without consulting Athenagoras they sent observers to the Council, thus apparently capturing leadership among the other Orthodox churches who were not represented until the second session.

Finally, John seemed to have turned an unseeing eye on the spate of books and articles by advanced theologians pouring from the presses – books by Hans Küng, Yves Congar, Xavier Rynne – that were highly critical of the curia and the conservative positions at the Council. They had been banned by Vatican action from sale in the bookstores of Rome.

In the opinion of his enemies, John seemed to have lost the sense of his own lofty dignity by accepting the Balzan Peace Prize and showing himself honestly in favor of the call for freedom within the Church – particularly the outlandish demands of the Dutch and other north European Catholics. In the minds of the curia, this Johannine extravagance had to be stopped and the Council either postponed or reoriented in Tridentine – strictly legalistic, ordered and controlled – fashion, thus enabling the curial faction to regain total hegemony over the reins of government within the Church.

At the beginning of June 1963, their worries suddenly ended. On June 3rd, recognizing that, at long last, he had got the Church turned in the direction of the twenty-first century, John XXIII peacefully shuffled off into eternity, mourned by the whole world.

5

Montini

Pope John's final agony had been followed by thousands of people crowded into St Peter's Square and by millions more with ears glued to radios and television sets all over the world. In the days before he lapsed into a coma, John had bid farewell to the members of his official household – the curial cardinals led by the dean, Eugene Tisserant, and their aides, then to his intimate assistants, his secretary, Mons. Loris Capovilla, his priest nephew, and the nuns from Bergamo who cared for his personal needs. He assured one and all that he would see them in eternity. Then lapsing into his prayers, he slowly drifted off into the embrace of death. At the moment of his passing, Cardinal Traglia, John's vicar in charge of the diocese of Rome, had just completed a public, televised mass for the dying pontiff on a platform fronting the great piazza of St Peter's. In the press, John's passing was reported as a 'Death in the Family of Mankind'.

Never before in the course of the Church's history had so much attention been paid to the passing of a pontiff. His demise brought telegrams of condolence from John Kennedy in Washington and Nikita Krushchev in Moscow; from the Orthodox patriarch Athenagoras in Istanbul and from the World Council of Church's Visser t'hooft in Geneva; from Buddhist monks in Korea and from the King of Basutoland. For John had not merely opened windows in the Vatican. He had actually turned the Catholic Church inside out for all the world to see its great strengths and weaknesses, to be spectators at the vast struggle within.

With the pope's death the vast machinery of the Church's control at the top had come to an immediate halt. Having officially ascertained

that John was dead, the cardinal *camerlengo,** the 84-year-old Benedetto Masella, put into motion plans for the deceased pontiff's obsequies. The pope's signet ring, the sign and seal of his office as successor
to Peter the Fisherman, was broken in two, and his living quarters were
promptly sealed off, awaiting the disposal of his successor. Under the
careful supervision of the dead pope's secretary, Mons. Capovilla, a
death-mask of the face and one hand of the pontiff was made by the
artist Manzu, and the body was handed over to the papal mortician for
embalming.

The next morning, a meeting of all the cardinals then present in Rome
was presided over by the camerlengo and the three ranking cardinals,
Tisserant for the rank of bishops, Tappouni for the presbyters, and Ottaviani for the cardinal deacons. Notification was sent to the eighty-four
cardinals in all parts of the world that they were to assemble in the
Pauline chapel in the Vatican on Wednesday morning, June 17, for the
mass *pro eligendo pontifice* (for the election of a pontiff) and be prepared to enter the conclave that evening. Specific instructions were
issued in keeping with immemorial custom as to the color of the cassocks and vestments they were to wear, and the rules governing their
personal needs, including the introduction of an aide or conclavist into
the precincts of the conclave.

Meanwhile the camerlengo and his aides had made proper disposi-
tions for the reception of the diplomatic corps and dignitaries coming
for John's funeral. Each morning during the nine days' formal mourning for the deceased pontiff the body of cardinals in Rome met in full
assembly and no decisions regarding the Church's daily routine or the
coming conclave were taken without their approval.

As the whole world paused in respectful awe, prelates, diplomats and
the faithful poured into Rome to pay a final tribute to the man who had
impressed the world as a father figure for mankind.

John's funeral was conducted in keeping with the ancient ritual for
the burial of a Roman pontiff. He was entombed in a vault close to the
shrine beneath St Peter's basilica where tradition said Peter had been
buried.

Electioneering on the part of cardinals before or after the death of a
pope is strictly forbidden by Church law. Nevertheless, the need for

*The cardinal appointed by the pope as chamberlain to take control of the Holy See as caretaker
and head of the college of cardinals between the death of one pope and the election of his successor.

discussion and consultation among the men responsible for providing the Church with a new Holy Father is inevitable. A papal interregnum – *sede vacante* – has always been a time of intense political action, exchange of opinions and above all, rumor-making among clerics, diplomats, journalists, and the purveyors of opinion inside and outside the Church.

Strict rules control the secrecy under which both the cardinals and the officials of a conclave operate. Entering the Vatican after arrival in Rome for the conclave, the individual cardinals are immediately put under oath to observe the proprieties of the election including the law of secrecy. The purpose of this procedure is to prevent interference of any type – political, ecclesial, or family pressures – that might curtail the complete freedom of the electors in choosing the new pope. Disastrous experience down the ages with royal families, political partisans, governments and pressure groups of all kinds, and internal deals among the electors – shades of simony, the taint of nepotism – have dictated the most severe precautions.

As the cardinals from the outside world descended on the Roman scene – Tatsuo Doi from Tokyo, Gilroy from Australia, Gracias from Bombay, Landazuri Ricketts from Peru, Silva Henriquez from Chile, Rugambwa from Africa, Spellman from New York, Feltin from Paris, Frings from Cologne, Wyszynski from Poland – the rhythm of political activity among the thousand and one people who one way or other fit into the ecclesiastical pattern of Roman life reached a high pitch.

Rumors regarding the eligibility of individual candidates flowed freely in the bars and dining rooms of fashionable restaurants and the attractive trattoria in the vicinity of the Vatican. In the headquarters and colleges of the religious orders – Jesuits, Franciscans, Benedictines, Dominicans, Oblates of Mary Immaculate, Redemptorists – and the elegant precincts of the embassies accredited to the Holy See, in the homes of influential businessmen and the palaces of the black Roman aristocracy,* there were gatherings of purple-clad prelates, monsignori with minor assignments in Vatican offices, canon lawyers from the Roman rota (the supreme ecclesiastical court), well-informed foreign journalists and minor diplomats, all busily discussing the prospects of the candidates.

---

*The families of previous popes who, given princely titles by the popes and having served in the Church (i.e. wore black), became known as the black Roman aristocracy.

'The time is ripe for a non-Italian . . .' 'Montini's chances are excellent . . .' 'Suenens will surely have a hand in selecting the next pontiff
. . .' 'Antoniutti looks good to me . . .' 'It will be a dark horse, Lercaro
or Roberti . . .' were among the clichés bandied about in salons and
ecclesial refectories, at cocktail parties, and in the intimate recesses of
Vatican households.

Among the journalists checking in from Jakarta and Sydney, from
Capetown and Montevideo, pools were being formed and odds laid.
Among the Italians Montini of Milan had the inner track; but Lercaro
of Bologna and Cicognani of the curia were not being overlooked.

Meanwhile on June 7th in the diocese of Milan the cardinal archbishop, Giovanni Battista Montini, preached a eulogy for the dead pontiff in which he said decisively that the deceased Holy Father's heritage
would not be buried with him in the tomb. Boldly acknowledging the
challenge for the Church occasioned by John's call for an *aggiornamento,* the cardinal of Milan said that the next pontificate would continue the program initiated by John. It would have to pursue the work
of the Council.

In the intricate Italian of a polished funeral oration, Montini said: 'If
we glance at the tomb now closed forever, we can speak of his heritage
which the tomb cannot enclose; of the spirit he has breathed into our
epoch that death cannot snuff out. And we are no more obliged to describe his past, but to look to the future that is born from him . . .'

To the Vatican, with ears and eyes wide open for the least hint of
electioneering, these words had a bold and significant meaning. Montini
was definitely in the running for the office of the papacy. There were
positive rumors that Pope John had actually said he wanted the cardinal
of Milan to succeed him.

Great significance was given to Montini's declaration in the outside
world as well. It was looked upon as an acknowledgement of the open
secret that the cardinal of Milan was Pope John's selection as the man
who could best carry out his revolutionary vision for the updating of the
Church. Though on more than one occasion, John was reported as having asked visitors from the north, jokingly, 'And how is your Hamlet
archbishop?', the portly pontiff had actually shown great preference
for Montini's support and advice. He was the only non-curial cardinal
to whom the pope had given a suite in the Vatican during the first session of the Council. And it was said that John had advised him to refrain

from actual participation in the debates so as to preserve his image of objectivity.

Montini had spoke only twice: once in the beginning and again just before the Council's close. But his latter intervention had been decisive. He had seconded the proposal of Cardinal Suenens that the coming session of the Council focus on two main areas: the Church *ad intra,* as it saw itself from within, and *ad extra,* in its relation with the outside world. Meanwhile, Montini had been writing weekly reports back to the Milan diocesan paper that were highly critical of the conservative curial group and its effort to hamper the Council's activities.

On this background alone, Montini's candidacy was a surety. It was further buttressed by the fact that he was the one cardinal with pastoral experience as head of a large archdiocese who could handle the intricate problems posed by the Vatican's administrative bureau, the curia, who made no bones about their determination to scuttle John's Council. Montini had been a member of that body from 1923 to 1954, serving as a confidential figure to Pope Pius XII for well over a decade. That experience had given him an intimate knowledge of the Church's power structure and the men who controlled it. But it had also earned him the implacable dislike of a number of powerful enemies.

Opposition to Montini's candidacy was strong and well organized. Its roots went back two decades when at the end of 1954 under severe pressure from the so-called *pentagono* – the five powerful cardinals of the curia (Mimmi, Pizzardo, Ottaviani, Micara and Canali) – Pius XII had promoted Montini to the see of Milan, thus removing him from the Vatican; but the pope had failed to give him the cardinal's hat associated with that ancient see for over a millennium. He had thus effectively prevented Montini's candidacy for the papacy in the election that brought Angelo Roncalli to the throne in 1958.

It was Pope John who created Montini his first cardinal shortly after his election. A close relationship had existed between the two men, going all the way back to the early 1920s when they met as junior Vatican officials newly arrived in Rome – John as Angelo Roncalli, in charge of collecting funds for the Propagation of the Faith, and Montini in the secretariat of state.

Their paths had crossed frequently thereafter when Roncalli was on the lower rungs of Vatican diplomacy in Bulgaria, Greece and Turkey, reporting into the offices supervised by Montini. They had become much closer when John as the papal nuncio in Paris after World War II felt he had a special friend in high places who understood his efforts to reorganize the French hierarchy, involve the Vatican in UNESCO, and salvage the worker-priest movement. Montini was one of the Italian cardinals called to Rome to visit John on his sick-bed shortly before the pontiff's demise – a fact not unobserved by the press and Vatican officialdom.

Most of the incoming cardinals had Roman connections. They had acquaintances among Vatican officials from their seminary or university days in Rome; among the so-called Roman nobility or ambassadorial community from the celebrations surrounding their elevation to the cardinalate and subsequent visits to the city; and among the families of the diplomats, businessmen or other acquaintances from their home country or diocese.

Former members of religious orders took up residence in the headquarters or college of their order. Others accepted hospitality in the clinics and convents conducted by nuns from their native land. And a few, to preserve their independence of movement, moved into hotels or pensioni. Cardinal Spellman, for example, had a suite in the Grand Hotel, while the other Americans resided at the American college. An old Roman hand, Spellman, as both a student in Rome in the early 1930s and a minor official in the Vatican had, on his own unabashed admission, cultivated highly-placed Vatican officials and their families. As a confidant of Cardinal Pacelli, the secretary of state, he had close contacts with the future Pius XII's nephews and with Count Galeazzi, the civilian governor of the Vatican City.

The other Americans – McIntyre of Los Angeles, Meyer of Chicago, Ritter of St Louis and Cushing of Boston – spent much time visiting Vatican officials of their acquaintance. Each paid several visits to Cardinal Amleto Cicognani, the former apostolic delegate in Washington and John's secretary of state, with whom they were on terms of intimacy. They were fêted at the Chicago House where a number of the American priests working in the Vatican resided, including Mons. Andrew Landi of Catholic Relief Services; and they were wined and dined by embassy officials and members of the Church of St Susanna, the American Catholic parish in Rome.

The cardinals of Spain had close relations with the Spanish embassy on the spacious Piazza de Spagna, a former stronghold of ecclesiastical intrigue and papal influence. Of a conservative cast of mind, they were still not curial men, despite the fact that Cardinal Arcadio Larraona, in the Congregation of Rites, was a Spaniard with an integrist involvement.

The German cardinals – Frings of Cologne and Doepfner of Munich – circulated in and out of the German College in the Vatican, while the Brazilian and Latin American princes of the Church were to be found at their respective national colleges. The more progressive among them were looking for direction to Cardinal Agostino Bea, the Jesuit ancient-of-days who resided in the Brazilian college on the Via Aurelia and had been one of Pope John's closest collaborators.

Bea's role in the days immediately preceding the conclave was inconspicuous but powerful. A German from Bavaria with an Italian-sounding name, he had taught scripture in the Jesuit Institute in Rome known as the Biblicum and, under Pius XII, became its rector. Considered mildly progressive but cautious, he had gradually led Pius toward an open attitude in the Church's pursuit of biblical studies. Under John, who made him a cardinal, Bea suddenly developed strongly liberal views in ecumenism and Church policies. There could be no doubt that Montini was now his man.

Among the cardinals from the non-European world, there was considerable concern over the rumors and gossip with which they were greeted by their co-nationals living in Rome and forming part of the social circles that surrounded the Vatican.

Journalists and officials of the curia were full of stories and anecdotes indicating that, with his demise, Pope John's revolution had come to a swift end. They cited unimpeachable evidence that the Roman curia, as it had boasted during the defeats it suffered in the course of the first session of Vatican Council II, would swiftly put an end to that unfortunate incident in the Church's history; that the new pope would quietly be advised or cajoled into closing the windows John had opened; that they would restore law and order within the Church's doctrine and discipline.

In the curia itself there was an air of suppressed but vigorous activity. Even before John's death, Cardinal Alfredo Ottaviani, the powerful spokesman for the Holy Office, had set his sights on the tall, imposing

Cardinal Ildebrando Antoniutti, the rigid aristocratic prelate from the mountains above Udine, whom John had created a cardinal in his final consistory of 1962.

Antoniutti was the exact opposite of Pope John – tall, lean, unsmiling. He had occupied first-class positions in the diplomatic corps, including Canada and Spain. In Spain he had favored the *Opus Dei* – an organization of devoted clerics and lay Catholics with promises of obedience and poverty, educated to enter professional and academic fields and bring the Church's social and political teachings into play. It had definitely rightist tendencies.

Within the Ottaviani sphere of influence were the cardinal members of the Congregation of the Holy Office – Micara, Pizzardo, Cicognani, Agagianian, Ciriaci and Confalonieri, kept well informed by the severe secretary, Archbishop Pietro Parente.

To consolidate their position, the cardinals of the curia had instructed the prelate in charge of the papal office for Latin Letters, Mons. Amleto Tondini – to whom tradition assigned the task of admonishing the cardinals with an exhortation at the electoral mass – to pull no punches in advising his audience that the deceased pope's policies had been a disaster, and that the next pope must be devoted primarily to restoring law and order within the Church.

In his oration Tondini did just that. In subtle Ciceronian phrases he said that to tax John's reign with the evils currently besetting the Church would be considered an act of pessimism; nevertheless, this had to be risked. Nor was John's reputation as a master in the realm of world peace above reproach.

John had sweetness and love, Tondini conceded, but not a few of his enthusiastic supporters lacked a true understanding of spiritual values. Hence, John's successor must take care to re-establish the metaphysical principles of Christian life. While John truly desired the unity of all people, his successor must be careful to expose the evils of the marxist approach to such unity; and the separated Christian churches must be made to realize that reunion could only mean a return to the one true Church of Christ.

Turning directly to the cardinals seated before him, he boldly exhorted them: 'You, most eminent fathers, have the duty to choose one from among you who will have the task of deciding whether the problems, the studies already undertaken and in particular the present state of mind of the Church are at such a maturity that we can hope for the results which the healthiest part of humanity awaits.' This last salvo was unpardonable. It was also a tactical mistake, giving the non-curial cardinals a direct indication of how bold and absolute the opposition to John's policies and the Council actually was.

There was more than one curial barb involved in these observations. The reference to pessimism was a direct riposte to John's remark at the opening of the Council when he called many of his advisors prophets of doom who knew no history and who constantly came to him with their pessimistic warnings. In questioning John's effect on world peace, the attack was directed against his dealing with agnostics and non-believers who had given his encyclical *Pacem in Terris* such an enthusiastic welcome.

As the Vatican observers weighed up the situation on the day the conclave opened, the curial bloc appeared to consist of twenty-nine cardinals directly attached to the Vatican, and it could count on a sure twenty votes for their candidate. These included Cardinal Ottaviani and the Italian Antonio Bacci, who detested the departed pope for having encouraged the downgrading of the Latin liturgy by approving the use of the vernacular languages in the Church's prayers and official rites. Equally opposed to John's regime was the Spanish curial cardinal Arcadio Larraona in the Congregation for Rites and the Italian octogenarian Pietro Ciriaci, prefect of the Congregation for Religious Orders; Cardinal Clemente Micara, seventy-nine, who had served as John's vicar for the diocese of Rome; and a spate of elderly cardinals whom John had known in his younger days. They included Francesco Bracci, Fernando Cento, Paolo Giobbe, Carlo Chiarlo, Efrem Forni, Francesco Morano, Giuseppe de Costa Nunes and Andrea Jullien – men who had promptly turned against John once he had made them cardinals and who would not submit to his request that they resign their curial positions. (John's secretary, Mons. Capovilla, has described the pope's consternation after a meeting with this old guard, when John kept murmuring to himself, 'But, they refused to obey the pope . . .', something he had never dreamed could happen before he took on that exalted office.)

Despite Ottaviani's vigorous attempt to line up the curial cardinals as a phalanx in the first voting and thus sweep the uncertain cardinals from outside onto the conservative bandwagon, he could still not be sure of a small number of the men from within. Gustave Testa, an octogenarian Bergamascan and boyhood friend of John's, was one such. Carlo Confalonieri, the former secretary of Pope Pius XI, was possibly another. Nor could the master of the Holy Office be sure of Paolo Marella.

Likewise uncertain was the stand taken by Cardinal Amleto Cicognani. John had made him a cardinal among his first appointees, rescuing him from exile in Washington after twenty-five years – what he had done to offend Pius XII is not known precisely – and making him his secretary of state upon the sudden death of Cardinal Tardini in 1960. While docile to John's wishes, Cicognani, who had been known in America as a gentle, mildly forward-looking prelate, seemed to have reverted to the conservatism of his youthful training, and definitely favored the curial line in the preparation for the Council and throughout its first session, when he played a behind-the-scenes role.

Nevertheless, Cicognani's links with Montini were ancient and intimate. In the early 1920s they had been associated as chaplains to the Italian university students at the old Roman College of the Sapienza. During Cicognani's sojourn in America, Montini was his principal contact in the Vatican. As an intimate friend and counsellor of the American bishops, Cicognani could not have been indifferent to their leaning toward the cardinal of Milan.

Similarly uncertain was the stance being adopted by the dean of the Sacred College, the formidable French cardinal Eugene Tisserant, who was disliked by most of the people in the Vatican for his imperious ways. A cardinal since 1937, he had won his spurs as an intelligence officer in the Middle East with the French army during World War I and had gone on to become a world-renowned scholar and member of the French Academy. Despite these accomplishments, his brusque manners were not appreciated by his colleagues, who referred to him derisively as 'The Frenchman'.

Nevertheless he too seemed to favor the curial line when matters of procedure were referred to him for a decision during the first session of the Council, where he served as president of the board of presidents. But where Tisserant stood on the Montini candidacy was unknown. He had been a strong opponent of Pius XII's policies; but he was well acquainted with the Milanese cardinal from their early days together in the Vatican under Pius XI. And when Montini was forced out of Rome, it was Tisserant who actually consecrated him Archbishop of Milan in St Peter's basilica, substituting for the pope himself who was ill. There were thus old and close bonds between the two men.

Of the cardinals coming in from outside Rome, it is all but certain that Spellman of New York was one of the first to rally to the Montini cause. On his way to Rome the New York cardinal had stopped off in Milan to call on Montini, apparently to encourage him to take on the tough burden of the papacy should it be offered to him. The two men were well acquainted since the early 1930s when Spellman had worked in the secretary of state's office as a junior official. He had become a close friend of Cardinal Pacelli and was selected by Mons. Montini as a courier entrusted with secretly carrying copies of Pope Pius XI's anti-Nazi encyclical *Mit brennender Sorge* (With burning concern) for distribution in Hitler's Germany. His reward was his consecration as Auxiliary Bishop of Boston, much to the annoyance of its imperious archbishop, Cardinal William O'Connell.

Created Archbishop of New York in April 1938, only two months after the election of Cardinal Pacelli as Pius XII, Spellman played an invaluable role as emissary between President Roosevelt and the Vatican, using his diplomatic immunity as well as his position as bishop of all the Catholics in the American armed forces to fly in and out of Europe and North Africa on missions of great import to both the Allies and the Holy See. And when the war ended it was his brain-child, (Catholic) War Relief Services, that was the instrument for feeding Italy, most of war-torn Europe and North Africa. He was likewise intimately involved in dealing with refugee problems all over the world, and in helping to rebuild the destroyed churches and ecclesiastical institutions in both Allied and Axis territories. In all these projects, Montini was Spellman's primary Vatican contact.

The New York cardinal had not been too well pleased with the open-window policies of Pope John, and particularly his call for major changes with the *aggiornamento;* for in 1958, upon John's election, the American Church seemed never to have been better off. Its churches were jammed with parishioners each Sunday morning; it did not have enough schools and colleges; it had no financial problems, and was making an incredible number of converts each year. Hence the Council seemed to the American prelate somewhat of a superfluous expense. Nevertheless he was sufficiently a son of the Church and a politician to have gone along with John's wishes. In supporting the candidacy of Montini, he thus felt that he was being loyal to John's heritage while likewise returning to the Pacelli tradition.

Located in the Grand Hotel to preserve his independence of movement, Spellman had the secretarial services of Count Galeazzi, including transportation, and was able to pay his respects to Cardinal Cicognani and take counsel with Bea and the curial cardinals in whom he had some confidence. Due to his frequent travels all over the globe, and his munificence both personally and through Catholic Relief Services, Spellman was considered a patron by a number of cardinals, including Valerian Gracias of Bombay, Laurean Rugambwa of Africa, Peter Tatsuo Doi of Japan, Thomas Tienchensin of China, Juan Landazuri Ricketts of Peru and Raul Silva Henriquez of Chile.

Likewise lined up on the Montini platform were Paul Emile Léger, the cardinal of Montreal, who had been associated with the Milanese archbishop when Léger was rector of the Canadian College in Rome, and the enfeebled Cardinal James McGuigan of Toronto. Also indubitably on the Montini bandwagon were the French cardinals – Maurice Feltin of Paris, Joseph Lefebvre of Bourges, Achille Liénart of Lille, Paul Richaud of Bordeaux, Pierre Gerlier of Lyons, Clement Roques of Rennes. Montini could likewise count on the so-called northern European bloc – Bernard Alfrink of Holland, Leon Josef Suenens of Belgium, Franziskus Koenig of Vienna, and the two Germans, Julius Doepfner of Munich and Joseph Frings of Cologne. In Italy he had the backing of Cardinal Agostino Bea in the curia and Giacomo Lercaro of Bologna.

It is quite possible that Montini also had the support of Cardinal Norman Gilroy of Australia, and perhaps William Godfrey of London and John d'Alton of Ireland, but there were countercurrents here, represented by the Scotch convert and curial cardinal, William Heard, and the intransigent Irish Dominican, Cardinal Michael Browne, who were definitely anti-Montini in sentiment. Out of the voting was Cardinal Josef Mindszenty, in exile in the American embassy in Budapest.

The non-curial Italians – Maurillo Fossati of Turin, Giovanni Urbani of Venice, Alfonso Castaldi of Naples, Montini himself, with the possibility also of Giuseppe Ferretto of the curia – had decided to support Cardinal Giacomo Lercaro of Bologna, who was considered a thoroughly pastoral bishop. In the post-war years, Lercaro had organized teams of priests capable of saturating a parochial neighborhood to offset communist appeals to the youth – apparently molded on the tactic employed by the Italian minister of the interior, Mario Selbas, of *celere* police – swift jeep-mounted carabinieri, capable of breaking up communist demonstrations before they got started. Considered a man of high spiritual motivation, Lercaro was rated as a compromise candidate between the intransigents of the right and left.

Solidly in the Antoniutti camp were Giuseppe Siri, the cardinal of Genoa, Clemente Micara, the Vicar in charge of the diocese of Rome, Alfredo Ottaviani of the Holy Office, supported by the Irish Dominican cardinal Michael Browne, Giuseppe Pizzardo of the Congregation of Seminaries and Universities, Ignace Tappouni and Gregory Agagianian, Ernesto Ruffini of Palermo, Manuel Cerejeira of Lisbon, Carlos Motto of São Paulo, and Ruffino I. Santos of the Philippines, and the group of septuagenarian conservatives of John's creation, together with Cardinal Giacomo Luigi Coppello, called to Rome as chancellor of the Holy Roman Church after the political gaffe of supporting Juan Peron's regime in Argentina.

Where the Spanish cardinals stood – Benjamin Arriba y Castro of Tarragona, Enrique Pla y Daniel of Toledo, Fernando Palacios of Compostella, Jose M. Bueno y Monreal of Seville – was not known. Several years earlier, as Archbishop of Milan, Montini had been persuaded to plead with General Franco for a young man apparently condemned to death for murder. Unhappily, the archbishop was given wrong information, and Franco rejected his plea with indignation. But whether the generalissimo's disdain influenced his cardinals is unknown. Nor was the position assumed by Cardinals Antonio Caggiano of Buenos Aires, Luis Concha of Bogotá and Jose Garibi y Rivera of Mexico discernible, although they were on the conservative side at the Council.

The cardinal of Milan arrived in Rome late on the afternoon of 16 June 1963 and, after taking the oath of secrecy at the hands of the camerlengo, made his way down to Castelgondolfo. He stayed there with the custodians of the papal summer palace, the Bonomellis, friends of the Montini family from Brescia. It was a frequent haunt of the Milanese archbishop, both when he was an official in the Vatican seeking solitude and rest, and on his infrequent trips to Rome after his installation in

Milan. Now he wanted to avoid the limelight that would certainly have surrounded him in Rome.

Though smiling and affable at the gathering of cardinals in the sacristy of the Pauline chapel before the mass for electing the pontiff on June 17th, he was seen with pursed lips and frowning obviously during Mons. Tondini's attack on John's achievement. At the end of the mass he disappeared quickly, only to reappear as the last of the cardinals to cross the line into the area of the conclave.

He was caught by a photographer in the dark purple cassock and biretta proper to a cardinal at the time of mourning, his hands clasped and eyes slightly downcast, a man obviously preoccupied with a great burden, following behind the aged, white-bearded Syrian patriarch, Cardinal Ignace Tappouni.

The Vatican palaces are a vast, imposing conglomeration of majestic-styled buildings, many going back to the late Renaissance. They are all interconnected and have been modernized with up-to-date facilities from plumbing and elevators to intramural heating and fire-proofing. In the spacious corridors connecting the papal quarters and the secretariat of state with the halls of benedictions, the papal Sistine Chapel, the Vatican Library and the museums, are a series of large apartments inhabited by major officials of the papal household. During a conclave, these suites of rooms are vacated by their occupants and individual rooms are turned over as cells to the cardinals.

In the final apportioning of rooms, Montini was given a 'cell' in the apartment of Father Alfonso Raes, the Jesuit prefect of the Vatican Library, whose other bedrooms were assigned to Cardinal Gregory Meyer of Chicago, Maurillo Fossati of Turin, and Jose Garibi y Rivera of Guadalajara, Mexico. What conversation took place between these prelates other than an exchange of pleasantries is unknown. Fossati was seventy-seven, Meyer notably taciturn, and Rivera in his seventies, while Montini himself seemed extremely preoccupied.

There is no doubt that Montini knew he was the prime candidate for the papacy, and that he felt that in some way or other he was predestined for this all-but-impossible task. His frank assertion of the necessity of carrying on Pope John's heritage and his certainty that this would be done must, he knew, have strengthened the determination of his supporters and at the same time have given him further grief with the intransigents in the curia. The latter were, in turn, fully aware of his potentialities as an administrator who knew intimately both the system and most of the individuals running it. They were also conscious of the mystical twist to Montini's personality, often taken for perplexity or hesitancy in making decisions, though it was not this at all.

What Montini suffered from was a humane and spiritual sensitivity, wholeheartedly desiring to be an authentic Christian and thus able to love his enemies as well as his friends. In this delicacy he did not want to appear unfriendly even to those who had caused his pain and trouble, particularly his opponents in the curia. They had been responsible for his removal from the Vatican in 1954, and were now definitely leading the opposition to his candidacy for the papacy. It was not with the aim of winning any of these men over to his cause that he wanted to show them deference. It was his normal, northern Italian temperament that desired bygones to be bygones.

Thus, instead of establishing himself in Rome at the Lombard College during the week before the opening of the conclave, and participating in the ebb and flow of gossip and maneuver, he had remained in Milan, then lodged with the Bonomellis at Castelgondolfo. As he entered the precincts of the conclave, there was an air of sadness mixed with resignation about him, almost as if he were saying within himself, 'Father, not my will but Thine be done.'

Into the election of John's successor was poured the full caldron of abrasive Vatican politics. Violently opposed to Montini's candidacy was the Cardinal of Genoa, Giuseppe Siri, a right-wing opponent of Pope John's Council, who held the powerful position of president of the Italian Bishops' Conference. Of a poor family – one of ten, his father served as janitor for a row of residences in Genoa – and ten years younger than Montini, Siri had been a brilliant clerical student who shortly after ordination achieved a reputation as a conferencier and counsellor to university students. There was an acknowledged rivalry between himself and Montini that was heightened when Siri was made an auxiliary bishop in 1944 in his native archdiocese at the surprisingly youthful age of thirty-eight, and then advanced to the cardinalate in 1953 at only forty-seven.

Siri's objection to Montini was precisely the fact that the cardinal of Milan would prove a champion of the Johannine line. He concurred in his opposition to the Milanese cardinal with the curial old guard, who were fearful of a communist takeover of the Italian government as a result of John's 'opening to the left', and felt that Montini with his pretentions to political astuteness would prove more of a fool in these matters than had Pope John. They were also conscious of Montini's determination to carry through a reform of the curia along the lines projected by his patron, Pius XII, over a decade earlier, but never achieved.

Montini was looked upon by the curia as a man from no-man's land, somewhere between peasant and aristocrat and thus doubly dangerous in his bourgeois determination to achieve his goals, and in his desire to accommodate the Church to the secularist ways of the outside world. Under Pius XII he had been the proponent of efficiency in the curia's operations, suggesting such monstrous innovations as punch-clocks in the Vatican offices, strict accounting of personal phone calls, travel expenses, and other immemorial perquisites.

The curial leaders had likewise taken the measure of Montini's theological competence and found it wanting. Though he had read widely, particularly in modern French theological literature, his doctrinal formation lacked depth. This accounted for his dilettante interest, they argued, in the new, existentialist approach to the great theological questions of the past – the divinity of Christ, His presence in the Eucharist, the twofold sources of divine revelation.

In contrast to the curial estimate of Montini's doctrinal abilities was their frank admission that he was a man of exceptional talent, quick comprehension and retentive memory for persons, places and events, all of which gave him the contours of great intelligence. They knew by experience that he had the courage of his convictions, could be easily approached, was benevolent when opposed in argument, generous in his judgments, and was all-embracing in his spiritual and worldly interests. They admitted he was capable of extraordinary, symbolic actions. They knew that he said his prayers with unfeigned fervor; and that in imitation of his great patron, Pius XII, he had mystical aspirations. But even these qualities were not sufficient to offset what they considered to be his disadvantages.

In the final days before the conclave opened, the formidable curial group did their best to line up the Spanish and Latin American cardinals on their arrival in Rome. They sought to gain their vote in favor of one of their curial candidates, more precisely, Cardinal Antoniutti, whom most of these Hispanic prelates knew personally from his days as papal nuncio in Madrid in the late 1950s.

The conclave assembled in the Sistine Chapel on the morning of June 17 for its first session. Each of the cardinals was seated on a wooden throne, over which hung a silk *baldacchino,* or protective covering – in purple for the cardinals created by Pope John; in green for the others. The ceremonies began with a reading of the rules for the election newly promulgated by Pope John in 1962. This was followed by the recital of the *Veni Sancte Spiritus* (Come Holy Spirit) and the selection of officials among the cardinals to collect and count the votes.

At the start of this session, all the clerical assistants, including the masters of ceremonies, were banished from the Chapel with the ancient, stentorian cry 'Exeant omnes' – and the eighty cardinals were left to the guidance of the Holy Spirit and their own devices.

On the first ballot it quickly became clear that sides had been chosen. Montini registered some thirty votes, Antoniutti twenty and Lercaro twenty. Scattered votes went to Roberti and Cicognani. The battle was on. There was little change in the second round that followed immediately that morning. After the burning of the ballots, the assembly broke for lunch, siesta and private prayer.

During the interval, the cardinals running Lercaro's campaign apparently decided to make a radical change, giving their votes to Montini. Thus in the third scrutiny, toward seven in the evening, Montini advanced to fifty votes. Antoniutti stood fast with twenty.

At this juncture, according to the well-informed journalist Giancarlo Zizola, a strange happening occurred. The eighty-year-old Cardinal Gustavo Testa, prefect of the Congregation for the Oriental Churches, suddenly rose from his chair and approached the thrones of Cardinals Carlo Confalonieri and Alberto di Jorio, the two most level-headed prelates in the curia. In a voice loud enough to startle the assembly, Testa charged his two addressees to do something about the scandalous intrigue that was being perpetrated by members of the curia. This sudden outburst came as a shock to the assembly. Cardinal Siri was on his feet at once, protesting the violation of the rule of silence. And the formidable dean of the college, Cardinal Tisserant, mumbled words of mild reproach to the Bergamese cardinal.

What possessed Testa to make this move is unknown. As a boyhood friend of Pope John, he had been one of the few curial cardinals to support John's revolutionary policies. Taciturn and intelligent, he had apparently little knowledge of, and less esteem for, Montini. In his perplexity before the conclave, he had gone to Archbishop Dell'Acqua, John's former right-hand man in the secretariat of state, and asked for advice regarding Montini as heir-apparent to John's policies. On Dell'Acqua's assurance that Montini not only had John's blessing but was capable of handling the task, Testa had decided to support the cardinal of Milan – 'But only because of your reassurance,' he told Dell'Acqua.

This interference did not immediately affect the vote. In the scrutiny that followed, Montini remained at fifty and Antoniutti retained his twenty votes. But it did evidently have an effect on the discussions among the cardinals as they gathered in small groups that evening.

It seems clear, for one thing, that Montini's primary support, including Cardinal Spellman, persuaded the cardinal of Milan to let it be known that he would not make any immediate changes in the major curial roles.

When this assurance was passed to Ottaviani, he apparently saw the wisdom of making a quick shift and thus functioning as the pope-maker. Dropping the candidacy of Roberti, with whom the curial leaders had decided to replace Antoniutti, he persuaded Confalonieri and di Jorio along with Micara and Marella to go along with him.

On the first ballot the next morning, Montini reached fifty-seven votes – three above the needed number. Immediately after the count was certified, the dean of the sacred college, Cardinal Tisserant, flanked by Cerejeira of the presbyters, and Ottaviani of the cardinal deacons, approached the pale, slightly trembling cardinal of Milan. 'Do you accept the election canonically made of you as Supreme Pontiff?', he was asked. To which Montini responded: 'Trembling and unworthy, I do accept.'

'By what name do you wish to be called?'

'I will be called Paul.'

The name, like John's, was an innovation. It had not been used in over two hundred years. It was also a program. It immediately conjured up the apostle Paul of Tarsus, born out of due time, to be an apostle to the gentiles. The new pontificate had already a new determination.

The three aged cardinals then bowed profoundly, as their colleagues broke into an applause that seemed like a release of a long-held breath.

Meanwhile, the secretary of the College of Cardinals and the papal master of ceremonies with two assistants had been introduced into the Sistine Chapel. They proceeded at once to lower the canopies over the heads of all the cardinals but Montini. Then they ushered the cardinals one by one to the platform before the throne of the newly elected Holy Father to perform the first *adorazione,* or act of obedience. Each one kissed his ring and received from Pope Paul the kiss of peace. When Cardinal Lercaro approached him, Montini said, 'See how life goes, your eminence; you are the one who should be in this post.'

By this time the papal master of ceremonies had observed the signing of the documents ascertaining the canonically correct election of Cardinal Giovanni Battista Montini as Pope Paul VI and his acceptance of that office. They were now ready to usher the new pontiff into the sacristy of the Sistine Chapel, where he was fitted by the papal tailor with the white cassock that henceforth would be the sign of his office.

Meanwhile, Cardinal Ottaviani had proceeded to the balcony over the entrance to St Peter's basilica. Where five years earlier he had announced to the tremendous crowd in the piazza the election of John, he now let the whole world know:

'*Gaudium magnum annuntiamus vobis* (A great joy we announce),' he thundered in his stentorian voice. The crowd seemed to hold its breath in tremendous anticipation . . . '*Habemus papam . . . Eminentissimum et Reverendissimum Dominum . . .*' Again the crowd paused. 'Giovanni Battista . . .'. The crowd let go with a gigantic shout. Montini was the one! 'He will be called Paul – *Paulus Sextus –* ', said the beaming ancient-of-days.

As journalists dashed for the news rooms of the Vatican, and crowds continued to pour onto the square, the newly elected pope appeared. He seemed to be in full possession of himself and his exalted position as he chanted '*Sit nomen Domini benedictum* (Let the name of the Lord be blessed)' – and then, extending his hand, gave his first blessing. The crowd broke into a sort of delirium, as the new Supreme Pastor of the Roman Catholic Church retired within the precincts of the Vatican.

After receiving the reverence of the various curial officials whose position gave them access to the papal palace, Paul returned to the dining hall set up for the conclave meals in the Borgia apartments for the

midday meal with the cardinals, and was offered the chair at the head
of the table by Cardinal Tisserant. He declined and took the place he
had occupied as cardinal.

Pope Paul, as was his wont, ate sparingly. At the end of the meal, he
confirmed Cardinal Cicognani in his post as secretary of state, and informed the other heads of Congregations that they were to carry on in
their positions. He then discussed the events that were to occur in the
next week – his television address to the world, the following day; his
coronation in St Peter's Basilica or, weather permitting, on the balcony
fronting that magnificent edifice, a week from Sunday; and his taking
possession of the Lateran Basilica, the Pope's church as Bishop of
Rome. Bringing the discussion to a sudden clc·e, he said 'We will do
the rest tomorrow.'

Meanwhile, the new pontiff had informed his secretary, Monsignor
Pasquale Macchi, that he would take possession of the papal suite on
the top floor of the papal palace at once. John's possessions were hurriedly displaced and the few belongings the new Holy Father had with
him were brought in from Castelgondolfo. Late that evening there was
a light in the room on the top floor of the papal palace that had been
dark for eighteen days. Romans took to their beds reassured.

The afternoon and evening were spent in receiving intimates of the
papal household, authorizing answers to the telegrams and messages of
congratulations flowing into the Vatican from all over the world, and
accommodating the papal tailors busily putting together the new pope's
wardrobe – cassocks, sashes, capes, surplices, shoes, socks, hats and
cloaks in white and red – a formidable collection.

Then the pope retired to prepare his message to the world for broadcast the next day. Meticulous in his composing habits, he had now to
give the Church and the world an assurance that his pontificate would
be at once a carrying out of the heritage he received from Pope John,
and an expression of his own pauline ambitions for the effective spread
of Christ's gospel that was the Church's primary *raison d'être*.

How the new Holy Father slept that night is not known. That he was
up betimes and at his prayers was part of his normal routine. Then he
turned his attention totally to the business at hand.

The man who emerged as Pope Paul vi from that brief but bitterly
contested conclave was a 65-year-old prelate from Brescia in the north

of Italy, and cardinal archbishop of Milan. Of medium build, balding, with jet-black hair and deep piercing eyes, he was a typical well-bred Italian of the north, and an ecclesiastic to his fingertips. From youth onwards his career had been a preparation for his assumption of the papal office. In his thirty years in the Vatican he had been privy to the policies and pursuits of two imperious pontiffs, Pius XI and Pius XII, having served each of them as a man of confidence. As Archbishop of Milan for about a decade he had lived the pastoral experience needed in a Roman pontiff.

For the second time in a half century the papal electors had ignored the ancient axiom: 'He who enters a conclave pope, exits a cardinal.' In 1939 Eugenio Pacelli, as secretary of state to Pius XI, had been the pre-conclave favorite. He was elected quickly, to carry out the tough anti-fascist policy of his predecessor on the eve of World War II.

Montini's election took place in the context of a major fracas within the Church itself. It was interpreted as a sign that a majority of the cardinals favored the revolutionary vision of his predecessor, Pope John XXIII. Actually, his failure to garner the curial vote – some twenty-three holding out against him to the end – was to trouble his pontificate and cause both the new pope and the Church unavoidable grief.

Amid the guesswork attempting to penetrate the secrecy of the conclave, a strange story emerged. The Italian periodical *Epoca* carried an account of the conclave's proceedings in which it maintained that Montini had actually been elected on the fourth ballot on Thursday evening – that would have been directly after Testa's intervention. But that the cardinal of Milan, in tearful confusion, had begged the electors to hold off the decision until the next morning. Obviously a fabrication based on Montini's supposed indecisiveness as Archbishop of Milan, this account had to be evaluated in the light of the no-nonsense attitude of Cardinal Tisserant, who would have brooked no such irregularity. The rumor did indicate, however, that some information regarding an extraordinary happening in the conclave had got out. It was presumed that it augured ill for the new pontificate.

In his televised message the next day Pope Paul assured the Church and the world that his pontificate would be devoted primarily to carrying out Pope John's heritage with a decisive Pauline initiative. To the satisfaction of most of his auditors, he said the Council would be continued; that the Church would turn its attention fully to the problems of mankind, particularly in their social and moral realities. He had no intention, he assured governments, of interfering in the affairs of nations, but his pontificate would be marked by the attempt to rejuvenate the Church and to have it take a leading part in turning the attention of the world's inhabitants to charity and justice in the search for unity. He did insist on the loftiness of his position as Supreme Pastor of the Church – one, holy, Catholic and apostolic – in succession to Peter, the prince of the apostles. It was a true Montinian speech, the obvious product of his own thinking. And despite an apparent insensitivity to the prerogatives of the other Christian churches, it was highly reassuring. This man meant business.

Later that afternoon, the new pope did something typically Pauline. Calling for the papal limousine, he set out for the Spanish College near the Piazza Navona where the aged Cardinal Pla y Daniel of Toledo was confined to his bed. Suddenly, as the papal vehicle passed the residence of the octogenarian Cardinal Gustavo Testa in the Vatican, the pope ordered it to halt. Alighting, he approached the apartment of the Bergamese prelate who, apparently alone in the house, answered the doorbell himself.

Too surprised to offer Pope Paul the courtesy of entering his parlor, Testa stood there abashed. The new Holy Father greeted him warmly and thanked him for his intervention at the crucial moment of the conclave. Then, in a characteristic gesture, Paul offered Testa the key to the private elevator which led to his own apartment in the papal palace. Finding his tongue, the baffled cardinal courteously refused the proffered symbol. 'No, Your Holiness,' he said. 'But should Your Holiness have need of me, you always know where to find me.' With that, he withdrew within the portal of his home. Pope Paul returned to his vehicle.

At the Spanish College the new pope was greeted with enthusiastic applause. Word had been spread among the faculty and students, and a handful of embassy officials had been hurriedly gathered. As the pontiff entered the courtyard, he received a wild welcome, and after greeting the octogenarian in his quarters, the new Holy Father stood and conversed with the rector and students. Word was quickly sent to Spain that the new pontiff had authentic Hispanic sentiments.

The following day was a Sunday, and at noon, in keeping with John's custom, the new pope appeared at the window of his library to recite the Angelus with the immense crowd in St Peter's Square below, and give them his blessing. He appeared at the portal with the Belgian Cardinal Josef Suenens smiling at his side. It was the Belgian cardinal whom Pope John had chosen to give a new direction to the Council in its forthcoming second session. Breaking through the curial log-jam that cluttered the agenda with an impossible program of topics to be discussed, Suenens had proposed a two-pronged approach – discussing the Church *ad intra,* in the internal structure, and *ad extra,* as it faced the world. And at this juncture, Cardinal Montini had broken his self-imposed conciliar silence to support Suenens's proposition.

Now the papal gesture certainly indicated that the Belgian prelate was to play an intimate role in Montini's pontificate. Rumors spread immediately that he would replace Cicognani as secretary of state, or that at least he would be given a directive office in the curia.

Taking to the rhythm of papal activities as if he had been pope all his life, Montini re-established the *tabella,* or table of official audiences, for the heads of the curial congregations or bureaus. On June 26th Paul announced the date for the resumption of the Council. The opening of the second session was set for September 29th, the feast of St Michael the Archangel. The swiftness of this decision and the brevity of the interval before the reopening took everyone by surprise, since the preparatory commissions had not functioned for over a month. But Pope Paul made it clear that the period of curial obstruction was over; the Council would get down to business with a set of schemas on the agenda that would be manageable. On Wednesday June 24th he held his first papal audience in St Peter's and told a group of Americans from Philadelphia that he would pursue his predecessor's ecumenical endeavors with vigor. On Saturday he motored to the church of St Charles Borromeo in the middle of the city to say mass in the Ambrosian Rite for a group of the faithful from Milan led by the mayor. He was presented with the tall, three-crowned gothic tiara, whose design he had approved and which was to be used in his coronation ceremony the next day. Meanwhile, Paul had settled into the arduous routine of papal business that confronted the pontiff each day.

In the first two weeks of his pontificate, Paul received in audience a number of political notables, beginning with King Baudouin and Queen Fabiola of Belgium, John Kennedy, the United States President, John Goulart, President of Brazil, Eamon de Valera of Ireland, U Thant of the United Nations, the *Capitani regenti* or Regents of San Marino, and

Antonio Segni, President of Italy, as well as the members of the diplomatic corps accredited to the Holy See.

On each of these occasions he delivered a short, formal speech of his own composition, in which he demonstrated a warmth of personal welcome and an awareness of particular relations with the lands and people his visitors represented. He told the Belgian royal couple, for example, of his joy at the pursuit of Christian social studies accomplished in their country and recalled the dialogue initiated by Cardinal Mercier and Lord Halifax on ecumenism, half a century earlier. Recalling his visits to the USA as a curial official in 1950 and more recently as cardinal, he assured Mr Kennedy of his great appreciation of the generosity of the American people. He reassured U Thant of his full support for the United Nations; and Mr Goulart, De Valera and the *Capitani regenti* of his affection for the religious spirit of their respective peoples.

The election of Cardinal Montini had been a considerable boon for the press. He was the man about whom they had the most information; his background in Brescia and his years as an official in the Vatican were easily exploitable. While reserved, his brothers and family members were helpful in supplying personal details about his youth and early career.

In his first audience with the press, the new pontiff was most affable. With considerable irony he referred to some of the stories about the conclave as 'unusual', echoing Pope John's comment on the accounts of his election – 'I could not find a word of truth in them.' Despite his long-winded affability, in which he claimed kinship with their profession based on the journalistic career of his father, Giorgio Montini, who had published a daily paper, *Il Cittadino* (The Citizen), in Brescia for many years, the journalists found the new pontiff an enigma. They thus joined the cardinals who had elected him and the majority of people who worked close beside him. The contrast between Montini and his predecessor was not merely one of physical proportions, looks and temperament. John and Paul were two totally different individuals.

Some of those who knew the new Holy Father intimately felt that within his own consciousness there was considerable confusion. But this estimate seemed belied by Paul's immediate actions.

A man of deep spiritual conviction, he was at once a visionary who desired to implement his predecessor's dream of making the Church the universal institution it claimed to be in calling itself 'Catholic'; and a realist, totally aware of the antipathy he would have to overcome within the household of the papacy and of the Church that he had just inherited.

Here he exhibited a personality trait that can be interpreted as an extreme sensitivity – a constitutional unwillingness to even appear to take vengeance on his opponents, or a character deficiency – an inability to rid himself of officials whose personalities and policies were inimical to his own person and to the well-being of the Church. There seemed to be deep down in Montini another trait whose elucidation was beyond his own and his observer's comprehension – it was a mystique rather than a truly mystical streak. In his eyes the papacy had always been an office immediately created by Christ to put into effect the redemption of the whole of mankind. As such, it was an office beyond the aspiration of the individual prelate. Its occupant was the selection of the Holy Spirit working through the incredible process of a papal election, surrounded as it was with political intrigue and personal contentions. In this conviction, Paul had the comfort of feeling that the popes of the last four centuries, whatever their shortcomings, had all been highly religious men devoted primarily to the spiritual well-being of the Church. He felt he could properly take his place beside them.

While Montini had not let himself run for the papacy, as one would seek political office or an academic position, there was within him a conviction that divine providence was on his side. He felt that he could handle the task; that his early experience in the ministry and his curial career as intimate aide to two pontiffs – he had served as *sostituto* to the secretary of state under Pius XI in 1937 and 1938, and under Pius XII from 1939 to 1954 – meant that he had a deep knowledge of the inner Vatican workings and saw these powerful popes handling the most difficult of religious and political problems. Finally, his nine years in Milan as archbishop of Italy's largest and most difficult diocese had given him a substantial pastoral awareness. All this experience had fitted him specifically for both carrying on Pope John's unfinished revolution, by bringing the Council to a successful end, and then implementing his predecessor's dream of accommodating the Church's teachings to the needs of the contemporary world.

As he took up the reins of papal government, Montini showed no hesitation in giving orders and making decisions that indicated well-thought-out patterns of development on his part. His decision to continue the Council at once was a clear message to the opposition. His determination to deal swiftly with the problems posed by the curia was another indication that, having become pope, Giovanni Battista Montini knew exactly how to function as the Supreme Pastor, Paul VI.

There were shadows and difficulties however. The first was the fact that his election had obviously been made possible by Ottaviani's swift shift; hence he owed some special consideration to the conservative policies advocated by that custodian of the Church's teachings. Likewise, his election was not backed by some twenty-three cardinals, a substantial number, particularly if they represented a curial bloc. What worried him particularly was the influence possessed by the man who had been runner-up in the conclave – Cardinal Ildebrando Antoniutti, in whom Paul recognized an intransigent opponent of John's revolution and of his own policies for reform.

There is no possibility of understanding the intricate thinking behind Pope Paul's decisions and activities without an attempt to comprehend the substance of his religious convictions. In turn, this analysis requires an inquiry into the metaphysical presuppositions upon which his spiritual awareness was based. And here, paradoxically, Paul was at odds with John. The distinction between the two types of personality was recognized by the early theologians who spoke of the man with *fides quaerens intellectum,* faith seeking understanding; and its contrary, *intellectus quaerens fidem,* intelligence seeking faith.

John's religious structure was characterized within the first category. His faith was basic and all-embracing. Paul's religious orientation was equally as fundamental to his being, but it had a different starting point. It was not a mere matter of religious conviction; it was something more fragile. It involved the elements of temperament and taste.

John's faith was essentially that of the peasant. It simply was, with no modifiers. Paul's faith had all the characteristics of his bourgeois education. It was surrounded with concerns of depth, breadth, actualization, and above all, a fearful desire to be authentic. John lived as a Christian; Paul behaved like a Christian.

To John, history was everything, the sacred history that explained the beginning and the end of all that is, from a recognition of God as a Trinity involved in creation, down to the *eschaton* – the restoration of all creation in God via death, judgment, heaven and hell; and secular history, the unfolding of human families and societies, including nations and the Church in a great disorder consequent on the human condition, or, in his terms, original sin. Behind this vast array of human experience, John recognized a divine providence that did not somehow directly interfere in human affairs but kept a hand on the general direction of individual lives as well as of the world and the universe.

Montini's approach was much more philosophical and speculative. He accepted the historical fact as such, but his version was more global than linear. He was seeking to penetrate categories of being and behavior that would bring some sort of logical order into his understanding of what existence was all about.

Where the truly paradoxical came into play was in John's total consciousness, at all times, of living in the presence of God, and dealing with the saints and angels who constituted his inner world. Prayer for John was not a 'lifting of the mind and heart to God.' He needed no such lifting. He lived on a level with the Almighty. To John, there was thus no dichotomy between the sacred and the profane. Whatever he turned his mind to in human concern – politics, people, public and private affairs – he did so as a Christian living in God's presence with his feet on the ground. John was in effect an aristotelian, beginning and ending with his experiences.

Montini was a platonist. Essentially, he was seeking direct contact with divinity in imitation of his acquired patron saint, St Paul. In the footsteps of his great model, Pope Pius xii, he was mystically oriented, but much more sensitive to the demands of public propriety. There would be no ecstatic experiences in his career as pontiff, such as Pius' claim to have re-lived the so-called Fatima experience – seeing the world engulfed in a final catastrophe, with the sun rolling loose in the heavens, under the inspiration of the Blessed Virgin Mary's appearance at the Portuguese shrine; or his claim to have seen Christ in agony.

Montini's mysticism was much more of a mystique. Like the fifth-century pope, St Leo i, he felt he had Peter breathing down his neck when compelled to make a final, delicate decision. The most obvious of these decisions would be in his judgment regarding the birth-control issue. But it had come into play numerous times before – for example in his very decision to accept the papal election. In John's case, the matter was simple and straightforward. Realizing the night before that he was certainly in line to be the next pope, John sat at his desk and wrote a speech indicating his reason for choosing the name John and laying out the general lines he would pursue.

Montini made no such provision. He had made up his mind to choose the name Paul and obviously felt that that would be sufficiently programmatic. But he would not presume on the good graces of the Spirit or the cardinal electors to let them see that he had anticipated divine providence.

Born of a bourgeois family in Brescia in northern Italy on 26 September 1898, Giovanni Battista Montini had a church-oriented childhood. His father, George, was a banker and agricultural entrepreneur who controlled a local newspaper, *Il Cittadino,* and championed Catholic causes. His mother, Giudetta, was a delicate but determined activist involved in social and charitable enterprises. Much of young Montini's childhood was directed by his paternal grandmother and aunt. Never robust as a boy, he attended private schools, came under the spiritual and intellectual influence of the Oratorian humanist, Father Giulio Bevilaqua (whom he created a cardinal in his old age), failed the physical examination when called to the army and spent most of World War I in charitable activities and studying theology at home, being ordained a priest in 1920.

He registered at the University of Rome in 1921 to take graduate studies in literature, but was quickly matriculated in the Vatican's College of Nobles when Mons. Giuseppe Pizzardo discovered that his father, Giorgio, was a member of the Italian parliament. A lasting impression was made on the young priest serving in the papal curia among fascist-leaning Roman prelates, when his father and the Aventine group of parliamentarians were literally assaulted by Mussolini's henchmen in 1924 after protesting the murder of the socialist deputy, Giacomo Matteotti. He later had his own difficulties with government repression in protecting the Catholic university students whom he aided as chaplain and spiritual guide.

A man of wide literary and religious interests, Montini collected the conferences he gave to Catholic circles in three books published as theological guides for university graduates before World War II. Well acquainted with French religious literature, he translated Jacques Maritain's *Three Reformers* into Italian, developed an ear for classical music, and was a voracious reader with a retentive memory, as Jean Guitton has demonstrated in his book, *Dialogues with Pope Paul.*

Limited to curial activities in 1937, Montini's world vision was fostered by his position of secretary to Cardinal Eugene Pacelli, accompanying him on a visit to Budapest in 1938 and becoming his factotum when the cardinal secretary of state emerged from the conclave of 1939 as Pope Pius XII. During World War II he was entrusted with organizing the papal information service for tracing prisoners of war and refugees in league with the international Red Cross, and supervising Vatican aid and relief activities.

In the post-war period, together with Mons. Domenico Tardini, Montini presided over the Holy See's internal and external affairs. With the death of Cardinal Maglione in 1944, Pius decided to serve as his own secretary of state, using the two monsignors as his 'inside and outside' men. Montini dealt with the conditions of the war refugees, international migration problems, and aid and rehabilitation projects, using US War Relief Services for direct contact with the United Nations organizations and the International Refugee Organization. He also supported the bid of the papal nuncio in Paris, Archbishop Angelo Roncalli, to have the Holy See involved with UNESCO despite the anti-religious bias of its original staff.

In December 1954, as the result of a power struggle within the Vatican – Montini had championed a gradual withdrawal of Vatican influence from Italian politics in keeping with the aim of premier Alcide de Gasperi and Don Luigi Sturzo – he was relieved of his position as personal adviser to Pope Pius and consecrated Archbishop of Milan. But he was not given the red hat of a cardinal. Though 'moved up in order to be moved out', his elevation to the see of Milan proved to be a stepping stone on his way to the papacy. It gave him necessary pastoral experience, and brought him into close contact with the patriarch of Venice, Angelo Roncalli. When the latter was elected pope in October 1958, his first move was to make Montini a cardinal. Shortly before his death, John indicated that the man who could carry out the Johannine revolution in the Church was the cardinal of Milan.

Unlike his predecessor in so many ways – he lacked John's insouciance, John's apparent neglect of unessentials, John's ebullient humor, and his ability to mollify opposition – Montini did share John's vision of a renewal of the Church, and his courageous determination to break out of the Vatican and see and be seen by the world. John's journeys were confined to walking tours in Rome, visits to hospitals, jails, orphanages, dying friends, and a train ride to Loretto in the Abruzzi mountains.

Paul, however, covered the globe. In ten major flights he visited the Holy Land, India, Turkey, the United Nations Assembly in New York, Bogota in Colombia, Kampala in Africa, and then a globe-trotting voyage to the Philippines, Australia, Samoa, Indonesia, Hong Kong and Singapore. He also visited Portugal and Geneva, and crisscrossed Italy from Taranto to Sardinia. On all these occasions he was accompanied by the press, went out of his way to visit poverty-stricken areas, and proved a most accommodating traveller.

His one great disappointment was the refusal of the Polish government under Gomulka to welcome him to Warsaw in 1966 for the thousandth anniversary of the founding of the Polish nation. He had served the first six months of his diplomatic career there in 1923 and wanted to return to demonstrate his affection for the Polish people. However, the communist regime, at odds with Cardinal Stefan Wyszynski and most of the nation's Catholics, feared his presence would destroy its credibility. It was correct. The pope had the satisfaction of seeing the papal proverb 'who bites the pope, dies of it' justified with the subsequent fall of the Gomulka regime, and the need that the new Gierek government felt of enlisting the political assistance of the cardinal of Warsaw.

In his dealing with the communist countries, Pope Paul followed John's example, distinguishing between an atheistic ideology that had to be condemned, and the historical evolution of an economic and political structure that the Church could tolerate.

Meanwhile Paul had inaugurated a political policy that continued John's so-called 'opening to the left'. He welcomed statesmen and heads of nations of every persuasion to the Vatican. His visitors included communists – Podgorny, Gromyko, Tito, Gierek, Ceausescu – revolutionary socialists from Asia and Africa, and representatives of the capitalist West. He exchanged diplomatic representatives with Cuba and Yugoslavia as well as with Algeria, Uganda and Indonesia. And he placed cardinals as residential bishops in almost every country where the Church was operating, including Korea, Sri Lanka, and Apia in Western Samoa. In his vision of the Church's obligation to preach the gospel to every nation, including continental China, Paul could not be faulted.

Within the inner confines of the Church's structure, the Pope showed himself likewise radically innovative. During the final session of the Council, he welcomed the concept of collegiality – the responsibility of the bishops with and under the pope for Church policy at the top – and took measures to implement this advance in ecclesiology by introducing the Roman Synod of Bishops.

He used his supreme authority in the Church to appoint a fifth of that assembly to balance out the ratio of openminded bishops elected by the national hierarchies. And while the structure of this new mechanism for Church rule still requires considerable development, it is a radical achievement, bound to affect the Church's presence in the world in an existential fashion.

On the day before the Council ended in December 1965 Paul telegraphed his intention to change the structure of the curia by abolishing the Congregation of the Holy Office with its Inquisition and Index of Forbidden Books. He replaced it with the Congregation for the Doctrine of the Faith. The significance of this move was enormous, though the fact was not immediately appreciated. It meant that Paul had accepted John's distinction between the 'truths of the faith' and 'the manner in which they are expressed' – the separation of the form from the substance of faith – that seemed close to heresy in the minds of most Roman-trained theologians.

Then, having achieved this, Paul hesitated. He did not change the personnel of the Congregation until three years later. He thus allowed the old guard to block the radical reform in the Congregation's operations and thinking called for by its change of name.

Paul's failure to make a clean sweep of the people who occupied the administrative offices in the Vatican when he assumed control of the papacy was an enigma. Most of the cardinals and prelates were no friends of his. Many of them had been involved in the machinations that forced him out of the curia in 1954. Only with the publication of his *Motu proprio* (On the Governance of the Church) in the spring of 1967 and the arrival of Archbishop Giovanni Benelli as the *sostituto*, or aide, later that year, did Paul inaugurate the essential change of personnel needed to implement the radical modifications in curial administration that he had in mind.

During the pope's convalescence from surgery in January 1968

Benelli began the retirement of six curial cardinals and the introduction of outsiders – Franjo Seper of Yugoslavia, Francis J. Brennan of the USA, Gabriel Garrone and Jean Villot of France, Maximilian von Furstenberg of Belgium and Jan Willebrands of Holland, among others – to give the curia an international façade at the top. It was too late. The change proved more nominal than real, for these outsiders gradually settled into the older curial style, seemingly determined to out-Roman the Romans.

On his arrival in the papacy, Paul could easily have achieved a total reorganization of the papal household. No one was better acquainted with its internal structure. With the full body of the Church's bishops before him in the Council, and with the obvious support of the conciliar leaders such as Joseph Frings of Cologne and Achille Liénart of Lille, who openly criticized the curia for its opposition to change, he could have retired the old guard and selected new men without disrupting the machinery of government.

That Paul was conscious of this possibility seems certain from the advice he offered his successors not to appoint curial officials in permanent positions until they were at least three months into the papacy. And to enable the next pope to be his own man, Paul established a rule of five-year tenure for all Vatican officials, without the right to reappointment and with the proviso that all should lose their positions with the death of the pontiff. With Pauline inconsistency, he then broke his own rule in 1973 by reappointing almost all the people installed in 1968. Meanwhile, however, in 1970 he had set the age of retirement for bishops at seventy-five, and for cardinals – from all offices, including the right to vote in a papal election – at eighty.

Among Paul's major achievements was the renewal of the hierarchies in Africa, the Far East and Latin America, where he has given a definitely progressive tenor to most episcopates. In the strictly social and political enmeshment of the Church in worldly affairs, he came down hard on the need for development as the path to peace. He condemned torture and repression on the part of governments, as well as terrorism of all types; stressed that governments that support or tolerate economic and social exploitation are unjust; and, without justifying violence, suggested that they are subject to overthrow.

Paul accepted the Council's changeabout in its definition of the nature of marriage, and while stressing the evils of abortion, divorce and sexual license, he allowed for a wide latitude of humane and psychological considerations in the handling of marital problems, and in the dissolution of impossible conjugal situations.

Paul's diplomatic policy did not enjoy the full support of the Roman curia, nor of a considerable proportion of the Church's hierarchy. To exiles from the communist countries he seemed to be selling out on their martyred brethren. From the start of his reign he had made overtures to the communist bloc, including continental China. He refused to allow members of the Vatican Council to pass condemnations on individuals or nations, thus gravely offending lay and clerical Catholics who had suffered for their faith. The Ukrainian cardinal, Josef Slipij, released from Soviet prison in deference to Pope John in 1962, openly criticized Paul's policies, declaring that in ten years of freedom in Rome he suffered more than in his twenty years in custody in Russia.

The Hungarian cardinal, Josef Mindszenty, who finally left his refuge in the American embassy in Budapest in 1971, defied the papal request that he resign his title as Archbishop of Esztergom, forcing the pope to remove him in order, as the Vatican stated, to allow for the proper functioning of the Hungarian Church. In general, Paul followed a policy of accommodation, careful however to have his voice heard in favor of justice and decency, and against oppression and genocide.

Paul's first encyclical letter, *Ecclesiam suam* (His church), had outlined the framework of the dialogue he felt it was the Church's duty to conduct with itself, with other Christians, and with the believers and non-believers of all the world. In his conduct towards the Council, he pursued this aim. From the start he championed the idea of clarifying the position of the bishops as successors to the apostles, and therefore as associated with the pope in a collegial responsibility for the governance of the universal Church. He wanted the Council to produce a clear program of development for the Church tomorrow. Hence he fought for unequivocal declarations on ecumenism, the attitude of Christians toward the Jews, and the identification of the Church's spiritual essence with its commitment to the social, economic and political problems of today's world.

The main thrust of the Council was directed toward a reorientation in the spiritual order. Nevertheless, it quickly became evident that the political elements of its earthly existence were a fundamental concern in any reconsideration of its purpose and function. To reverse the axiom of Emile Durkheim, behind every major religious conflict there is a political problem. Thus the Council found itself influenced by the practical difficulties of the Arab-Jewish conflict as it attempted to clarify Christian attitudes toward its Hebrew ancestry, its centuries of anti-semitic thinking, and its relations with the rest of the non-Christian world from Muslims to atheistic communists.

Of even more pertinence was the need to confront actual political structures in its teaching regarding property, justice, the exploitation of the poor and destitute, and the rationalizations involved in the justification of modern warfare.

What is truly extraordinary about the Catholic Church as a political organization is not the fact that it is actually undergoing a revolution in its internal structure and ideology, but the impression that its leaders have been able to project over the centuries that the Church is the one institution that does not change. Actually, the opposite is true. The Church is continually concocting new traditions not only in political and organizational spheres, but in its doctrinal and disciplinary projections as well. Even a superficial acquaintance with the history of the Church's theology will testify to great divergencies in the explanation of its teachings. During the debate on Holy Scriptures at Vatican II, Cardinal Gerlier of Lyons said: 'The Church is so enamored of tradition that it is always creating new ones!' A fair knowledge of its institutional development indicates clearly that it is only by adapting itself to the exigencies of time and space that the Church has survived the ravages of nineteen centuries of history.

Dealing explicitly with the political order, the Council's Pastoral Constitution discussed the proper view of relations between the political community and the Church. Disclaiming the identity of the Church with any state or political system, this document claimed that the Church's function is to contribute to the wider application of justice and charity within and between nations. In acknowledging that the Church does employ temporal means in pursuing its spiritual and secular ends, the Council announced a clean break with past policies. It asserted that the Church 'does not lodge her hope in privileges conferred by civil authority,' and stated that 'the Church stands ready to renounce the exercise of certain legitimately acquired rights if it becomes clear that their use raises doubts about her sincerity . . . or new conditions of life demand other arrangements.'

This is a revolutionary statement compared, for example, with the attitude assumed by Leo XIII in his encyclicals dealing with the political order, even though in their day the Leonine documents were considered to contain a definite radical development. Certainly the Pastoral Constitution provided a striking contrast to the assertions of Pius XI in his encyclical on Christ the King (*Quas primas,* 1925) where the pontiff maintained that as the Church was divine in origin, its rights were inviolable, above and beyond the judgment of secular society – almost a throwback to the medievalism of Innocent III or Boniface VIII. This imperious approach was modified by Pope Pius XII who, while not repudiating the divine right theory of his predecessor, took a pragmatic attitude towards the Church's political problems.

In bringing Vatican Council II to a successful close on 8 December 1965, Paul seemed determined to pursue its immediate implementation. Two days before, he had replaced the old Holy Office with the Congregation for the Doctrine of the Faith. However, he retained the old staff with the conservative 'watchdog' Cardinal Ottaviani at its head. Then, instead of taking advantage of the momentum created by the Council's activities, he was persuaded to slow down its implementation. A man of precise and orderly administrative procedures, Paul evidently felt that the less theologically aware and more staid members of the Church should not be exposed to the shock of immediate change in the liturgy, new attitudes to non-Christians, and a fundamental reorientation in seminary training, the religious life of monks and nuns, and the overall workings of the Church.

Many people were convinced that this sudden change of pace was a fatal mistake. It disappointed activists within the Church who had been reading the conciliar documents and preparing for swift action. Paul's calculated risk in declaring a cooling-off period resulted in a reaction whereby adventuresome clerics and laity began innumerable experiments in the liturgy, a worldwide series of confrontations with bishops, and revolt in the seminaries and within religious orders and societies. These people had jumped to the conclusion that the Council's constitutions and decrees now constituted the mind of the Church. They attempted to force a showdown between traditionalists and innovators. Thus, much of Paul's pontificate was plagued with rebellious actions, leading him frequently to deplore the fact that the pope was not being obeyed. His habit of touching on all aspects of a question in his sermons and speeches worsened his public image, for the press invariably reported a pessimistic sentence or paragraph, whereas his message was usually uplifting and hopeful.

Paul's vigorous though orderly pursuit of the reform of the papal household was an important achievement. One of his first acts was to abolish the titles of nobility bestowed on their families by former popes and known as the black or old Roman aristocracy, telling its members, many of whom were involved in societal scandals, that the Church could no longer do anything for them. He reduced the pomp and circumstance of Vatican protocol. Gone were the flamboyant retinues, the papal zouaves and guards, the glittering ceremonial that accompanied papal functions in St Peter's or the reception of political luminaries.

The pope now appeared in elegant but modest robes, carrying a reed-like crozier on liturgical occasions, accompanied by only a few necessary attendants and usually on foot. During the 1973–4 energy crisis, he drove to the Lateran basilica in a horse-drawn carriage. And in his visits to local parishes he tried to get as close to the people as possible.

By 1967, four years after assuming the papal office, Paul had changed the complexion of his administrative organs, known as the curia, to which he gave new titles designating these offices as papal household members rather than bureaucratic offices. He reduced the number of Italian heads of curial congregations – the equivalent of cabinet officers – to four, brought in a Frenchman, Cardinal Jean Villot, as secretary of state; appointed a Yugoslav, Cardinal Seper, as prefect of the Congregation for Doctrine; a Brazilian, Cardinal Rossi, in the Congregation for Evangelization; an American, John Wright, in the Congregation for the Clergy; and a Canadian, Maurice Roy, as head of both the Secretariat for the Laity and the Papal Commission for Justice and Peace.

Meanwhile, in keeping with recommendations of the Council, he had instituted the Roman Synod of Bishops, which in 1967, 1969, 1971, 1974, and 1977 brought to the Vatican diocesan cardinals and bishops from around the world to discuss and help settle specific problems facing the postconciliar Church. Elected by national or regional Conferences of Bishops, these prelates convened with the heads of the curial offices under the guidance of the pontiff. In 1967 they decided that heresy was not an immediate danger; in 1969 they discussed the use and abuse of authority; in 1971 they dealt with problems of social and economic justice; in 1974 and 1977 they considered the Church's call to evangelization and its catechetical practices.

To give permanency to the bishops' assembly, Pope Paul instituted a synodal secretariat in Rome, to which fifteen prelates selected by the bishops on a revolving basis were attached and given the task of implementing the decisions of former, and preparing the agenda for future, synods.

In his creation of cardinals, Pope Paul attempted to give the Church a truly international look. He made cardinals in such sparsely Catholic areas as Karachi in Pakistan, Osaka in Japan; Nairobi in Kenya, Seoul in Korea, Hanoi in Vietnam, Brazzaville in the Congo, and Apia in the Samoan Islands.

Paul defused a series of confrontations posed by the progressive wing of the Dutch Church, by individual theologians such as Hans Küng and Ivan Illich, and by priest groups in Latin America, Europe and Italy. He gave no encouragement to rightist movements, and opposed so-called Catholic countries, such as Spain, Portugal, Brazil, for their intransigent capitalistic attitudes. He removed the conservative cardinal, Giuseppe Siri of Genoa, from chairmanship of the Italian Bishops Conference, and gave free rein to the Conference's deliberations.

Although at the start of his reign, curial officials did interfere in Italian political affairs, Paul himself made a great effort to withdraw. But he did not succeed completely. Clearly enunciating the Church's opposition to divorce, he felt compelled to interfere directly in the battle over Italy's introduction of a divorce law. Even after the defeat of the attempt by conservative Catholics to overthrow the divorce laws via a referendum, Vatican officials continued to interfere in the inner circles of the Christian Democratic party, using a subtle veto power to block candidates for public office who did not conform to their demands. The kidnapping and death of the ex-premier Aldo Moro greatly saddened Paul in his last year, and he personally tried to comfort the Moro family by attending the private funeral service. Concerned with the sad state of his own diocese of Rome, he induced the Archbishop of Spoleto, Ugo Poletti, to become his vicar, and on making him cardinal, gave him *carte blanche* to do a radical job of pastoral reorganization.

Although offended by the stance taken by the Belgium cardinal,

Suenens, who in 1969 demanded a more profound implementation of
the Council, reform in the selection of bishops and a democratization of
papal elections, Paul considered the call for a new papal elective system. He suggested, but did not put into practice, the possibility that
bishops who were not cardinals, but had been elected members of the
secretariat for the synod of bishops, and non-cardinal patriarchs of the
Oriental churches, be allowed to vote in a papal election. This suggested move pointed to a further democratization of the Church's hierarchical structure and might be used in a future federation with the Oriental Orthodox and the Protestant churches.

In an interview granted to the Milanese journalist Alberto Cavalleri in
1966, the only one of its kind on record, Pope Paul confessed frankly
that he was thoroughly confused on the birth-control issue, not knowing
which way to turn. Cavalleri states that the subject was broached by the
pontiff himself, for, out of a sense of respect for the highly sensitive
religious leader, the journalist had decided not to bring up this difficult
matter. So extraordinary were both the interview and the papal admission
of confusion that the editor of Milan's *Corriera della Sera* refused at
first to publish the piece, fearing they might have something of a hoax
on their hands. When finally the article appeared on the front page of
the Milanese journal, it caused a sensation. The pope's admission to
perplexity over the birth-control problem was grasped eagerly by the
progressive theologians, who immediately interpreted the papal stand
as confirming their conviction that the Church was in a state of doubt
concerning this important moral problem. Hence, married couples were
free to use contraceptives, since an uncertain law could not bind them
in conscience.

Vatican officials were furious over both the interview and Pope
Paul's indiscretion in admitting to uncertainty in such a grave matter.
In several successive issues, *L'Osservatore Romano* did its best to dis-
abuse the world and the Catholic faithful of the validity of the inferences
drawn from the papal statement.

Meanwhile within the papal commission on the family, the debate
mounted toward a climax. Gradually it became clear that the opposition
to the possibility of change in the Church's attitude had reached a rock-
solid foundation. Four priests proclaimed themselves irretrievably com-

mitted to the impossibility of accepting an alleviation of the Church's traditional position. Pushed to an ultimate stage in the argument, they admitted that they could not prove the prohibition on the grounds of the natural law; nor was there any absolute evidence one way or another in the scriptures or in divine revelation. Nevertheless, the word of the Church had been so consistent and recent popes so positive in condemning the use of artificial means of contraception that the teaching had to have had the sanction of the Holy Spirit. On that stand they simply would not budge. The committee was finally persuaded that further discussion was useless. A report was put together indicating that a consensus had been reached by the overwhelming majority (64 to 4) of theologians, legal experts, historians, sociologists and family members, advising the Holy Father that a change in Church's stand was both possible and advisable.

When this conclusion was submitted to the commission of cardinals and bishops, it caused great perplexity. Forced to a vote, six of the prelates abstained, eight voted in favor of recommending the report to the pontiff and six voted against it.

Within the Roman curia there was consternation. In his determination not to budge on the issue, Cardinal Ottaviani persuaded the four intransigent theologians – the Jesuit Marcellino Zalba, the Redemptorist Jan Visser, the Franciscan Emenegildo Lio and the American Jesuit John Ford – to draw up their conclusions in the form of a special report. This document was submitted to the pope along with the commission's report, as if it were a minority recommendation of dissension. When news of this maneuver reached the notice of the English Cardinal Heenan, he was furious. As one of the two vice-presidents of the pontifical commission, he denied that a minority report formed part of the commission's work – for justice had been done to the opinions of the dissenters in the official report.

Cardinals Heenan and Doepfner had in fact encouraged the Bishop of Albi in France to prepare a paper that should be submitted to the pope by way of a preface for the statement they expected the Holy Father to make. In this tract, full justification would be supplied for the change in the Church's attitude.

Pope Paul's agonizing became all the more acute. While the principal members of both the bishops' and the experts' commissions returned to their homes, or exercised great restraint in not approaching the pontiff personally to persuade him to accept their position, the opposition did no such thing. Fiercely determined not to allow the pope to betray what they considered the Church's heritage, they waylaid him personally day after day – Ottaviani, Cicognani, Browne, Parente and Samore – never letting an opportunity pass.

Paul finally decided to take the matter totally into his own hands. Calling Archbishop Agostino Casaroli from the secretary of state, he removed the problem from the competence of the Holy Office. Then he sent for the French Jesuit Gustave Martelet and returned to Castel-gondolfo, where he worked over the final draft of an encyclical. When it was published on 24 July 1968, he had Mons. Lambruschini of the Lateran University explain its significance to the press, and state explicitly that it was not an infallible document. Nevertheless the pope insisted, to the end of his reign, on its validity as a traditional solution to a moral problem, within his competence as pope.

Few documents in the course of the Catholic Church's long and turbulent history caused such immediate and widespread consternation as Pope Paul's encyclical *Humanae vitae*. Contrary to the desires of a large proportion of the Catholic faithful and the expectation of the outside world, the pontiff repeated the Church's traditional ban on the use of artificial contraceptives. To be non-sinful, he asserted: 'every conjugal act must be open to the transmission of life.'

This statement was immediately challenged by a group of young theologians at the Catholic University of America (in Washington D.C.) and repudiated by groups of responsible Catholics around the world. It was deplored by individuals and organizations struggling with the world's vast overpopulation problems.

While the pontiff admitted that it was not an irreformable pronouncement, he insisted that in his office as supreme guardian of faith and morals he had used his prerogative to settle a controversy raging in the Church for half a century. And he settled it in favor of the Church's traditional stand. A deliberate interference with the biological process involved in *coitus* was a violation of God's law. No matter what the motive, it was wrong and therefore sinful.

This decision was seen as a reversion to a position abandoned by Vatican Council II, which in its teachings on marriage maintained that the morality of a human act had to be taken from 'the nature of man and his actions' and not only from his biological structure.

Paul's reputation as a progressive pope was seriously damaged by his *Credo*, or Declaration of Faith, in 1968 with its conservative theology, his encyclical *Humanae Vitae* and his decision to hold the line on clerical celibacy in the Western church. And while he favored the employment of women in ecclesiastical offices and decision-making, he strenuously opposed their ordination to the diaconate or priesthood.

In the birth-control decision Paul had gone against the official advice of a papal commission on population and family life, and raised the charge that he was indifferent to the miseries of individual married couples and the unfed masses of mankind. The pontiff did back the few bishops who severely disciplined priests for opposing the encyclical, although he did not indulge in such condemnations himself. While he seemed to feel a mystical need to uphold the Church's pro-natalist position, he did little to curb the conferences of bishops who interpreted the pastoral teaching of the encyclical broadly, telling their people that the pope proposed a high ideal; but that if, in conscience, they could not live up to that ideal, they should not consider themselves in sin. This was the stand not only of the Dutch and Canadian bishops, but also of the French and Italian bishops.

Paul's concern for traditional papal authority and the right to life confused his attitude toward the problem of overpopulation. He ran the risk of having the Church accused of failing mankind at a crucial crisis. He did call for a 'rational control of births', insisting on the right of parents and not governments to decide the number of children they should have. On the tenth anniversary of the encyclical in 1978 he maintained he had made a correct decision, but cautioned pastors and confessors to a pastoral implementation of the teaching.

Meanwhile Paul's truly progressive attitudes were revealed in his encyclical on the *Development of Peoples* (1967) and his apostolic *Call to Action* (1971). These were radical documents, dealing with the world's social, economic and political structures. Not merely did he deplore war (at the UN General Assembly in New York in October 1965 he had cried: 'No more war! War, never again!'), but he condemned injustice, governmental violence and economic exploitation. In 1968 he flew to Bogota in Columbia to preside at the opening of the Latin American Bishops' Conference (CELAM) and encouraged the delegates in their attempt to reach fundamentals in discussing that continent's problems involved in the exploitation of the poorer classes. He said plainly that governments that supported economic systems which kept the majority of their people in degradation were guilty of violence. Asked in Bogota if this meant that the revolutionary overthrow of such regimes was justified, he replied that 'violence was not in keeping with the Gospel'.

Pope Paul did condemn the use of torture, the deprivation of civil rights, and the continued exploitation of the poor in Latin America, where once the Church was identified with the establishment. In 1969 in Kampala, Uganda, he called for the africanization of the Church. He warned against the possibility of genocide after the civil war in Nigeria; condemned the savagery of civil strife in Uganda, and showed great displeasure over the failure of the American bishops to follow his lead in condemning the bombardment of Vietnam. Following his trip to the Holy Land in 1964 he exhibited a carefully balanced attitude toward the state of Israel. He welcomed Golda Meir and other Jewish leaders to the Vatican, and called for a special status for Jerusalem, but did not accept diplomatic relations with Israel, mainly out of deference to the oriental-rite Catholics – Copts, Maronites and Melchites – in the Arab countries. On most theological matters Paul followed a traditional line. Nevertheless, he strongly encouraged ecumenical relations with other churches and religions, himself praying with their leaders.

Unlike his two predecessors – the aristocratic Pius XII and the jovial friend to mankind, John XXIII – Paul's personality did not come across to the Church as a whole or to the general public. Nevertheless, he had worked harder than any of his predecessors at being a pope of the people. In the innumerable public audiences where he received thousands of pilgrims and tourists, Paul went out of his way to accommodate his visitors. He used eight or nine languages to greet them, paused to let individuals or groups get a good look at him, and tried to shake the hands of newly-weds, babies in arms, children and the handicapped. In his talks he referred to events of the day from sport to politics, not neglecting earthquakes, plane crashes, kidnapping, tourism, inflation, housing problems, starvation and the thousand and one human happenings he read about in the seven or eight papers at which he glanced each day. But Pope Paul was still considered a relatively faceless pontiff.

The strength of the Catholic Church can be measured by the vast agglomeration of religious orders and congregations of men and women whose lives are dedicated to giving witness to the presence of Jesus Christ in each age. In keeping with the upheavals of the last two decades, most of these institutions experienced a revolution from within. Encouraged by the Vatican Council to bring their rules and lifestyles up to date, many of the orders went through an identity crisis. Members challenged the validity of their objectives as teaching, nursing, preaching, missionary and social-service institutions; and not a few priests, nuns and brothers departed from their commitment to the vows of poverty, chastity and obedience upon which the structure of their organization had depended.

A similar phenomenon attacked diocesan priests. When the first wave of defections from the ministry came to the pontiff's attention, he reacted with anger and shame. In a sermon on Holy Thursday, 1966, he referred to the 'new Judases'; but then, examining this situation with his usual good sense, he realized that attempting to hold priests, monks or nuns to their original commitment once the spark of a religious vocation died, would be futile.

Before Pope John had died he had informed the congregation of the clergy that he desired to give a dispensation to marry to priests who had left the ministry to get married, and who had achieved a stable Christian family life despite the handicap of being cut off from the sacraments. This information had been spread orally through the apostolic delegates and nuncios without achieving public notice. By way of precedent for his extraordinary action, he could point to the decision of Pius XII to ordain as priests, married men coming as converts to Catholicism from other Christian churches, particularly the Lutherans. This was a decision totally at odds with the attitude of his predecessor, Pius XI, of whom it was said that to a petition for laicization from a dying, married priest, he had answered, 'Let him perish!' Pope Paul gradually began granting dispensations to marry. Only at the insistence of curial officials did he surround the petition with difficult, and at times humiliating, conditions such as an admission that the petitioner could not and had not observed the vow of celibacy. There was evidence that during the Roman Synod of 1971 the pontiff had seriously considered granting the privilege of a married clergy to the African and Asian churches. But debate on this issue was refused at the insistence of both curial officials and bishops, primarily from the English-speaking world, who considered the matter too delicate and too dangerous for public discussion.

Besides, the churches who might have welcomed this facing of the facts of life did not want to create a situation in which their clergy would assume the rank of second-class citizens in the Church's priesthood. The problem of clerical celibacy had not reached its critical point of maturity before Paul's passing.

A large part of the difficulty in the efforts at renewal of the religious orders was created by the man Pope Paul inserted into the Congregation of Religious Orders as its prefect in order to shunt him off from possibly succeeding the elderly Cardinal Cicognani, who was serving as the pope's secretary of state. This was Cardinal Ildebrando Antoniutti, who had been the runner-up candidate in the conclave. A hard-headed churchman with service in the diplomatic corps, Antoniutti attempted to block the progressive movements in the religious orders. He went so far as to dictate the length of skirts that nuns should wear and refused to authorize changes in an order's rules that had been voted on properly by chapters or constitutional assemblies in keeping with the Council's dictates. He had favored the hard line followed by Archbishop Marcel Lefebvre in his attempt to dominate the postconciliar development of the Congregation of the Holy Spirit Fathers, of which Lefebvre was elected the Superior General in 1962, almost splitting that religious congregation in half; and when Lefebvre was voted out of his post, Antoniutti used him in his repressive activities.

Of all the religious orders whose reaction to the Council caused consternation, the hardest hit seemed to be the Society of Jesus, the largest of the congregations and supposedly the best trained to withstand the fashions of the hour. Nevertheless, despite the heroic efforts of their Basque Superior General, Father Pedro Arrupe, to stabilize the order while allowing experimentation in the lifestyles of its members, during these years the Jesuits suffered great losses in personnel and institutions.

To face up to a threatened split between the conservatives and progressives in the order, as well as to lay out a program for recovering the losses, the Superior General and the procurators of the Society with the pope's acquiescence called a chapter to meet in Rome early in 1975. The assembly represented the second phase of a program of interior renewal for the Catholic Church's most prestigious religious order, a phase begun in 1966 in keeping with Pope John's call for a 'leap ahead.'

In preparation for close to four years, the General Congregation had to confront the order's current problems and prepare its members – down from 36,000 in 1966 to 29,600 in 1975 – for the year 2000. In a preliminary press conference, Father Arrupe emphatically denied that he had any intention of resigning under pressure from conservative Jesuits; and described the Society's principal need as an authentic commitment to justice.

This direction had been confirmed by Pope Paul in an extensive allocution to the delegates on 3 December 1974. Telling them not to worry about their identity, Paul instructed the members not to tamper with the inner structure of the Society of Jesus. Instead they were to concentrate on furnishing the Church with answers to the problems of a loss of faith and a breakdown of decency in today's world.

At intervals during the discussion on the need to update the Society's apostolate and authenticate its lifestyle by a new approach to the vows of poverty and obedience, Father Arrupe was asked to comment on the Society's activities. Referring to an 'Ignatian radicalism' that he attributed to the Society's founder, the sixteenth-century Ignatius of Loyola, Arrupe said its members would have to preach, and also practice, justice. Injustices in the political and economic order, he remarked, were often the doings of their own friends and relatives. Were Jesuits ready, he asked, to risk the accusation of Marxism and subversion, and the loss of financial support, in their zeal for the pursuit of justice?

What bothered the Superior General was the lack of internal loyalty on the part of discontented members who felt justified in running to the press with every detail of the order's inner problems, even accounts of conscience or privileged communications. He seemed to feel that disgruntled arch-conservatives were the worst offenders in this regard. He accused them of rendering the rule of the Society almost impossible when every conversation of a superior was liable to be reported to some Vatican official, or repeated outside the Society.

Vatican rumblings had accompanied the assembly's discussion of the fourth vow of loyalty, that to the pope, administered to only some 30 or 40 per cent of the priest members who were chosen for their talents or accomplishments. This vow thus creates an elitist group, excluding the majority of priests and brothers from holding key positions, such as rectors of institutions, provincial superiors and staff assistants. Even though the strictness of selection had broken down drastically in recent years, as was attested by the number of younger men serving as delegates in the assembly, a straw vote was taken that favored the granting of the vow to all the Society's members.

Retribution was swift. The pope sent the assembly a letter indicating his displeasure, and chiding the delegates for not paying sufficient attention to the tasks he had set before them. Prolonging the assembly an extra week, the somewhat stunned delegates made heroic efforts to align their resolutions with the papal strictures.

The General Congregation had in fact already accomplished a great deal, turning out directives concerned with the 'Jesuit need to achieve its goal in self identity' and the formation of its new aims; spelling out the Society's charter for pursuing social and political missions; and describing the *diakonia fidei,* the service of faith through justice. In reconsidering the order's vow of obedience, the delegates laid down directions for the formation of future Jesuits and discussed ways of dealing with tensions and dissent within the Society.

During a private audience at the close, in which Father Arrupe gave the Holy Father the Congregation's documents, he found the pope most cordial. Half apologizing for having interfered to preserve the Society's original structure, the pontiff assured the Superior General and his four assistants of his trust in the Society.

Troubling Pope Paul were genuine worries about the faith and religious consciousness, a reflection of the rigid theological training of his youth and early priesthood. Only peripherally involved in the theological stirrings after the end of World War II, he was ill prepared for the radical thinking behind many of the doctrinal advances demanded at Vatican Council II. It was with reluctance that he allowed the substantial changes in the Church's traditional teaching on religious liberty, on marriage, and on the nature of divine revelation to become conciliar doctrine. Though he promulgated the documents, he was easily persuaded by the fearful cardinals and conservative theologians in his entourage to declare a holding-off of their implementation until the Roman curial offices could give these constitutions and decrees an official and restraining interpretation. Then, in 1968, in preparation for his encyclical on birth control, he published his *Credo,* read by critics as a reactionary document hardly in keeping with the advanced thinking of the conciliar theologians.

Heading into his eightieth year, Pope Paul was confronted with speculation regarding his possible retirement. After all, he had deprived cardinals of their posts, and the right to vote in a papal election, on their eightieth birthday. But word from the Vatican's upper echelon was a simple: 'The father of the family does not retire.' Nor was there any reason for such a move. Though troubled with arthritis, the pontiff was still capable of a full day's work and very much alive mentally.

In June 1977 he created four cardinals, beginning with the man who had served as the aide in the secretary of state's office and the pope's executive officer, Archbishop Giovanni Benelli. Benelli's promotion, at the same time, to the archbishopric of Florence brought to mind Montini's own banishment from the Vatican in 1954 when he was sent to Milan but without the cardinalatial dignity.

Like Montini then, Benelli had been a controversial character in the curia, wielding great power in carrying out the pope's policies. Strong-minded and blunt, he had accumulated the enmity of not a few curialists, and rumors were circulated that his promotion was another case of the Vatican's far-from-subtle removal process. The reality was quite the opposite. The pope was rewarding a faithful collaborator by making him eligible as his possible successor in a future conclave, and at the same time giving the Italian episcopate a cardinal who would quickly rise to a position of leadership. Events were to prove the pontiff correct.

In the fall of 1977 Pope Paul assembled the fifth Roman Synod of Bishops, setting them to the discussion of the Church's catechetical methods in spreading the Gospel. Difficulties in confronting the modern world with the Church's teachings were affecting the 'third' as well as the 'first' world, and the pope was seeking a solution by collegial consultation that would take in all the varied factors affecting this principal task: to preach the gospel to every creature.

In most parts of Asia and Africa the faith had been implanted primarily by full-time catechists, whose conversion from paganism had been to a total devotion to Christianity with a Pauline passion for spreading the faith. For more than a century, the system was almost self-supporting, minor financial assistance from abroad allowing most of the money received from overseas to be used for building mission compounds, schools, clinics and other conveniences. But as the contemporary world economic system caught up with them, the self-sustaining catechist was disappearing, making the vast work of conversion still confronting the Christian churches in the third world very difficult.

In addressing this difficulty a number of prelates from the communist and Muslim lands pointed to the curial insistence on orthodox teaching as extremely unhelpful. Theological niceties were a luxury in which only the leisured class of Christians had time to indulge. Under circumstances of political exploitation or simple backwardness, missionaries were intent upon putting across the Christ of the gospels. They found these primitive documents extremely adaptable to the various cultures in which they were operating, without worrying whether they were given a fundamentalist or sophisticated interpretation. What was essential was forming Christ in the recipients. Only the real conviction of Christ's actuality gave their people the courage to live their faith under political harassment or economic exploitation.

Also of considerable interest to the synodal observers were events on the Italian ecclesiastical scene. The gathering of bishops seemed to be an auspicious moment for the Communist leader, Signor Berlinguer, to publish an open letter to Bishop Bettazzi of Ivrea, the comparatively youthful prelate who had questioned the Communist boss the previous year. Bettazzi's queries concerned the sincerity of the Party's vaunted adherence to democratic government, and the trust that could be put into its guarantees of religious freedom. These worries were paramount in the minds of Church authorities as the ranks of Communist voters continued to grow.

Berlinguer's answer to Bettazzi was both long in coming and long in explanations, eliciting a 'methinks he doth protest too much' response from most commentators. His assurance that Italian communism aimed at a state that would be neither 'theist nor atheist but democratic and humane' was pounced upon by the editor of the Catholic daily paper *Avvenire* as obviously a lie. This attack was powerfully reinforced by the recently created Archbishop of Florence, Cardinal Benelli, in a talk to an association of Catholic schools. Challenging Berlinguer's assertions, Benelli said that what counted in such matters were facts not words. And he pointed to the Communist-inspired new Law 382, for the reform of the country's social assistance system. This proposal to put the total responsibility for aid to the poor, the social security system and institutions caring for the indigent, sick and handicapped, in the hands of the regional governments would eventually eliminate the Church and other private institutions from works of charity. The declared aim of the law was to eliminate waste and possible chicanery. It stemmed from the Communists' reaction to the past misuse of charitable funds under Church auspices. But as Benelli pointed out, the elimination of the Church and other private institutions would immediately deprive the country of the services of well over a million devoted clerics, nuns and lay people who received a pittance for their unsparing labors. Not merely would the new law be costly, the cardinal continued, but it was obviously aimed at destroying the idea and the practice of charity – hence it is obviously unchristian in intent, and fully in keeping with the procedure of Communist regimes in the Iron Curtain countries.

The newly created cardinal's intervention in this political *mise en scène* confirmed the impression that he had been made Archbishop of Florence to give the Italian episcopate strong and clear leadership.

One unquestionably joyful experience occasioned by the Synod was the celebration of a papal mass in St Peter's for the pope's eightieth birthday on Sunday, 21 September 1977. Though obviously slowing down with age, the Holy Father was in excellent spirits. Seated on the *sedia gestatoria* and receiving the uproarious acclamation of the crowd, he showed his usual animation. Taking his cue from Paul's Epistle to the Colossians, where the apostle speaks of his own sufferings as a contribution to those of Christ for his body, the Church, the pontiff made several observations concerning old age, which brings with it venerability but also definite limitations, such as the inevitability of an end. The import of this statement was suddenly caught by the crowd, as the pope broke into a wide smile. Far from lugubrious, he referred to speculation about the possibly imminent termination of his reign as in no way implying that his labors were slowing down. The only resignation he would admit, he implied, was that of accepting God's will. Addressing himself to the people of Rome, the Pope insisted on a *romanitá*, a concept of Roman culture that was not merely a classical inheritance but an authentic Christian tradition. The apostle Paul's appeal to his Roman citizenship had played a mysterious but real part in the Church's primitive consciousness, and contributed to the early universality of the Christian presence in the world.

Nine months later, on 6 August 1978, Pope Paul took leave of the Church and the world. He had been on his feet conducting a papal audience only the day before. With his great model, the Apostle of the Gentiles, he could truly say: 'I have run the course, and I have fought the good fight. I have kept the faith.'

6

The Empty Throne

Seldom will history record a more poignant sight than that of a simple wooden coffin lying on a plain oriental rug on the hard stones of the entrance to St Peter's basilica in the Vatican, with a stately Easter candle its sole sentinel as it lay beside the open-air altar, waiting for the requiem mass of the resurrection on Saturday, 13 August 1978.

That unadorned cypress box contained the remains of Pope Paul VI, who the previous Sunday in his summer residence at Castelgondolfo had suddenly breathed his last. Conscious almost to the end, he is reported to have whispered, 'See, so the pope dies like any ordinary man.'

Pope Paul had been ill since early in March when he caught a cold that he simply could not shake off. Nevertheless, despite the increasing pain given him by a debilitating arthrosis in his hip and leg he had carried on with his demanding schedule.

Paul's sudden demise caught the Roman Church, Italy, and the world by surprise. Immediately word was passed to Vatican officials who came rushing from Rome and nearby villas to Castelgondolfo. There chaos reigned. Although the pope had set out explicit procedures to be followed for his death and funeral, no one seems to have thought them through into a plan of action. Certainly no one knew how to handle the press and the hundreds of curiosity-seekers who immediately descended on the papal summer palace, which stands high above the Via Appia overlooking Lake Albano, some twenty miles south of Rome.

Thus confusion prevailed both outside the castle and also in the antechambers, where important ecclesiastics were held at bay by the Swiss guards under strict orders from Cardinal Villot, who hurriedly summoned the pope's doctor and the papal master of ceremonies to draw up documents certifying the pontiff's death.

Paul's last will and testament left instructions that his obsequies be extremely simple. He asked the college of cardinals to celebrate a mass of the resurrection in the piazza of St Peter's before the entire world; and he wanted to be buried deep in the crypt beneath the Vatican basilica, close to the tombs of his predecessors Pius XII and John XXIII, and near the grave of St Peter. A simple stone slab should mark his burial place with the inscriptions *Paulus P.P. VI* – Paul Pope and Pontifex VI. So it was done.

Despite an inadequate embalming, Paul's body, vested in the dark red *chasuble* proper to papal mourning, with a white mitre adorning his head and red slippers on his feet, lay in state at Castelgondolfo for two days. In mid-afternoon, on Thursday, August 11th, it was transferred by hearse to Rome within a tight cordon of police, on the alert lest the Red Brigade use the occasion for a terrorist incident similar to the attempt made by anti-clerical radicals in 1878 to throw the body of Pius IX into the Tiber.

The transfer, televised to millions in many parts of the world, was without incident. The body was then exposed once more on a plain catafalque before the main altar in St Peter's basilica.

The funeral mass on Saturday evening in the piazza in front of St Peter's drew over 100,000 Romans and visitors. Included in this immense throng were heads of state and their personal representatives, ambassadors, diplomats, civic officials and representatives of the world's religions. In formal attire the notables of church and state flanked the altar, around which were gathered a hundred cardinals in red chasubles and white mitres, led by the thin, aristocratic dean of the college of cardinals, Carlo Confalonieri.

Chanted in Latin with readings in Aramaic, Greek, French and English, the liturgy was conducted with dispatch. In his simple Italian eulogy, Cardinal Confalonieri cited the deceased pontiff's constant endeavor to serve the Church and the world in simplicity and holiness. And when the group of pall-bearers – the *portatori* who regularly carried the pontiff on the *sedia gestatoria* – lifted the simple casket to their shoulders and slowly disappeared into the dark atrium of the basilica, a wave of mild applause swept across the vast square. It was a spontaneous recognition that in death the troubled pontiff had finally reached the serenity that he had vainly sought in life.

With the Pope's death and by Paul's explicit instructions, the heads of the curial congregations or cabinet officers lost their jobs. This included the secretary of state, Cardinal Jean Villot, and the prefect of the Holy Office, Cardinal Franjo Seper, as well as the Utrecht-based Dutch cardinal, Jan Willebrands, in his function as head of the Secretariat for the Promotion of Christian Unity. Authority for the running of the Church was in the hands of the college of cardinals, who were to meet twice each day and settle by majority vote matters requiring immediate attention, under the chairmanship of the dean of the college. More immediate discretion was exercised by Cardinal Villot in his capacity as papal chamberlain, charged with caring for the Church's properties and carrying out the decisions of the cardinalatial college.

Provisions for the caretaker activities of the curial offices were in operation, but Cardinal Willebrands found himself in the embarrassing situation of being the recipient of over 400 letters of condolence from religious leaders all over the world, but without the authority or means to respond officially. With authorization of the college of cardinals, his former office was put to work answering these messages under his signature.

In the daily general congregations or meetings, the cardinals discussed procedures for the interim running of the Church. They elected two three-man committees to supervise the physical layout of the conclave area in the Borgia apartments surrounding the Sistine Chapel, whose interior furnishings had to be dismantled for the introduction of long conference tables and chairs that would accommodate the one hundred and eleven cardinal electors. Gone were the thrones and the *baldacchinos* that on election in the past were lowered over the place of each cardinal except that of the newly elected pontiff. And in front of the altar there was a simple faldstool on which the next pope would be seated to receive the obeisance of the cardinals immediately after his election.

The second committee was charged with the interpretation of the rules and procedures to be followed in the balloting, and for policing the area of the conclave to make sure that no communication devices of any kind were introduced into the precincts. In anticipation of the conclave, the apartments occupied by high Vatican officials and scattered through the halls and corridors of the Borgia palace had been evacuated, and the rooms were converted into 'cells' with a simple bed, table and washstand. These were numbered and apportioned to the cardinals in keeping with each prelate's rank, age and date of creation as cardinal.

Ordinarily warm, this vast area of the papal palace that had to accommodate the cardinals and some sixty officials caring for the household chores and other necessary services was being turned into what the Belgian cardinal Leon Josef Suenens termed a sauna by the carpenters instructed to shut it off completely from contact with the world outside. This meant blocking doors and windows with any aperture whereby a signal could be given to someone outside.

In the daily meetings of the cardinal electors before the conclave, some attention was given to the status of the Church in various parts of the world, but there was no attempt at electioneering, nor was there any mention of particular candidates.

In fact during the three-week interval between Paul's death and the opening of the conclave on 25 August 1978 the principal campaigning seemed to be conducted in the Italian and world press. Shortly before the pontiff's passing, a group of United States laymen had called for a 'responsible' election of the next pope – as if papal elections were not usually responsible; and a consortium of international theologians prepared an Identikit of the ideal pontiff. But neither of these projects proved of interest to the cardinal electors.

Pope Paul's death came at a most inconvenient time for Romans, who promptly on August 1st had fled the city for the mountains, the sea or overseas touring. It had also caught the Vatican officials and the coterie of curial cardinals totally unprepared. For years they had been criticizing Paul's governance, as bringing the Church to ruin, yet at this critical moment they themselves were without a plausible candidate for the papacy.

The first cardinal of the curia to arrive back in Rome was Pericle Felici, the rigid representative of the Church's preconciliar legal line. He managed to get a plane from Barcelona to Rome on August 7th and went straight to Castelgondolfo to pay his respects to the dead pope's remains. He was also interested in discovering who among the curialists were back in town. On reaching his lodging in one of the Vatican palaces across the piazza of St Peter's from the papal apartments, Felici, a camera and telescope enthusiast, turned his gaze on the living quarters of the other cardinals in nearby palaces. He then began arranging a meeting with Cardinals Corrado Bafile, Alfredo Ottaviani, Pietro Parente and Ferdinando Antonelli, of whom the last three were excluded from the conclave by their age.

In this meeting and in a meeting with the curial cardinals Sergio Gerri, Paolo Marella and Umberto Mozzoni, it was decided to organize a quiet campaign insisting that the next pope be an Italian. It was based on the supposed desirability of having a new Bishop of Rome able to understand Italian politics from the inside. This would, for example, better equip him to ward off the danger of a communist takeover of the Italian government – the first step toward the victory of eurocommunism.

But the curialist strategy backfired, for this very involvement with Italian politics disturbed most churchmen in and outside Italy, who were becoming disgusted with the running of the papacy as if it were an appanage of the Italian state.

On the Sunday following the pope's funeral a meeting of sixteen Latin American cardinals had considerably disturbed the curial groups. These third-world prelates had composed a letter for distribution among the electors urging that the new pontiff be a pastoral figure who would eschew Italian politics and would pay full attention to the problems of people in underdeveloped areas of the world, as well as in the vast missionary territories of Africa and Asia where the Church's greatest growth was taking place. With these needs in mind, they hinted, the time might be ripe for a non-Italian pontiff.

This gathering proved to be the only obvious caucus attempted by a regional group of cardinals. For on the next day, the curial prelates with Cardinal Felici at their head persuaded Cardinal Villot to caution the electors against meetings and gestures that could be interpreted as political or aimed at electioneering. He suggested great prudence in making television appearances or giving interviews or press conferences.

Villot's intervention had no effect on the cardinals, many of whom were anxious to co-operate with the journalists and television interviewers from their homelands – the Belgian, Leon Suenens; the Dutch, Jan Willebrands; the Germans, Joseph Hoffner of Cologne and Joseph Ratzinger of Munich; the French, François Marty of Paris and Alexandre Charles Renard of Lyons; and the American cardinals, Terence Cooke of New York, John Carberry of St Louis, John Dearden of Detroit and Humberto Medeiros of Boston, were all most accommodating. They were aware of the value of massive media coverage of Paul's funeral and, now, the coming election. As a shrewd monsignor from the *Propaganda Fide,* the congregation for evangelization, remarked, it would be ridiculous not to let the secular media do a professional job of placing the Church and its message before the entire world.

The death of Cardinal Paul Yu Pin of Nanking created a minor stir during the pre-conclave period. As an exile in Taiwan since 1949 with General Chang Kai Shek, Yu Pin had forced the Holy See to exchange plenary ambassadors with Taipei, thus providing an impenetrable obstacle to relations with continental China. Yu Pin had been stricken during the funeral for Pope Paul and died two days later. His passing was considered a blessing and an omen by the Church's China watchers.

Five years earlier, despite Yu Pin's violent protests, Pope Paul had made a subtle gesture toward Mao Tse-Tung's China by sending the papal nuncio in Taipei, Mons. James Cassidy, from there to Bangladesh without relieving him of his title. From Bangladesh, he seemed prepared for a move into Peking, once relations between the Vatican and the Chinese were re-established.

On the communist issue itself, there was not much immediate anxiety among the cardinals. During the 1977 Synod of Bishops the Archbishop of Saigon followed Pope John's lead in distinguishing between the atheistic marxist theory and the actual working out of the communistic system in political, social, and economic matters in the historical order. He said that in his country the Church would have to adapt itself to the marxist language and marxist analysis of historical situations. Otherwise it would not be able to preach the Gospel to its people who were all, including himself and the cardinal of Hanoi, being re-educated in that idiom.

He hinted that just as the original message of Christ had been preached in Hebrew or Aramaic, and had been adapted to the Greco-Roman culture and mentality, so now it could be fitted into a marxist culture without the loss of its true meaning or message for mankind. Pope John had certainly said as much in his encyclical *Pacem in Terris* (Peace on Earth); and Pope Paul had agreed in his *Populorum Progressio* (The development of peoples) – even though Pope Paul had frequently shown signs of stepping back from the essential pluralism in theology that this distinction implied.

That the cardinal of Hanoi was on hand for the conclave indicated that the Church in the Far East would survive with the so-called 'historical compromise' – the acceptance of the communist elements in political systems – just as it had survived the ancient Roman imperial absolutism and the medieval feudal system.

What soon became obvious to seasoned Vatican observers was the fact that nobody outside the curia was sure either of the major issues or of the criteria for choosing a new supreme pastor; nor had the cardinals descending on Rome a truly unswappable candidate in mind. All were making frequent and annoying reference to the need for inspiration by the Holy Spirit. Considered at first as a stratagem to protect inner convictions, this reference to the Spirit was eventually recognized as a sure sign of political naïveté on the part of those who used it.

In contrast the curia was well aware of its own political objectives. Their first aim was to block the principal 'pretenders' to the papal office – Cardinal Sebastiano Baggio, the 65-year-old head of the Congregation for Bishops, and Cardinal Sergio Pignedoli, 68, considered the last pope's favorite, who was in charge of the secretariat for the Church's contact with non-Christians. These two prelates had been clearly running for the job for the last four years, and were thoroughly disliked by the old-guard curial potentates. Baggio had been in the diplomatic service in Brazil and France, and had functioned briefly as Archbishop of Cagliari in Sardinia before being called to Rome as a curial cardinal. He claimed pastoral experience and hoped for support from the French and Latin American electors.

Pignedoli had been a naval chaplain who was brought into the office of the secretary of state by Pope Paul during his own days there. As Archbishop of Milan, Montini made him an auxiliary bishop of Milan, then released him to serve in the diplomatic corps in East Africa and in

Canada. Hence, he felt he could count on some African support and the three votes from the north – Cardinals Flahiff of Winnepeg, Roy of Quebec, and Léger, the retired cardinal of Montreal.

But all was not well with Pignedoli's candidacy. Three years earlier he had accepted the hospitality of Colonel Gaddafi for a conference between Muslims and Catholics in Libya, and let himself and his advisors be bested. In the final resolution published by Qadaffi were definite anti-semitic statements that had to be repudiated by the Vatican. This gaffe confirmed the curia's opinion that Pignedoli was a man of little substance.

The curia's second objective was to elect an Italian pope, preferably one whom they could trust. Their first choice had been the seventy-year-old Paolo Bertoli, known in the diplomatic service for his intransigent honesty. But when it became clear during the final week before the conclave that, Italian or not, the outsiders wanted a pope with pastoral experience and no direct links with the curia or the diplomatic service, they shifted to the Archbishop of Genoa, the 72-year-old Cardinal Giuseppe Siri. This move caused a split with Pericle Felici, the 66-year-old canonist, who decided to join the unpretentious rally for the Cardinal Albino Luciani of Venice that had suddenly surfaced in the Italian press.

Cardinal Siri was known for his opposition to the changes introduced by Vatican Council II. He was widely quoted as having said at the end of that revolutionary Church experience: 'the decrees and constitutions will never bind us.' He had unfairly proved a rigid opponent of the Council and in the end Pope Paul had reluctantly to relieve him of the presidency of the Italian Conference of Bishops.

During the three weeks after Paul's death, the cardinals from outside Italy had been meeting in small groups at dinners and other gatherings. They also visited the curial cardinals in the various Vatican offices – those dealing with doctrine, education, sacraments, rites, bishops, priests, religious and the secretariats concerned with ecumenical matters – both to settle particular problems in their own territories and with an eye to stumbling on rumor or gossip of curial interest.

On the Tuesday of the second week after Paul's death Cardinal Cooke's remarks during a television interview in Rome about the need of a pope whose first interest would be the third world came as a shock to the determined men of the curia. The cardinal of New York had insisted that since all the cardinals travelled, they knew each other and the needs of the Church in various parts of the world much more intimately than was generally realized. And while he gave no hint as to what this meant, he did gradually involve his two companions in the interview, Cardinals James Manning of Los Angeles and Humberto Medeiros of Boston, in his obviously deep concern for the poor and exploited in other parts of the world. Cardinal Manning had revealed that in the last ten years he had travelled widely in missionary territories and he agreed that his interests were in an authentic attack on poverty and exploitation at home and abroad. To have these two American cardinals forced to take a progressive stand by the Archbishop of New York struck the Italian journalist Giancarlo Zizola as highly significant and he played up this move to the hilt in his Milanese paper, *Il Giorno.*

As the Cooke-Manning-Medeiros trialogue came closely on the heels of the interview given in *Messagero* by the African cardinal Hyacinthe Thiandoum of Dakar, about the importance of the Church in the third world and the growing dynamic of its non-Roman elements, the tough cardinals of the curia, from Pietro Parente and Antonio Samore to Pietro Palazzini and Silvio Oddi, abetted by the over-eighty-year-old cardinals clamoring to be let into the conclave, showed some signs of panic.

They stepped up their campaign, pointing to the inability of a non-Italian pope to deal with Italy's governmental situation. But that was precisely what was on the minds of the majority of Latin American, African and Asian cardinals as the greatest disservice to the Church of today. These outsiders wanted the Holy See divorced from Italian political entanglement once and for all. Such involvement had nothing to do with the governance of the universal Church, yet it had so frequently interfered with the proper conduct of the papacy as to have constituted a standing scandal before the Christian world.

Among these cardinals there was little sympathy for Italian fears of a communist takeover on the Italian peninsula. More than one outsider remarked that it might not be the worst thing in the world, certainly no more deleterious than the muddling capitalist exploitation of government and labor pursued by the Christian Democrats in the last thirty years. To the objection that once the communists got control of the government it would be impossible to dislodge them, a shrewd monsignor remarked, 'a good dose of Italian communism has practically cured Naples and Bologna of the idea that they are any different as corruptible Italians than Christians or agnostics.'

Why Cardinal Suenens of Belgium did not play a guiding role in the preconclave policies in Rome is not clear. With Montini, he had been Pope John's confidant and both men had planned the structure of the last three sessions of Vatican Council II. But after the Council he had gradually broken with Pope Paul over the slowness and recalcitrance that the pontiff demonstrated in implementing the Council's decrees, and in 1969 he gave a famous interview, publicly embarrassing pope and curia for their regressive policies.

The result of the ensuing brouhaha was a face-to-face confrontation between the cardinal and Pope Paul, in which the Belgian prelate was invited to resign. He refused, telling the Holy Father that his conscience would not allow him, but assuring the pope that if he took the cardinalate and the archdiocese of Brussels away from him, he would be happy to submit.

The pope calmed down and Suenens retained his position despite severe criticism from both the curia and his fellow bishops in Belgium. A theologian in his own right who had also seen eternity face to face (he was about to have the rope put around his neck by the Germans in 1944 when the American forces entered Louvain), Cardinal Suenens had recently turned his attention to the doctrinal foundation of the charismatic movement. Eventually peace was restored between him and Pope Paul. It was given public expression when Paul, during an October 1976 audience with members of the charismatic movement, praised the cardinal's book on charismatic experiences.

Suenens' absence from Rome was considered by some a tactical error. He had no hopes of being elected pope himself, although because of his world vision, personal benevolence, prayerfulness, ability at languages and his actual physical appearance, he would have made an ideal candidate. But he could have been a key figure in encouraging the northern European block – Alfrink and Willebrands of Holland, the four or five French cardinals under Marty of Paris, the Germans with Ratzinger of Munich, Volk of Mainz, Hoffner of Cologne and, hopefully though doubtfully, Bengsch of Berlin and Koenig of Austria – in reaching out for a candidate who would represent an undoctrinaire middle-of-the-road position, and for whom Suenens could have garnered the support of many of the Latin American cardinals, possibly some twenty votes – about ten out of the native African cardinals, and possibly another ten between the North Americans and Canadians.

The man most in the limelight of the north European contingent had been the 69-year-old Cardinal Jan Willebrands who had replaced Cardinal Alfrink as Archbishop of Utrecht while retaining his position in Rome as head of the secretariat for promoting Christian unity. He seemed to have restored a certain peace to the turbulent Dutch church following the policies of his predecessor. Against him was the fact that in his ecumenical contacts, particularly in his early dealing with the Russian Orthodox patriarchs in Moscow, he had won the enmity of the conservative cardinals in the curia who could not stand his apparent disregard of their charges that he was consorting with heretics and exposing the Church to the vanguard of the communist menace. His lack of what the Italians called *presenza* in his public appearance was also an obstacle. The world as well as the Church wanted a man who would give them the reassurance of the smile and the laughter of the good Pope John.

Cardinal Benelli's absence from Rome also seemed to have a political bias. The 57-year-old-Tuscan had served for nine years as Paul's *sostituto* under the secretary of state and as his confidant. He had thus won the bitter enmity of the curia, and was looked upon as the pontiff's hatchet-man.

A good omen for the conclave was seen in the arrival of the Russian Orthodox archbishop, Nikodim of Leningrad, for the funeral of Pope Paul and the subsequent installation of the new pope. Representing the Orthodox Patriarch of Moscow, Nikodim was given hospitality by the Jesuits in their summer villa near Frascati, where he was joined by two Orthodox Russian priests who had just finished special courses in theology at the Jesuit-run Oriental Institute in Rome.

Nikodim's affection for Pope Paul was genuine. And the pontiff's sudden death moved him greatly. His own health was precarious; he had already suffered several heart-attacks. His hosts were worried lest they have an international situation on their hands if he were to die while staying with them. And this was precisely what was to happen during a meeting with the new Holy Father two weeks later. He died after receiving the last blessing from Pope John Paul I.

Nikodim had made no secret of the fact that while apparently unconcerned, the Russian government would appreciate a new pontiff who would be as openminded and benevolent in his thinking about the Russian people as had been both Popes John and Paul. In this respect, the candidacy of the Dutch cardinal Willebrands, who had been John's emissary to Moscow to obtain Russian Orthodox observers for his Council, got a slight push forward.

In the end what the cardinals seemed to want was a Holy Father who would both have a comparatively long pontificate and prove acceptable to all factions within the Church. Apart from anything else, the death of Pope Paul and the subsequent conclave was costing in the area of ten million dollars, so there were good financial incentives in favor of electing a pope who would last for some years.

Recent statistics indicated that there were some 725 million Catholics among the world's more than four billion inhabitants. Catholics formed sixty-one per cent of the population of the Americas (in Latin America, from Chile to Mexico, the majority were Catholic, at least in name; in the United States, some sixty million; in Canada, some ten million). Catholics claimed to represent forty per cent of Europe; twenty-five per cent of the Pacific Islands, including Australia; twelve per cent of Africa, and two and a half per cent of continental Asia.

The new pope would be confronted with an awesome situation. The world he was called to evangelize was largely incapable of listening to that message. According to a recent report of the World Bank, by the year 2000 there would be over 600 million people living in absolute destitution among an overall population of close to 5 billion. And with the world's demographic growth, that number would double in another four decades. In view of this enormous, threatening calamity, the problems the pope would face within the Catholic Church itself and the body of Christendom seemed peripheral. Nevertheless, his immediate task would be so to reorientate that Church that it could tackle the problems of world hunger and degradation with a truly charismatic and effective policy.

The Church that Pope Paul had left behind him was a vast conglomeration of peoples scattered literally all over the globe, the greater majority of whom were what might be called marginal Catholics. They were either too poor, or too disaffected, to comprehend fully the nature of the Church and the essence of its belief. Most of these people lived in the third world. They were the object of tremendous missionary effort that had in mind not merely their conversion to Christianity, and Catholicism in particular, but their uplifting in the social and economic order. Here, the Church was running into tough problems. In the past, the priests, nuns, brothers and committed lay apostles who labored in this area were also purveyors of hygiene, education, law and order, giving a hand to the colonial powers who had taken over in Africa and Asia particularly, to exploit national resources and natives – both human and material – under the guise of bringing them civilization and modernization.

Only gradually did the missionaries come to realize that they were being used by the capitalistic enterprises taking over these lands. And only recently, due in good part to the encouragement of Vatican Council II and Pope Paul's revolutionary encyclicals, *On the Development of Peoples* (1967) and *Call to Action* (1971), had they rebelled. They began a process of making people aware of their human dignity and rights at the same time as teaching them to read and write, add and subtract, work and pray.

Eventually, the missionary priests and nuns, aided by a vast system of native catechists who taught the elements of the faith to their people, began to break with the local governments. They demanded that the rights of peasants, indigenous natives, slum dwellers and the poverty-stricken in general, be respected. They protested the exploitation and degradation of the oppressed classes.

The rich and the powerful took umbrage at this rebellion. Clerics, priests and nuns were berated, maltreated and persecuted by local police and vigilante squads organized to protect the rights of the rich. Gradually the hierarchy – bishops and cardinals – got involved in the front line of these economic, social and political problems. From being a nice, safe, government-supporting institution, the Church was suddenly getting totally involved in the revolution that the twenty-first century was demanding.

The whole system of evangelization in Africa, Latin America and Asia was changing radically. Due to a new awareness of the desire for local autonomy, the Church's local governance was quickly being taken over by native bishops, priests and nuns. This indigenization was also due to the rapidly diminishing number of foreign missionaries from Europe and America, whose numbers had declined because of the lack of vocations and, not infrequently, difficulties with the xenophobic attitudes of local governments.

Nevertheless, the Church was still engaged in a tremendous proselytizing effort. What was more, the great rivalry between Catholic and other Christian denominations in what had been considered missionary fields in Asia, Africa, and the Pacific areas was turning into co-operation. Former antipathies between Christian churches that had been the cause of grave scandal among the peoples they were trying to evangelize, were being gradually overcome, as a result of the great ecumenical movements given *droit de la cité* by Vatican Council II, where the representatives of diverse Christian and other religious groups had been recognized and given the opportunity not only of observing, but of contributing unofficially to the great debates.

This Christian co-operation was itself being challenged in peculiar ways – in Africa, for instance, by the tremendous number of breakaway churches, started by native preachers and evangelical leaders who created their own forms of church assemblies out of a conglomeration of native religious beliefs and practices interlarded with Christian teachings and organizational forms. They claimed an indigenous heritage and repudiated the expatriate missionaries.

During the first fifty years of the twentieth century the missionary efforts of both Catholics and Protestants had prospered miraculously. Despite the eruption of two world wars and countless limited local fracas, the Christianization of Africa and parts of the vast continent of Asia had made great progress. It had to contend with the assistance, and also the interference, of colonizing governments. It was confronted with the growing consciousness of its own missionary activity by Islam, stretching in a great semi-arch from the center of Africa out to the tip of Australia – although the Moslem presence had frequently been exploited, particularly by the British colonial masters, as an antidote to Christian notions of individual liberty.

With the tremendous movement for independence that suddenly affected all these lands immediately after World War II, the churches were caught in the middle. But Rome had acted with fair success to get native bishops and priests in a position to take over these churches – a bit late and a bit slow – but, in the end, sufficiently effective to save the basic situation.

There were cardinals scattered all over the globe: twelve in Africa, from the aging Owen McCann in Capetown to the youthful septuagenarian Pierre Duval in Algeria; and including the native Hyacinthe Thiandoum, successor to the rebel French prelate Marcel Lefebvre as Archbishop of Dakar; Cardinal Paul Zoungrana in Alto Volta; Maurice Otunga in Kenya; Victor Razafimahatrata in Malagassy; Laurean Rugambwa in Tanzania; Emmanuel Nsubuga in Uganda; Joseph Malula in Zaire; Ignatius Ekanden in Nigeria; and Stephen I. Sidarouss in Egypt. Besides these, there was the former Archbishop of Benin, Cardinal Bernadine Gantin, in the Roman curia who had been given attention as a possible candidate for the papacy. All these men had had troubles with their native governments, either because of tribal rivalries or because they posed a threat to the popularity of a truculent leader – Amin in Uganda, who had jailed Nsubuga; Mobutu in Zaire, who exiled Cardinal Malula – and there was the case of Emile Biayende of the Congo, whose strange death had all the marks of martyrdom.

These native cardinals were symbols of the well-organized native Catholic hierarchies and churches that, with large amounts of aid from America and Europe – Germany in particular, with its vast development funds organized under two tightly regimented but generous institutions, *Adveniat,* the countrywide pre-Christmas collection, and *Misereor,* its Lenten effort, which could be tapped for educational facilities, medical and development projects of all kinds – had made incredible progress since the close of World War II.

Ironically in the Church's missionary efforts in Africa much of the successful organization in the francophone territories of West Africa from Senegal to Madagascar was due to the impressive efforts of the now rebel French Archbishop Lefebvre, who served as the papal apostolic delegate there from 1948 to 1958. Lefebvre utilized his political skills in negotiating with the French colonial authorities to organize over thirty new dioceses and four ecclesiastical provinces. He had fallen out of grace, however, when, to General de Gaulle's horror, he had sided with the rebellious generals of the OAS in Algeria.

A situation parallel to that of Africa was true in regard to the heroic efforts of the missionaries in Asia. On hand for the election of the next pope were fourteen native cardinals scattered between Joseph Cordeiro in Pakistan and Reginald Delargey in New Zealand. They included Joseph Parecattil of Ernakulam in Kerala, India; Lawrence Picachy of Calcutta and (not in the conclave because of grave illness from which he died on September 20) Valerian Gracias of Bombay; Stephen Sou Hwan Kim in Korea; Joseph Trin-Nha-Khue from Vietnam; Thomas Cooray from Sri Lanka; Julio Rosales from Cebu and James L. Sin of Manila from the Philippines; Justin Darmojuwono of Semarang in Indonesia; Pio Taofinu'u of Samoa; and James Freeman of Sydney in Australia. Another Australian, James Knox, had served in the Roman curia; and, on the conclave's eve, Paul Yu Pin of Formosa had been eliminated by death.

Once again, these men were symbolic of the tremendous spread of the Church all over this vast territory. They witnessed not merely to its good interior organization but also to its involvement in the social, economic and pastoral problems of this immense portion of mankind. Except for Vietnam and the Philippines, the Church was a small minority in most of these countries. But it was recognized almost invariably as an educational and developmental instrument and, for the most part, tolerated.

It was, however, in considerable trouble with the governments in India, Sri Lanka, Cambodia and Burma, but seemed quite capable of survival. In Vietnam it was under great pressure to change some of its ways and adapt itself to the communist way of thinking. During the Roman Synod of Bishops in October 1977 the Archbishop of Ho-Chi-Minville, Paul Nguyen Van Binh, testified that the Church was making an heroic effort to adapt its message to the marxist language and the communist attitude to social justice as the only way of surviving in a world that was forcibly creating a new mentality. He felt the Christian message could be accommodated to this new cultural pattern. This contention had shocked many of the curial cardinals and the bishops of the capitalist world. But it had not been rejected by Pope Paul, nor repudiated by the curial offices of the Vatican.

The Vietnamese experiment might prove the key to the gradual adaptation of the Church's teaching to the oriental mentality and help solve the challenge posed by China, where some two million Catholics with a well-organized hierarchy of some hundred bishops had simply disappeared in the 1950s, due to the intransigence of the anti-communist curial drives under Pope Pius XII.

Advised by premier Chou en-Lai in the 1950s to indigenize the Catholic Church – employ a native clergy, native customs, and native financing, while staying in close conjunction with the pope for doctrinal matters – the local Catholic hierarchy was forbidden to take this advice by the apostolic delegate, Antonio Riberi, who was eventually expelled not as a religious representative, but as a native of Monaco engaged in subversive activities in China. He had caused the imprisonment of countless priests and people after advising them to oppose the Maoist forces as 'red devils.'

When the local churches conformed to the government's suggestions and elected their own bishops, following the customs of the early Church, and sent telegrams to the Holy See requesting confirmation and communion, they were frozen out by Pius XII. This Roman intransigence eventually gave the Chinese authorities the right to close off communications, saying that their peaceful efforts had been rejected by Rome.

In this folly Pius XII was repeating the stupidities of the Roman curia four hundred years earlier, when it destroyed the great missionary effort of the Jesuit Matteo Ricci in his adaptation of Mandarin customs and his translation of the Christian doctrines into the Chinese mental patterns and ritual comprehensions. Pursued with jealousy by the less successful Dominican and Franciscan missionaries, his efforts were finally condemned by the Holy See in the early 1700s. The Church lost a great opportunity of converting the whole of the Pacific area through the Chinese merchants and migrants, whose Christian beliefs were condemned as being based on 'ancestor worship' – as if Rome did not cultivate the memory of its ancestors in the almost idolatrous attention paid to its saints.

Meanwhile remnants of the Chinese church had been moved to Taiwan under Cardinal Paul Yu Pin and provided an insurmountable obstacle to relations between the Vatican and Peking. Ironically, three hundred years after the condemnation by Rome of Father Matteo Ricci, Cardinal Yu Pin was reported as having conducted an 'ancestor worship' ceremony in the Cathedral of Taipei. The death of the Chinese cardinal, following his sudden cardiac failure during the funeral of Pope Paul VI, could be taken as a fortuitous omen.

In Latin America the new pope would again be faced with a tremendous aggregation of churches, made restless with the stimulus given by Pope John's meetings with the hierarchies of Central and South America in 1958 and 1962.

Throughout the nineteenth and the early part of the twentieth century the Church in all these countries was considered part of the established political structure, along with the army and the government. It was one of the three pillars of Latin American society. This was only partially true. Clerics, with the acquiescence and occasionally the aid of local bishops, had frequently been behind the revolts of the nineteenth century. And more recently the Church had been under fire, indeed persecuted, in Uruguay, Argentina and Mexico. The encouragement of Pope John and the experience of the Vatican Council had been decisive for the vast majority of the Latin American bishops. Despite a rearguard effort by the papal nuncios and apostolic delegates in these countries, a major group of the new hierarchies were focused on total reform within the Church and a dedication to poverty and justice among the clergy.

But the Latin American Church was facing a great number of breakaway churches. In Brazil, for example, hard hit by losses of priests, nuns, brothers, and lay apostles, the Church was also up against a tremendous proliferation of movements that combined Christian elements with some of the worst features of a superstitious paganism. These religious groups controlled between 175 and 200 radio stations and transmitters and attracted unnumbered millions of the lower classes, with a sprinkling of aristocrats and moneyed interests.

The breakaway movement reflected in part a dissatisfaction with the failure of the old official Church to adapt its liturgy to the deep emotional needs of these people from mixed cultures and hybrid genealogies. In part it was due to the older hierarchy's refusal to confront the living conditions and injustices of the social, economic and political situation.

With few exceptions that situation had changed radically with the formation of the Latin American Bishops Conferences (CELAM) and their revolutionary declarations regarding the social order. The tenth anniversary of the first CELAM conference at Medellin was to be observed at the end of October 1978 at Puebla in Mexico, and the new pope would be invited to attend this important gathering of the Latin American hierarchy.

There were nineteen Latin American cardinals who participated in the papal election. Politically on the right were the archconservative Brazilian cardinal Angelo Rossi (removed by Pope Paul from Sao Paolo for attempting to cover over the repressive activities of the Giesel government, and given a function in the curia) and the intransigent cardinals Mario Casariego of Guatemala, Anibal Munoz Duque of Bogota and Juan Carlos Aramburu of Argentina. All the other Latin American cardinals, from Landazuri Ricketts in Lima to Clemente Maurer in Sucre, Bolivia were involved in the terrible problems facing the majority of their people. Most of them were suffering from the harsh repressive measures of their governments who were threatened with revolutionary violence, a reaction to the horrible conditions of the great majority of their people. The priests, nuns and bishops were thus on the firing line in their pursuit of social justice, this pursuit being labelled 'Liberation theology'.

Just how a new Holy Father would attempt to confront these almost insoluble problems in the third world Church was impossible to predict.

At the mass preceding the conclave, Cardinal Villot, the papal chamberlain, gave the homily. It was a simple exhortation reminding the electors of the great privilege and obligation they shared to be open to the suggestion of the Holy Spirit in voting for the next Holy Father.

When the one hundred and eleven cardinals filed into the Borgia apartments that Friday afternoon, there were a few among them who had an absolute commitment to a particular candidate. Among the others there seemed to be an air of serene patience, a sort of listening and awaiting for a sign from the Spirit.

The English cardinal, George Basil Hume, seemed to have a premonition as to how this might come about. In a homily at an evening mass in St Silvester's church, the parish for the English colony in Rome, he said: 'There will be a moment on Saturday morning next . . . when each cardinal will stand before the altar of the Sistine Chapel, and say aloud for all to hear, "I call to witness Christ the Lord who will be my judge, that my vote is given to the one who before God I consider should be elected." He will then vote.

'Rarely does God interfere in human affairs with that immediacy which would make momentous and grave decisions so much clearer, and response to them so much easier. His delicacy of touch is to pay man the compliment of being his collaborator.

'It is through the human instrument then that the divine purpose will be worked out and achieved.'

In view of the conduct of the conclave two days later, the British cardinal's words seemed to be strangely prophetic.

7

The September Pope

In the conclave that began on 25 August 1978 the intransigent curialist cardinals had decided that if the 72-year-old Cardinal Siri could not garner thirty-five or forty votes on the first two ballots – enough to give him a chance of blocking Cardinals Baggio and Pignedoli – they would abandon him in favor of whichever Italian cardinal seemed to have the best chance.

On the first ballot Siri got twenty-five votes, an astonishingly high number considering his reputation as a rigid traditionalist. Immediately behind him with twenty-three votes came the cardinal of Venice, Albino Luciani, also a surprise to those electors unfamiliar with the Italian press. Pignedoli had eighteen, and Baggio only twelve. Koenig of Vienna garnered nine; Bertoli got six; Pironio, the Argentinian of Italian parentage, got four; and Lorscheider of Brazil and Felici of the curia got two each. There was a scattering of votes for favorite sons.

During the silence that prevailed between the first and second ballots there was a slight shift in loyalties. Cardinal Siri's total mounted to thirty-three, while Luciani's rose from twenty-three to thirty-one. The curialists had successfully blocked Pignedoli: his vote dropped to fifteen. Lorscheider received twelve votes, Baggio, ten, Felici, eight and Cordeiro of Pakistan, four. At noon the black smoke pouring from the Sistine chimney indicated that the cardinals had yet to elect a new Holy Father.

Voting for Luciani on the first ballot were almost certainly five of the Italian residential archbishops: Pellegrino of Turin, Ursi of Naples, Poma of Bologna, Pappalardo of Palermo and Colombo of Milan. The Brazilians voted for him and, under the guidance of Volk of Mainz and

Hoffner of Cologne, the Germans did likewise. Also, Luciani had the support of Cardinal Giovanni Benelli, Pope Paul's right-hand man. Benelli, from the safety of his archepiscopal palace in Florence, had telephoned friends among the non-Italian cardinals to assure them of Luciani's soundness. Among the French, it is almost certain that Marty of Paris and Renard of Lyons voted for him. So also did Cardinals Malula of Zaire and Nsubuga of Uganda.

On the second round, having probably picked up a scattering of Spanish and North American votes, Luciani reached what he himself was later to describe as the 'danger point'. Siri's strength had peaked.

When the cardinals assembled for their midday meal and those from outside Italy got a better look at Luciani, the conclave was for all practical purposes over. Cardinal Silvio Oddi of the curia is credited with breaking whatever tension remained. He remarked that the name 'Luciani' bore a resemblance to the Italian word for the rising of the moon, thus reminding his colleagues of the legendary prophecy of the Irish seer Malachy, that this pope would rise *de medietate lunae,* from the half-moon.

The third vote in the late afternoon was impressive. As Cardinal Hoffner observed the next day, the only name that seemed to echo through the counting was Luciani, as he bounded to over sixty-five votes. Siri, Pignedoli, Lorscheider and Koenig each retained a dozen or so. Then on the fourth and final vote, Luciani shot up into the nineties and there was one vote for Lorscheider, that of Luciani himself. The clamorous applause that greeted the official announcement was taken as a total acclamation, so that in their indiscretions the following day Cardinals Suenens and Koenig spoke of a 'unanimity'.

Asked officially by Cardinal Camerlengo, acting for the dean of the college, whether he accepted the election, Luciani said without hesitation, 'I do'. Then after a pause, he announced that he would be known as John Paul I, a name that caused no little surprise among the electors.

Immediately upon Luciani's acceptance, the junior cardinal deacon, Luigi Ciappi, summoned the secretary of the college of cardinals Mons. Ernesto Civardi and the papal master of ceremonies Virgilio Noe into the Chapel to notarize the documents certifying the election. At the same time the Gammarelli brothers, tailors to the Holy See, were brought into the sacristy of the Sistine Chapel where they had three white cassocks in readiness. They quickly fitted the new pontiff in his papal white, and he returned to the Chapel and was seated on a faldstool. After a few nervous remarks, thanking the cardinals for the high honor thrust upon him, he received the obeisance of the cardinals, who approached him one by one, kissed his ring and received a warm embrace. To his amazement, the next day, he read in the papers that some of the cardinals took his remarks of gratitude as a reproof. As he explained later, he was using the words of St Bernard of Clairvaux, the twelfth-century terror of kings, emperors and popes, who on hearing that the cardinals had selected one of his former – and not so apt – pupils as Pope Eugene III, exclaimed, 'And what is this that you have done in regard to me!'

With this ceremony completed, the cardinals broke into the *Te Deum* as the papal master of ceremonies and Cardinal Pironio gathered up the ballots, notes and promemoria of the electors to burn them, as prescribed in Pope Paul's regulations. To make sure that the eager crowd in the piazza below them, and all the world, should get the message loud and clear, the cardinal threw a batch of chemical candles intended to create unmistakable white smoke into the stove. The actual result was an agonizing uncertainty outside that lasted for well over a half hour as smoke poured out of the chimney in great blobs, billowing between white, gray and black, not helped by the glowing sunset against which the smoke was viewed.

Vatican Radio, considered the most trustworthy of observers, admitted confusion. Father Roberto Tucci, its Jesuit director, was detected making a beeline for the Bronze Door of the papal palace across the piazza; and someone phoned both the home and office of the Gammarelli brothers, but got no answer. After what seemed an endless interval, lights appeared in the Hall of Benedictions over the basilica, and the doors to the balcony were opened to let courtiers drape a papal rug over the balustrade. Soon afterwards Cardinal Felici, the senior cardinal deacon, appeared and in his sonorous Latin announced: '*Gaudium magnum . . . habemus papam . . . cardinalem Albinum.*' The crowd drowned out the 'Luciani'. Joy and consternation intermingled as the crowd reacted vociferously. 'A new pope . . . Another Italian . . . An incredibly quick choice . . . A man from Venice . . .'

When the Holy Father himself arrived he took the crowd by storm. The broad smile, his obvious enjoyment of the encounter, and the hearty voice as he intoned the blessing *Urbi et Orbi* were accompanied with gestures of great joy and benevolence. It was Pope John all over again – just what the Church needed. In a flash he was gone, only to return for a moment to receive the salute of a battalion of Swiss Guards and Italian soldiers who suddenly appeared in the piazza. Then he disappeared again. By ten o'clock, despite the begging of the television newscasters who had given the event such elaborate coverage, the great lights blanketing the piazza went out.

That evening, taking the obedience of all the cardinals and keeping the conclave in session, the pope dined with his colleagues. He decided to deliver his televised message the next morning, immediately after the mass they were to celebrate in the Sistine Chapel. Pope John Paul I set the following Sunday for his installation and, despite the alarm of several cardinals, he accepted the document that the curial officials had prepared for the occasion. But he radically altered several key paragraphs, giving the document a genuine Luciani twist.

The next morning John Paul received the greetings and obediences of the cardinals excluded from the conclave and led the college of cardinals in a dignified mass of thanksgiving. Then he gave his message to the world.

His pontificate, he said, would vigorously pursue the goals of Vatican Council II, joining with the bishops in an authentic collegiality. He would bring back into force the Church's grand discipline but in a pastoral fashion. He would implement ecumenism without compromise of the Church's teachings but also without hesitation; and he would cooperate with the rest of the world in the pursuit of peace through dedication to human rights and human dignity.

With the conclusion of the mass of thanksgiving ceremony, the conclave was officially over, and the workmen began dismantling the elaborate superstructures they had completed only two days earlier. With the *portone* cleared, scarlet cassocks appeared in the cortile of the Borgia palace, where small knots of nuns, chauffeurs, porters and valets had assembled to return their respective cardinals to their Roman lodgings.

The first to exit was the unsmiling cardinal archbishop of Genoa, Giuseppe Siri, who for a second time had felt the wind of the Spirit pass him by. An intransigent traditionalist, he had also been a candidate in the conclave from which John XXIII emerged as pope. Now, valise in hand, he brushed past would-be greeters and left the papal palace in his priest-driven Lancia.

Behind came the German cardinal Hoffner of Cologne, only too happy to be reminded of his prophecy that the conclave would be brief. Yes, he was delighted with the conclave's results. No, he couldn't say anything about the voting . . . A flock of cardinals descended into the cortile, its members relieved of their baggage by the nuns and priests who hurried over to kiss rings and take possession of their scarlet-clothed masters. All were in excellent spirits. *'Contentissimo!'* was the sentiment of Cardinal Guerri ; *'Felicissimo . . !'* 'A magnificent stroke . . .', said Cardinal Bertoli, 'it's a sin that we are not able to tell you what went on.' Asked directly, 'How did it go?' Cardinal Silvio Oddi, the loquacious diplomat, replied: 'I'd say it was definitely an inspiration. So many electors, from so many parts of the world; and *voilà,* all over in a few minutes.'

'And the new Pope, how did he react?'

'Moved, greatly moved. But no, no, I did not see him cry.'

One of the first victims of the incredibly brief conclave was the secrecy with which Pope Paul had tried to invest it. The almost paranoiac character of the oath of secrecy made the penalty for its violation – excommunication – highly unrealistic. Elegantly trained Roman consciences lost no time in disposing of the oath via casuistic argument. From the Holy Father on down, indiscretion about the proceedings was almost the rule. The day after the conclave, before reciting the Angelus at noon, the pope shared with the crowds in St. Peter's Square his reaction to his awareness during the voting that 'danger' was threatening – the danger that he might be elected. (He also explained why he had chosen the singular name of John Paul I. It was as a mark of love and respect to Pope John, who had ordained him a bishop, and to Pope Paul, who had made him a cardinal.)

A day later, Cardinal Malula confirmed the first of these confidences. He and Cardinal Luciani had occupied neighboring cells. After lunch and the siesta, and just before the third round of voting, Malula had accosted Luciani with an encouraging greeting. According to Malula, Luciani's reply was, 'A great storm is troubling me.'

By Monday morning there were at least three oracles where authentic information was available. Not all the numbers were the same, since the ballots and the notes of the electors had been burnt. But the pattern was similar, with Siri receiving all those votes on the first and second ballots, and Luciani coming up closely behind him. Astonishingly, very few of the journalists covering the conclave realized that the eleven octogenarian cardinals excluded from the balloting, and resentful of the exclusion, had taken no oath of secrecy. These cardinals were only too anxious to question their cronies among the electors, and many of the latter were bursting to explain the surprising result and the even more surprising speed with which it had been attained. In the comfortable surroundings of Vatican apartments, under the emollient influence of an excellent cuisine and fine wines, tongues were loosened and the details of the voting were revealed.

Of the hundred biographies prepared by the Vatican press office in anticipation of the conclave, that devoted to Albino Luciani was the shortest. Born in Forno di Canali, near Belluna in the Dolomite Mountains southwest of Venice, on 17 October 1912, Luciani was the son of a poor laborer who did seasonal work in Argentina, Germany, France and Switzerland before settling down in his native town as a glass-blower. Luciani senior was a socialist by conviction. But his second wife, Bartola Tancon, marched him off to church each Sunday, and he had no objection when their son, aged 10, entered a minor seminary as a first step to the priesthood.

Ordained a priest on 7 July 1936, Don Albino Luciani served in Belluna as a curate, a teacher of theology and sacred art, and a diocesan official. There is some evidence that he gave spiritual assistance to the Italian partisans during World War II. After the war he was dispatched by his bishop to brush up on his study of theology at the Jesuit-run Gregorian University in Rome, where he wrote his doctoral dissertation on the outspoken nineteenth-century priest-philosopher Antonio Rosmini, at least one of whose books was placed on the Index of Prohibited Books and whose *Five Wounds of the Church,* published in 1848, was an explosive critique of Catholicism's failure to capture the majority of the people in keeping with Christ's command to preach the Gospel to every nation. The fact that he chose to write on so controversial a character indicated that Luciani had little desire for conventional advancement in the Church's hierarchy.

In 1958 he was consecrated Bishop of Vittorio Veneto by Pope John himself. He followed Vatican Council II with an open mind, unlike most Italian bishops who resisted the changes the Council introduced. Transferred to Venice as its Patriarch in 1969 and created a cardinal by Pope Paul in 1973, Luciani had been uncompromising toward dissidents from the official Italian episcopal position on the Communist Party's attempts to run Catholics as independent candidates for Communist seats in parliament. He was nevertheless loved by the laity and respected by most of the clergy as a man of culture, literary competence and devotion to the cause of the poor. Soon after entering Venice, for example, Luciani sold a precious pectoral cross and other church treasures on behalf of a sanitarium for handicapped children; and he urged his priests to do likewise with their unneeded ecclesiastical treasures. Even as he attacked the communist and socialist communes of Meghera for their anti-religious attitudes, he held the Church responsible for its own failure to build proper facilities for the needy. A book he had written while he was still Patriarch of Venice revealed more about the man than did the details of his parentage, youth and education. *Illustrissimi,* the Italian title of polite address, was the name of the book, and after the election it became an instantaneous bestseller. In a serious of fictional letters to famous personages, the then-archbishop discussed contemporary problems with insight, wit and understanding. Addressing himself to Charles Dickens and Mark Twain, Sir Walter Scott and Maria Theresa, Pinocchio and Figaro, before turning to Jesus Christ, Luciani displayed a grasp of world literature unusual in a priest and remarkable in an Italian prelate. (As a young priest, he spent two years in a tuberculosis sanitarium. There he read omnivorously.) He also revealed his acute awareness of the problems contemporary society poses for its young, its families and its aged.

The new pope spoke good German and fair French. His reading knowledge of English was excellent, and for two years before his election he had been studying conversational English. He read his Breviary in that tongue, and employed as his personal aide Diego Lorenzi, a 34-year-old priest who had studied theology and been ordained in England.

The patriarchate of Venice can be a confining office, but Luciani took pains not to let himself be confined. At the behest of Cardinal Willebrands, head of the Vatican's secretariat for the promotion of christian unity, he had sponsored (and paid for) a series of five ecumenical conferences. Of these, two were meetings between Catholic delegates and members of the World Council of Churches; another was a dialogue between Catholics and Pentecostal Christians; a fourth, a meeting of Catholics and Jews. The fifth meeting brought Anglicans and Catholics together and produced a notable statement on Church authority. In the fashioning of this, Luciani had a hand.

In addition, Luciani paid at least one visit to Uganda as the guest of a group of missionaries from Venice. Late in 1975 he spent a month with Cardinal Lorscheider of Fortaleza, Brazil, visiting the numerous Italian parishes and studying the phenomenon of *communidades de base* – new types of Christian experiences at the ground level – and other projects for the re-Christianization of Latin America. On friendly terms with the German Cardinal Hermann Volk, he had visited Mainz in 1978. And of course, Luciani frequently played host to the senior ecclesiastics who made their way to the City of the Doges.

On the morning after his election, he impulsively picked up the telephone and dialed his old number in the bishop's residence in Belluna. To the astonishment of the bishop, it was the pope himself who was calling. The new pope said he was lonesome for his people and wanted them to know he had called.

During John Paul's first working days as pope, he had a large number of audiences to give. On Monday and Tuesday, he saw relatives and friends from Belluna, Vittorio Veneto and Venice, as well as members of the papal household and the Roman curia. On Wednesday, he received the cardinals as a body, and tossing aside as 'too unctuous' the speech prepared for him, he told them that he expected their full cooperation. This, he said, 'would require, at times, sacrifice and a change of viewpoint on their part.' To the cardinals of the curia, he made it clear that their function was to administer. He, not they, would govern and determine Church policy and its implementation. In an aside he admitted that, uninformed as he was about the Church's executive structure at the top, and about the people working for the papacy, he had been paging through the *Annuario Pontificio,* the papal yearbook, for 1978.

Acknowledging the genial presence of Cardinal Felici, he said that during the final balloting, Felici had approached him with a 'message for the new pope.' When he opened the envelope it contained a *Via crucia* – a symbol of the way of the cross.

Much of his talk was devoted to his desire to make collegiality gen-

uine within the Church. When he turned to his written discourse for the
final blessing, he again discarded the text, saying, 'This is much too
officious.' He said that he felt out of place to be blessing a group of
bishops who were like himself successors of the Apostles.

Instead of this informal talk, *L'Osservatore Romano* published only
the official text; and complained that the pontiff's actual remarks, recorded by Vatican Radio, had later been pirated by a private station. In
this and several other minor matters – for example, changing John
Paul's use of 'I' to 'We' in reporting informal remarks – the newspaper
seemed intent on exercising the traditional curial censorship over the
pope's public utterances.

In his speech to the diplomatic corps later the same day, the pope
asserted that the Church had no designs on civil states and no interest in
political rule. He justified its close contacts with secular governments
through ambassadorial exchanges as a means of guaranteeing the
Church's catholic or universal presence in the world. He left no doubt
that he would pursue vigorously the Church's obligation to proclaim
justice and to protect the downtrodden and the persecuted at no matter
what price. Quietly but firmly he said that his primary obligation was to
guarantee everywhere the protection of human rights and human decency.

In an audience with eight hundred members of the press, radio and
television on Friday he expressed his satisfaction with the very wide
coverage given to Pope Paul's funeral and his own election. Arriving
promptly but a bit dishevelled, with his *zucchetto,* or white skull-cap,
askew, John Paul read a text that exhorted this less than worshipful craft
to pursue truth and to respect justice. He interspersed his prepared remarks with anecdotes, after assuring his audience that he was not without some knowledge of their activities, and promising them a fresh,
honest and frank collaboration. Then, he repeated the advice that an
editor had given a young Italian journalist about to interview Napoleon
III: 'Don't worry about what the Emperor said to the King of Prussia.
Find out the color of his socks and what kind of cigars he smokes.' And
he asked his audience that when its members dealt with religion and the
Church they keep in mind its mission and speak of it with respect.

Earlier John Paul had announced that his installation as pope would
be a simple mass before which he would be invested with the *pallium*
– the white woolen stole decorated with six black Latin crosses. Gone

was the coronation ceremony, the tiara, the throne and all the other appurtenances of worldly grandeur. Once a royal pageant lasting as long as six hours, this ceremony had in recent times been reduced to a mere three hours. Now it was no more: the Church could return to the simple Gospel concept of itself. When Pope John XXIII spoke of returning the Church to the form it had when it left the hand of Christ its founder, he had this concept in mind. John Paul, too, wanted a pristine simplicity. No longer should Catholic apologists have to waste time explaining why the Church was an institution with the pomp and splendor of earthly majesty when Christ had said so explicitly, 'My kingdom is not of this world.'

John Paul I was hardly in office when he received a polite but unmistakable reminder that one worldly sector of his domain was in considerable disrepute. In an open letter to the new Holy Father, the editor of Italy's foremost financial review, *Il Mondo,* Paolo Panarai, asked the pope if the Church should be involved in financial exchanges of a purely speculative character; and if the Vatican Bank should be the instrument for the expatriation of funds and the evasion of Italian currency-control laws. Though a non-believer, Panarai said he was concerned that the Church should be a credible religious organization truly dedicated to the poor and the exploited, and not involved in enterprises contributing to exploitation. He hoped, further, that by setting a good example the Church might improve Italian fiscal practices. To spare the Holy Father intricate research in this field, his weekly was publishing an analysis of Vatican finances as they appeared to the banking and commercial world.

As Panarai's rhetoric reminded the pontiff, controversy has surrounded Vatican finances ever since the Lateran Treaty of 1929. Under its terms, Mussolini's government turned over to the papacy about 90 million dollars in cash, securities and credits. Restrictions on the withdrawal of these funds (which were paid to indemnify the papacy for the loss of the Papal States and other Church properties in 1870) involved the Vatican in the Italian domestic economy. Panarai went on to say to John Paul that his predecessor, sensitive to the 'scandal' of the Vatican's holdings in the 'vast' construction and realty firm, *Societa Generale Immobiliere* (in fact worth a total of 200 million dollars), had attempted to liquidate these and other domestic investments. But Pope Paul, in entrusting the task to Sicilian financier Michele Sindona, had blundered badly. Sindona's own financial failure, Panarai assured John Paul, had cost the Vatican 'unacknowledged losses' in the millions of dollars.

Il Mondo, ploughing valiantly into the complicated accounting and budgeting procedures of the various bureaus and departments of the Vatican, uncovered no real scandal, only inefficiency and a remarkable lack of up-to-date information. Panarai, indeed, found himself in rather the same position as Cardinal Egidio Vagnozzi. Installed by Pope Paul as a sort of comptroller, but with no authority over actual expenditures, Vagnozzi has had his problems. In his attempt to obtain an overall picture of the Holy See's financial position, Vagnozzi found himself up against the reluctance of the officials in the Congregation for Evangelization, the *ancien Propaganda Fidei* (Propagation of the Faith) and the Congregation for the Oriental Church, as well as the heads of the Vatican City State and the Vatican banks (each of which had its own resources), to give a complete account of their financial holdings and expenditure.

On 5 September, in a special audience for the Orthodox prelates present for his installation, Pope John Paul was given a shocking lesson in the caducity of mortal things. The Russian Orthodox Archbishop of Leningrad, Nikodim, suddenly slumped in his chair. A few seconds later, after receiving final absolution from the quick-thinking pope, Nikodim died in the Holy Father's arms.

The 49-year-old Nikodim, a bishop at thirty-two, had had real affection for Pope Paul. Despite his frail health – he had suffered five previous heart attacks – Nikodim had persuaded the Patriarch of Moscow, Pimen, with the agreement of the Soviet authorities, to allow him to attend Paul's funeral and the convocation and election to follow. Before releasing Nikodim's body for transport home, John Paul celebrated a mass of the resurrection for him in the Vatican parish church of St Anna. In death, the pope and the Russian prelate had achieved a unity in the Eucharist that evaded both religious leaders during life.

This incident revealed much about John Paul's attitude toward the ecumenical movement. No one could question his predecessor's genuine desire to put an end to the great scandal of Christian disunity. Nor could anyone doubt the brotherly feeling he expressed in his unfeignedly warm welcomes to leaders of other churches. But Paul had let curialists, of the type Pope John described as 'prophets of doom', persuade him that before true Christian unity could emerge, doctrinal and disciplinary issues had to be resolved. Accordingly, Paul refused to countenance intercommunion between the Catholic Church and the non-Catholic Christian churches. He seemed never to understand that the grace of joint worship would serve the cause of unity far better than would haggling over theological trifles.

There were some signs that Pope John Paul would set aside the cerebral notion of the faith projected by the Roman curia and would return to the Johannine attitude that unity could be won through the exercise of co-operation and charity among Christians in 'feeding the hungry, clothing the naked and consoling the disconsolate.'

How the new pope would handle the more immediate problems troubling Catholics was of course unknown. But his insistence that his rule would be collegial rather than monarchical was one indicator. The reliance on collegiality meant that in dealing with the birth-control issue, the problems raised by divorce and homosexuality, the call for married priests in the Western Church (the Oriental Catholic churches have had married clergies from the beginning) and the agitation for the ordination of women, the pope would be seeking the mind of the whole church. Collegiality would also mean acting on the advice of the bishops in directing the Church's involvement in the political, social and economic realms.

Regarding the issue of birth control, reliable reports indicate that during the early 1960s Luciani, then Bishop of Vittorio Veneto, commissioned a detailed study of the use of artificial means of contraception. This study, embodying the findings of doctors, sociologists and theologians, was supposedly forwarded to the Holy See by Cardinal Giovanni Urbani, then Patriarch of Venice, as representing the opinion of the bishops of the Veneto district. It advised Pope Paul to refrain from reasserting the traditional ban on contraceptives.

Father Henri de Riedmatten, the Dominican priest who was secretary of Pope Paul's *ad hoc* commission on the issue, categorically denied that such a document ever existed. He maintained that if Luciani had presented the study he himself would have seen it. The denial, however, is couched in the kind of curial language that usually signifies the exact opposite of what it says.

In any event, Luciani is said to have received Paul's decision on birth control obediently, with the classic phrase of acceptance: Rome has spoken, the case is closed. This, however, did not keep him from help-ing to hammer out the statement that the Italian Bishops' Conference offered in interpretation of Paul's encyclical *Humanae Vitae,* a state-ment that greatly softened the impact of the Pauline pronouncement at the pastoral level. (The bishops had praised the pope's statement of the inseparable unity of the sexual and procreative functions in the coital act, calling this a great ideal. They then assured their flocks that no one can live up to ideals unfailingly, and if they failed to do so in this instance and were in good faith, they should not consider themselves in sin.)

Only a month before his election as pope, Luciani had commented publicly on the 'test-tube baby' born in Britain. He had offered the child his 'cordial wishes'. He had no right, he said, to criticize its parents, who 'might even have deep merit before God for what they encouraged their doctors to carry out'. But he added that not all such developments were helpful to mankind. If 'baby factories' were to result, these might produce many more malformed babies.

Amid the simple splendor of Pope John Paul's inaugural as Bishop of Rome were the heads of state and their representatives from some 110 nations. The one ominous note was the presence of General Jorge Rafael Videla, the president of Argentina, whose participation in the ceremonies was protested by several activist groups and an open letter to the Holy Father from Amnesty International.

Videla and his consort were escorted throughout the ceremonies by Archbishop Agostino Casaroli, the pope's assistant in charge of the public affairs of the Church, in what seemed to be an obvious gesture of preventive goodwill by the Holy Father. During the ceremony a large red balloon floated high above the piazza, carrying a large white streamer with the message, 'Videla, butcher'. No one has reported what the Holy Father said to the general in the ten-minute audience he was granted on Monday along with other heads of state. But it was likely to have been a message protesting the injustices, the torture and the mur-ders associated with Videla's rule – infamies already condemned by prelates, priests, nuns and laity, as well as by many international wel-fare organizations.

Amid the thousand and one details that surrounded John Paul I's first few days in the Vatican, there were indications of personal preferences

and tastes totally different to those of his predecessor. Taking possession of the papal apartments that had been sealed until his arrival, he
threw open the windows and turned off the air-conditioner. He was a
montanaro – a man of the mountains. He loved the height at which the
pope's quarters were located in the papal palace, and wanted to breathe
the fresh air blowing in from the sea and down from the hills surrounding the Eternal City.

Gone was the triumphalism, the temporal power, the pomp and circumstance of the Church. In taking formal possession of the see of
Rome by having himself invested with the simple *pallium,* an ancient
symbol of pastoral care, John Paul gave notice of his intention to pursue
the pastoralization of the Church. With the text of Vatican Council's
Dogmatic Constitution on the Church, *Lumen gentium* (the Light of the
Nations) in hand, he set out on a task that no pope in centuries had
dared even to dream of realistically.

The question was: could he come anywhere close to accomplishing
even the beginnings of this anarchical program? Both his predecessors,
John and Paul, had honestly desired to put the Church back on the long
road to the simplicity and honesty of its earliest experiences. Both pontiffs had gradually to give way before the entrenched realism of the
immense political structure that the Church had become over the past
nineteen centuries, and the vested interests of the prelates and people
who totally identified with this institution.

How could this comparatively unknown man from the Veneto, who
had hardly any experience of the world and very little of the Church's
incredibly complex existence all over the globe, think that he could
revolutionize its outlook so as to completely reorganize its structure?
Yet, this was what he seems to have had in mind.

He was evidently a dreamer who, in the eyes of the cynical Vatican
officials, would soon have to wake up and face the reality of evil, the
forces of destruction that were besieging the Church, and against whose
attacks only its governmental structure was capable of preserving its
institutional integrity.

John Paul was not in office a week when the instinctive curial control
began to assert itself. Even in his first few hours he had been faced with
a difficulty. In anticipation of the need for an immediate papal message
to the Church, the secretary of state's office had prepared just such a
document in good curial Latin. Having decided to deliver his televised
message the next morning, the new pope accepted this canned docu-

ment despite the objection of several cardinals who felt that he was setting a bad precedent for himself. But since there was no time to compose such a document on his own or even to dictate it, John Paul took the curial text and, with major modifications, particularly his insistence on collegial rule and an expedited ecumenism, he delivered it. As events would prove, this kind of document was hardly in keeping with his style or way of doing things.

While minor curial incidents were taking place at a level certainly below the concerns of the new Holy Father, they represented the kind of surreptitious control that had paralyzed genuine papal efforts at reform in the past. How was Pope Luciani going to ferret out the men responsible for this curial recalcitrance? And what was he going to do about it if and when he caught up with them?

In his first few weeks in the Vatican it was all he could do to find his way around. As he jokingly told the cardinals, he had had to consult the Vatican yearbook, which lists the offices and officials of the Church around the world, to find out who was actually working for him and what was the Church's inner structure at the top. (He did not, however, repeat Pope John's remark, who, when asked how many people worked in the Vatican, replied, 'Oh, about half.') Despite Pope Paul's explicit admonition to his successor that he should not reappoint any officials for the first three months of his pontificate, John Paul felt the need to regularize Vatican operations at once. He appointed Cardinal Jean Villot as his secretary of state; then he reinstated the other curial officers in keeping with their position in the five-year appointments established by his predecessor. What he was apparently banking on was the assistance of the Holy Spirit and the attrition of age to let him introduce, in time, the people who would share his vision.

In reducing the Church to the basic structure of a refuge of the poor, how would he be able to confront the nations and rulers whom the Church had been able to intimidate to some extent in the past by a show of political as well as spiritual force? How would he face up to Idi Amin of Uganda, who had thrown Cardinal Nsubuga into prison and arranged the fatal accidents that did away with other Church dissidents? Or the government of Brazzaville that had a martyr on its hands in the sudden, unexplained death of Cardinal Emile Biayende, two years before? How was he to handle Arturo Pinochet in Chile? The Marcos family in the Philippines? General Somoza in Nicaragua? – to mention some of the so-called Catholic dictatorships that were challenged by their Catholic bishops, clergy and laity. And what of the Church's daily dealings with the communist leaders in Poland, Hungary, Yugoslavia and the other Iron and Bamboo Curtain countries, and its attempts to push its way into continental China by way of Bangladesh, if the Church did not retain at least the appurtenances of a strong parapolitical entity?

Somehow, John Paul would have to face that situation. Behind him, of course, was a long tradition in which the Church had survived persecution and, despite great losses, had not only buried its enemies, but preserved their names from oblivion. In the last century, as he was well aware, the French Catholic publicist Louis Veuillot had called public attention to the fact that *'qui mange le pape en meurt'* ('who bites the pope dies of it').

It was from within the Vatican itself, with its vast tentacles reaching round the world in nunciatures and apostolic delegations, that some of the pope's most obstinate opposition would come. Already concern had been growing among the archconservative cardinals, many of whom voted for him in that quick changeover after the second ballot of the conclave, that John Paul I really meant to turn the Church upside-down in the Johannine sense. They felt that, as the new Holy Father, he must try his wings, and make noises in the direction of reform. But they expected him to remember the traditions of the Italian Church from which he sprung – its doctrinal integrity, to the extent of boasting that no heresy ever got its start in Rome (a thoroughly untruthful statement); and its disciplinary security, based on *romanita*, a consciousness of law and order derived from the halcyon days of the Roman emperor Augustus and the *pax romana* which, it was believed, had been arranged by divine providence in consideration of the birth of Christ (another doubtful legend).

At a crucial point in the old, discarded, papal coronation ceremony, the pope's penitentiary would burn a flaxen cord before his master, uttering as he did so: *sic transit gloria mundi*. As he settled into his job, John Paul would notice that the attention of the world, like its glory, is, even for a pope, a fleeting matter. The focus of extraordinary attention for the few days after his election and inauguration, John Paul then disappeared from view into the depths of his job. His pontificate would be watched with routine vigilance for significant words or deeds;

otherwise, he was simply part of the world's daily scheme of things.

Then, suddenly, he was gone. On Friday September 29th, only thirty-three days after his election, the world awoke to discover that Pope John Paul I was no longer with them.

8

John Paul II

The sudden death of John Paul I shocked the Church and the world. The Venetian pope with the gracious smile had in a very short span managed to give the papacy a new vigour of simplicity and joy. In his symbolic actions banning the final vestiges of the Constantinian era and in his pastoral attention to the crowds who flocked to greet the new supreme pastor (he did not want to be called a pontiff), he set a new style, and one very much in keeping with Pope John's desires for a simplification of the papal presence.

Just how the Luciani pope would have faced up to the complex exigencies of Vatican government will never be known. Well before he could show his hand, death had called him. Sometime after eleven o'clock on the night of 28 September, while sitting up in bed reading a speech for delivery the next day, he died of a massive heart attack. That very morning he had been in good spirits, welcoming a group of Philippine bishops on their official visit to the Holy See, and he had delivered one of his catechetical talks to a vast public audience in St Peter's. He had retired at ten. When he failed to appear for mass at 5.30 the next morning his anxious secretary, Father John Magee, entered his room to discover that he had slipped off into eternity.

John Paul's funeral, which took place in St Peter's Square, was a much sadder affair than that of Pope Paul. The weather was inclement. And cardinals and dignitaries – the Holy See suggested to heads of state that they should not interrupt their schedules for a third time – and an immense crowd of mourners withstood driving rain that only ceased during the communion of the mass. Once more the aristocratic octogenarian Cardinal Confalonieri led the ninety-five cardinals in a dignified if rain-dampened mass of the resurrection and pronounced a fitting eulogy. Then, as the pall-bearers lifted the simple wooden coffin to their shoulders the vast crowd applauded like the beat of muffled drums, and they marched the tiny corpse up the *scalinata* of St Peter's into the darkened atrium of the basilica. John Paul I was no more.

Arriving in Rome for the new conclave, the cardinal electors decided to enter the conclave with all speed, and the date of their assembly was set for 14 October. No longer new to the parts they would be playing, they cut back the excessive preparations for secrecy, giving themselves room to breathe within the confines of the conclave area surrounding the Sistine Chapel. But despite the scurrying of a thousand or more journalists, radio and television reporters maneuvering for tidbits of pre-conclave action, there was little information as to what was going on in the minds of the assembling electors.

Cardinal Jean Villot's homily at the mass for the election of a pontiff, preceding the entrance into the precincts of the conclave, was a commentary on St John's Gospel not substantially different from the brief sermon he had delivered before the election of John Paul I. He did not comment on the strangeness of the event that seemed to indicate so direct an interference by the Holy Spirit, nor did he speculate on the possibilities now open to the electors.

One thing seemed certain in the mind of the cardinals as they gathered for the voting. They wanted another pope who would project to the world an air of confidence and joy. But, this time, they had better seek out a younger man whose health and strength could withstand the enormous weight of the papal office. Despite the persistent questioning of the newsmen and the speculation of Vatican observers, there was precious little evidence that the cardinals, other than the men of the curia, had a specific candidate in mind. And the skirmishing during the first day and a half of the balloting proved that the majority entered the conclave awaiting the nod of the Spirit. It came to them, as usual, in a most unexpected fashion.

The election of the Polish cardinal on 16 October 1978 came as a complete surprise. It is known that during the first day of voting, a duel was fought between the curial supporters of Cardinal Giuseppe Siri and the partisans of the former aide to Pope Paul VI, Cardinal Giovanni Benelli of Florence. On the third ballot Benelli had come within some fifteen or twenty votes of the necessary two-thirds plus one (eighty-five); but he had peaked, and on the next ballot many of his supporters switched to the older Italian residential cardinals such as Colombo of Milan and Ursi of Naples. Meanwhile the name of Wojtyla had sounded sporadically (Cardinal Koenig of Vienna acknowledged voting for him from the start; but it is not known when the English Cardinal Hume and the eight American cardinals gave him their vote, although Krol of Philadelphia and Baum of Washington had been his guests in Krakow during the early spring); and when, on the sixth ballot, the Italians failed to produce a pope, the outsiders switched to Wojtyla, having had a good look at him as a candidate during lunch (as in the case of Luciani a month and a half earlier). On the seventh voting he bounded into the sixties, and was in, with over ninety votes, on the eighth ballot.

In the switch to Wojtyla no thought was given to the political implications of a man from behind the Iron Curtain. As Cardinal Hume remarked, 'We would have voted for him even if he were an Italian.' Despite a mild amount of electioneering among the cardinals, most of the political speculation had been carried on in the press. On the Sunday immediately following John Paul's death Cardinal Benelli had given a sermon at Lisieux in France in which he said that the qualifications for the new pope should include comparative youth, robust health, and keen administrative abilities, throwing in for good measure that he should be an Italian from the provinces with pastoral experience. The cardinal of Genoa, Siri, seemed to take this as a direct attack on his candidacy and in a series of statements protested that he was neither an archconservative nor anti-conciliar. And on the Thursday before the conclave, in an interview with a Florentine journalist embargoed until the following Sunday, Siri criticized John Paul I as a creature of the secretary of state. The interview was published on Saturday in the *Gazzetto del Popolo di Firenze,* and when Siri denied its contents a cassette was produced. He was an unhappy man entering and leaving the conclave.

John Paul II's comparative youth and vigor, and his immediate tradition-breaking reassurance to the Romans and the world that although 'a man from afar', he was the Bishop of Rome and would do his best to speak 'your – no, our [the slip seemed deliberate] – language,' won him spontaneous and universal acceptance.

Nowhere in the world was greater consternation registered than in

Poland. But after a short period of official perplexity, shared with the news media who were faced with the need for instant biographical information, the Polish government reacted properly. When a Polish television team arrived the next day in Rome, to the joshing of their on-the-spot Western colleagues, they could only reply, 'We had no idea that a Pole would make it!'

The quick and unexpected election of a Polish Holy Father confirmed the feelings of the majority of the cardinals that in their choice of a new pope they had been influenced if not managed by the Holy Spirit. For on their entrance to the conclave not many had Wojtyla's candidacy in mind. That the cardinal of Krakow had some presentiment of what was to happen is hinted at by his reaction to the sudden death of his predecessor John Paul I. In August, Cardinal Wojtyla had taken the death of Pope Paul in his stride and on departing for Rome made his usual round of farewells to his household. This time it was different. He seemed to have suffered some sort of shock. Dropping the business at hand, he left for Rome with his secretary almost surreptitiously. And upon arrival in the Eternal City he fled to the Polish Shrine of the Madonna at Montorella, high in the Apennine mountains, where he spent several days in retreat. When during lunch on the second day's balloting he realized that the choice would fall on him, he seemed to recede into himself and had to be reminded by Cardinal Wyszynski that should the Holy Spirit choose him he had no option but to obey. When on the eighth ballot he received the election, he was prepared.

The new pope had been involved in the preparation for Vatican Council II both as bishop and theologian. Noted as a man of culture and quiet ways – he was a working poet as well as a philosopher – the Polish government had accepted him as Archbishop of Krakow in 1964 hoping to play him off against the intransigence of Cardinal Wyszynski, only to discover that while he encouraged the other Polish bishops to stand up to the primate in their episcopal meetings, he was equally difficult in his dealings with the government. His mettle was demonstrated when in the course of a long campaign he forced the authorities to allow the construction of a church in Nowa Huta, the modernistic steel center outside Krakow which had been intended as a model of scientific realism, with no room for religion. In a ten-year struggle Wojtyla led the communists' hand-picked workers in their determination to construct the huge futuristic edifice that now adorns the city's periphery. At Vatican Council II, Wojtyla contributed to the revolutionary teaching on the nature of the Church as 'the people of God' rather than the juridical institution described by Cardinal Bellarmine after the Council of Trent and the 1918 code of canon law. He then concentrated on the adaptation of this teaching in the Council's Pastoral Constitution that dealt with the practical needs of today's world. His approach to the problems of love, marriage, religious freedom, humanism and culture was phenomenological, demonstrating the need to comprehend the actualities of a situation before seeking Gospel-based solutions to moral dilemmas.

As a young bishop in the late 1950s he had published a book on *Love and Responsibility,* an up-to-date discussion of sexual pleasure with an analysis of the female psyche in relation to the physiological aspects of marital relations. It proposed an idealistic solution to the problem of birth control via natural methods, based on a realistic description of the elements involved in married love (the factual nature of this description seems responsible for the unfounded rumor that he had been married and widowed before entering the priesthood).

Not only was Karol Wojtyla not an Italian, but his youthful experiences differed considerably from those of most of his predecessors over the last two centuries, cut out for Church careers almost from childhood. Born in the small industrial town of Wadowice in the Tatra mountains, he lost his mother at three, and a sister and older brother before he was eighteen, when he moved to Krakow with his father and registered for studies in literature at the local university. Interested in acting, he joined a group called the Rhapsodic Theatre, but had to support himself and avoid conscription in a labor camp by working first in a stone quarry, then in a chemical factory. A tall, strong, blond-haired youth with good religious sentiments, he caught the attention of Cardinal Sapieha of Krakow, who took him and several companions into the episcopal residence on the outbreak of hostilities in 1940. They spent the war there, studying theology and aiding that courageous churchman in his refugee and resistance projects. Little is known about Wojtyla's actual involvement in clandestine activities; but with the war's end he helped reorganize the local seminary and was ordained a priest in September 1946. He was then dispatched to the Dominican house of studies in Rome known as the Angelicum, for graduate work in philosophy.

Living at the Belgian College in Rome with a group of American and other students, Wojtyla studied under the famous Father Reginald Garrigou-Lagrange, known as the most decisive of the Thomistic theologians – in 1950 Lagrange had a principal part in authoring Pius XII's encyclical *Humani generis*. He was also exposed to the teachings of the Irish Dominican, Michael Browne, and the Frenchman Paul Philippe, both of whom later opposed, as cardinals, the progressive decisions of Vatican Council II.

Wojtyla had come to Rome with an interest in the seventeenth century Spanish mystic St John of the Cross, the friend of the famous St Teresa of Avila. Despite the fact that John had spent time in the prison of the Inquisition, he was eventually canonized. Wojtyla wrote his dissertation on the notion of faith in John's mystical writings. Meanwhile he was employed by Catholic War Relief Services to give spiritual assistance to the numerous Polish refugees in Rome, Italy, Belgium, France and Germany, thus obtaining a wider view of the world, meeting prominent ecclesiastics, including Monsignor Giovanni Battista Montini, and perfecting his knowledge of modern languages. An actor by talent and training, as he was to demonstrate by his ability to mesmerize immense crowds in his jet pilgrimages as pope, he mastered Russian and Slavic, as well as German, French, Spanish and English.

Returning to Krakow in 1948, he served as a parish priest and then as university chaplain while teaching at the Catholic theology faculty of Lublin University. Turning his attention to some of the immense moral and ethical problems of the post-war years, he answered the call for a new approach to Catholic moral teaching by studying the German phenomenologist ethician, Max Scheler, and the Polish Roman Imgarden, attempting to achieve a synthesis between their value-oriented judgments, his own Thomistic formation and the personalist philosophies of the French Catholic existentialists Maurice Blondel and Emmanuel Mounier. Gradually he immersed himself in the problems of the 'human', partly as a response to the marxist challenge that maintained that man's worth was determined by his labor. Going back to Kant's insistence that human nature was an end in itself demanding recognition of its dignity and liberty, and never to be used as a means, Wojtyla turned out a large number of erudite monographs and papers on technical aspects of these problems. In the process, he won himself academic degrees from the state university. His love for sports and choral activities made him an ideal chaplain for the university students with whom he went on skiing, canoeing and hiking expeditions even after being consecrated an auxiliary bishop of Krakow in 1958, archbishop in 1964 and cardinal in 1967.

As an auxiliary bishop in Krakow, Wojtyla did the leg-work at the beck and call of the civilian authorities. On becoming the Archbishop in 1964, however, he would deal with no one in the government below politburo rank. While often in full agreement with the indomitable Cardinal Stefan Wyszynski of Warsaw, Wojtyla frequently urged his fellow bishops to speak their minds in meetings with the tough-minded primate of Poland. Wyszynski had suffered imprisonment as a confessor of the faith in the later days of the Stalinist era, and had stood up to Pius XII in his political dealings with the Polish government. Paradoxically, Wyszynski's courageous confrontations with both the Kremlin and the Vatican had made him almost the king-maker for the communist politburo.

The Warsaw cardinal's support enabled the Gomulka government to be formed, and assisted in its replacement by Edward Gierek's regime in 1970, despite violent disagreements over repressive policies harming the Church's liberty. The cardinal had to step in to calm down rioting for food and higher salaries in the mid-1970s that would have toppled the Gierek government. Between the two cardinals there was an almost son-to-father relationship expressed in Wojtyla's *bon mot,* 'In Poland only forty per cent of the cardinals ski', acknowledging Wyszynski's domination of the ecclesiastical scene. Nevertheless the government were not happy at the prospect of Wojtyla's succeeding the cardinal of Warsaw as primate. The latter's reaction to communist harassment was violent but predictable; whereas Wojtyla's was subtle and more dangerous. On the latter's election as pope, sardonic wits maintained it was an answer to the politburo's prayers.

Wojtyla had been one of the last bishops appointed by Pius XII in July 1958, and was consecrated a month before the election of John XXIII later that year. When the Vatican Council was announced, Wojtyla became a member of the preparatory commission and then attended the four sessions between 1962 and 1965 as a working theologian, renewing friendships formed in his Angelicum days and receiving invitations to lecture first in Italy, then in Germany, France, and, in 1969, in the United States. Through the auspices of Anna-Teresa

Tyminiecka, head of the Institute of Phenomenology in Belmont, Massachusetts and editor of the *Analecta Husserliana,* his reputation as a cardinal philosopher was given world-wide prominence and he lectured at Harvard, Princeton, Stamford and the Catholic University in Washington. He travelled as far as the University of Canberra with stopovers in New Zealand, Indonesia and other parts of the Far East. In 1976 he attended the Eucharistic Congress in Philadelphia and spent three months travelling through the United States and Canada. Meanwhile, he became a permanent member of the council of the Roman Synod of Bishops, as well as of postconciliar committees that brought him back and forth frequently between Krakow and Rome. He took an active part in all the Roman synods of bishops except that of 1971, when he refused to leave Poland in protest against the government's withdrawal of Cardinal Wyszynski's passport.

A confidant of Paul VI, whom he would claim as his mentor in his first encyclical, John Paul II seemed to have adopted that pontiff's progressive attitudes toward the modern world without Montini's painful, scrupulous sufferings in attempting to balance postconciliar theology between the liberal and arch-conservative camps.

It seems clear that Wojtyla's outgoing nature spared him the psychological anxieties over the burdens of the priesthood and the self-imposed austerities of a profound spirituality that have proved so difficult for a large number of priests today, forcing them to leave the ministry for other lifestyles. Instead, his deep Marian piety and his momentous energy have enabled him to balance a total involvement with the priestly life, including the challenge of governing the vast archdiocese of Krakow in the face of government hostility, with escapist travel to foreign lands for meetings with intellectual and religious leaders, as well as his sporting excursions with university students – activities which continued right down to the month before his election as pope.

In his inaugural address, John Paul insisted that his pontificate would carry out faithfully the decisions of the Council in keeping with the positive attitudes of the two popes whose names he had adopted. He assured his audience that his papacy would be joyful and effective. And during his first few weeks in the Vatican he had given every indication that this was the *élan* he would introduce into the Church's affairs.

No one expected the new pope to take a neutral attitude toward ecclesial issues, and in his first public audiences he sounded alarmingly conservative, as he stressed the beauty of motherhood to fifteen thousand young women, advised priests and nuns to wear clerical garb in public, and ignored the suggestion of the Anglican primate, Donald Coggan, present for the pope's installation, that he immediately declare communion between the Catholic and Anglican churches.

Opposition leaders in the Italian parliament tried to portray his condemnation of divorce and abortion as an interference in Italy's politics; but the pope was not fazed by that ploy. Nor did he interfere with the negotiations between the Italian government and the Vatican for an accord that would abolish the Concordat of 1929. Addressing the diplomatic corps shortly after his election, John Paul assured some hundred ambassadors, ministers and personal representatives of governments accredited to the Holy See that the Church had no desire for special treatment by states or any intention of meddling in politics. But it did demand freedom to conduct its affairs on its own terms and in its own way.

In keeping with this declaration, the Polish Holy Father acquiesced in the revision of the 1929 Concordat which provided for the disestablishment of the Catholic Church, freedom of conscience, civil marriage, the abolition of special privileges for the clergy, and the cancellation of obligatory religious instruction in the schools. Violently opposed by rightwing Catholics and superannuated members of the papal household, the new agreement had the blessing of the majority of the Italian bishops.

A similar situation existed in Spain where a new constitution was voted in by a large majority in December 1978. Supported by two-thirds of the nation's bishops under the guidance of Cardinal Vicente Enrique y Tarancón of Madrid, this document was violently attacked by the cardinal of Toledo, Marcelo Gonzalez Martin, who said that it was an agnostic constitution foisted on a nation of the baptized. The absence of any reference to God and the natural law, said the prelate, would lead to a nefarious permissive society. This was the Francoist stand, and had been repudiated by Vatican Council II in its constitution on the Church in today's world. *Ya,* the conservative Catholic daily, supported the new constitution. 'It is a political text,' it noted, 'not a philosophical or dogmatic statement. Hence it begins with its feet on the ground and offers liberty, justice, equality and political responsibility to all. To speak of the Constitution as atheistic is to reveal a mania for tilting at windmills.' And Mons. Gardia Faiode, a Vatican legal expert in the Madrid nunciature, told *Il Pais,* 'the Constitution contains nothing a Christian conscience should reject'. His remarks seemed to reflect the new pope's conviction that older conflicts between church and state were *passé.*

But this attitude did not apply *in toto* to John Paul's native Poland, where the pope's Christmas message to Krakow had been senselessly mutilated by a local censor who removed his reference to the eleventh-century martyr St Stanislaus as a champion of religious liberty. The following Sunday an indignant pope blasted the Polish regime for its continued repression of religious liberty in his midday appearance at his window, and ordered the powerful Vatican Radio to turn its attention on Poland, broadcasting, among other services, a weekly mass for those who were tied to the home.

Among the questions put to John Paul II during his first audience with journalists were 'Are you going to Poland ?' 'Will you visit Ireland?' 'What about Russia?' and, most of all, 'Will you go to Puebla ?' To all of these interrogations, the new Holy Father replied in a bantering mood, 'Yes, if they let me.' On John Paul's desk were invitations to visit every corner of the world. But the most pressing of these was a request to attend the meeting of the Latin American Bishops' Conference (CELAM), scheduled for Puebla de Los Angeles, Mexico, in the fall of 1978 – the meeting had been postponed twice by the deaths of Popes Paul VI and John Paul I.

In preparation for over two years, the Puebla meeting was to be a follow-up of the great conference at Medellin in Colombia, opened by Pope Paul VI in 1968. That meeting had given the Church in Latin America a new lease on life. In a famous *'Medellin Manifesto'* the cardinals and bishops of the South American continent had told the world that their vast Church was henceforth dedicated to preach the Gospel to the poor and neglected. With that declaration, a revolutionary change was introduced into the image of the Catholic presence. No longer to be identified with the rich and powerful, the Church's prelates and priests, nuns and lay activists were to teach the Gospel by living close to their people. To put this decision in practice, strategists in the Church concocted a 'Theology of Liberation' – a manner of interpreting the Gospel as the call to freedom from government oppression, social injustice and financial exploitation. Liberation Theology analysed social and economic conditions with tools that greatly resembled marxist methods while demanding social improvement in keeping with Christ's injunctions in the Gospel. This program had been accepted by Pope Paul VI and initiated by a majority of the Latin American clergy and laity. But it met opposition from old-fashioned churchmen, dictatorial governments, and well-to-do Catholics, fearful that it would lead to socialism and eventually to a communist takeover, as had happened under Fidel Castro in Cuba and, abortively, under Allende in Chile. The meeting in Puebla was to analyse what had happened to the Church in Latin America during the ten years following the Medellin Declaration, and to set new goals of evangelization for the continent's three hundred million Catholics. As the cardinal of Krakow, Karol Wojtÿla had of course been aware of these preparations; as Pope John Paul II he was confronted with the request to authorize the Puebla meeting and fly to Mexico to inaugurate its proceedings.

First drafts of the Puebla agenda had been severely criticized as the work of conservative prelates under the control of the curial cardinal Sebastian Baggio and his lieutenant, Mons. Alfonso Lopez Trujillo, auxiliary bishop of Bogota and executive secretary of CELAM. Eventually, with the aid of outside pressure, the majority of Latin American bishops and experts forced the Rome-dominated committee to ameliorate the agenda. Nevertheless an air of potential controversy hovered over the proposed meeting.

Under these circumstances the presence of the pope at Puebla became an important issue. The new Holy Father set the date for the Puebla Conference for late-January 1979. After listening to Cardinal Baggio among others, who advised against the pope's journey saying it was dangerous and could backfire, and to the Bishop of Cuernavaca, Mexico, Mons. Mendez Arceo, who urged the Holy Father to encourage Latin American Catholics with his first overseas pilgrimage, John Paul decided to make the voyage. Leaving from Rome's Fiumicino airport on 26 January, the Polish pope mingled with journalists and answered their innumerable questions in a challenging fashion. He told the representatives of the communist *L'Unita* that he read that paper first each morning, wanting to know what opposition the Church had to face that day; confirmed the fact that he had spoken to the Polish president Jablonsky about a trip to Poland; and expressed great hopes for his Latin American journey.

The Polish pontiff arrived in Mexico City on 27 January. The papal pilgrimage had begun the previous day in Santo Domingo where, in the footsteps of Columbus, allegedly buried in the local cathedral, the Holy Father had kissed the ground and told a vociferous crowd of some 300,000 in the Plaza de la Independencia during a late-afternoon mass that he was a voyager of peace and hope. Received with full diplomatic honors by the President, Silvestro Guzman, the Holy Father had to be rescued from a group of seminarians intent on stripping him for souvenirs.

The next day, Mexico's constitutionally a-religious president, José Lopez Portillo, gave the pope a brief, formal welcome before handing him over to the Church dignitaries and fading from the scene.

To permit the Holy Father to wear his ecclesiastical garb and celebrate mass in public, Portillo had threatened to force a constitutional change through the national assembly and allay the fears of businessmen who believed that the papal visit would stir revolutionary ideas among the peasants and provide guerrillas with a platform to preach rebellion. In contrast to President Carter's polite but grim reception two weeks later, John Paul's welcome was noisy and chaotic, with immense crowds trying to get through the cordon of police and soldiers to see and touch the Holy Father. Whisked by open vehicle under the guidance of Mexico City's Archbishop Ahumada to the cathedral of the Assumption – the oldest major church (1531) in the New World – the pope celebrated mass and delivered one of some twenty discourses in which he urged fidelity to the Church's teachings while 'discarding secondary things valid in the past but now outdated'. John Paul then visited the Polish colony in Mexico City, indulged a personal piety with a visit to the shrine of the Virgin of Guadalupe where on 9 December 1531, ten years after the conquest, the Virgin Mary had appeared to a converted Indian, leaving her image on his tilma and requesting that a church be built on the site that once housed the ancient shrine of the Aztec deity Teotinantzin – mother of the gods – thus furnishing the infant church in New Spain with the earliest example of acculturization.

Eleven years earlier, at Medellin, Paul VI had sanctioned the

Church's commitment to the social and economic uplift of its people through 'conscientization' – a spiritual and political awakening induced via literacy. But his caution, 'violence is not in keeping with the Gospel' had haunted the struggle for justice in Latin America for over a decade. Under Medellin's inspiration, the continents' clergy and laity, nuns and prelates had gradually repudiated the military juntas that were playing into the hands of oligarchs and multinational corporations who were robbing these countries of their wealth and resources, exploiting the poor and depriving the peasants of their livelihood. All but a few of the cardinals – Casariego of Guatemala, Duque of Colombia and Aramburu of Argentina – had broken with the dictatorships and made heroic efforts to protect their people. In the decade and a half since Vatican II, the gap between rich and poor in Latin America had widened, with right-wing associations for the protection of Family, Property and Tradition hounding the Church's activists. Puebla was intended as a solution to the continent's problems by initiating a movement to re-Christianize both the extremely rich (on several occasions John Paul II said that the Church had a duty to others besides the poor) and the abandoned.

On January 29th the pope motored the eighty miles to Puebla, standing in a specially constructed vehicle, greeting the thousands of peasants and indians in native dress, the police and guardsmen who lined the serpentine highway, and arrived at the luxurious Palafox seminary on the outskirts of the city. Started by Bishop Menendez Palafox in the 1550s, this large complex had been reconstructed through the generosity of Cardinal Cushing of Boston in the 1950s and now housed the Puebla Conference's bishops and experts.

John Paul's speech opening the conference was long and complicated. It gave rise to a number of ambiguities. Though he emphasized the Church's involvement with the liberation of man as man, he deliberately avoided the term 'Liberation Theology,' and while insisting that man's plight in the political and economic order was intimately involved with his spiritual well-being, he made it clear that in the Christian catechesis Christ had not been a revolutionary seeking to overthrow a colonial power. The Holy Father insisted that politics was the business of the laity, thus seeming to discourage priests from involvement in political action. Praising the Puebla meeting as 'A wonderful hour in the history of the world,' John Paul said it should not re-examine the problems solved at Medellin, but should renew the spirit of that gathering 'in a new way, at a new pace, and in a new moment of history'. In pursuing this task, he said, 'clerics were not to be social directors, political leaders, or functionaries of temporal power'.

Lifted from its context, this latter sentence was interpreted as a definite prohibition to priests to get involved in politics and, as an editorial in a Mexican journal remarked, 'the pope's prohibition could easily be used by governments and paramilitary goons in beating up clerics demonstrating for their people's rights.' This criticism obviously got through to the Holy Father and the next day he was seen busily rewriting the speech he was to give to some 40,000 Indians at Oaxaca.

Moved by the extreme poverty he observed everywhere, at Oaxaca the pope delivered a vehement condemnation of the greed and exploitation that deprived these impoverished people of their right to land and a decent livelihood. He told his listeners: 'we want to be the voice of the voiceless; the defender of the oppressed who have the right to effective help – neither charity nor the crumbs of justice.' Obviously enjoying his contact with the hundreds of thousands of people who greeted him everywhere he turned, John Paul proved tireless in moving about the country while the conference delegates battled through a complex program, calling for justice in the social and economic ordinance of the continent.

John Paul's balanced approach represented an attempt to avoid the brouhaha initiated by Cardinal Baggio's efforts to control the gathering upstaging his co-presidents, Cardinal Lorscheider of Fortaleza, Brazil, and Archbishop Ahumada of Mexico City. Twice passed over for the papacy, Baggio desired to function as the savior of the Church in Latin America, working through his trusted lieutenant, Mons. Alfonso Trujillo, the auxiliary bishop of Bogota, whom Baggio promoted to the archbishopric of Medellin. He was aided by the Belgian Jesuit Roger Vekemans, who had played a strategic role in Chile, funnelling millions of US aid and, it is said, CIA money into social and development projects for President Frei's Christian Democratic Party in the late 1960s (asked by the curial archbishop Antonio Samoré why he visited Washington before checking with Rome for his projects, Vekemans replied: 'In Washington one gets cold cash; in Rome, hot air'), before fleeing Chile upon the election of the Allende government in 1970. Welcomed to Colombia by the hard-nosed Cardinal Duque of Bogota, Vekemans was used by Bishop Trujillo to offset the apostles of social and economic reform, particularly among the junior clergy working in slum areas, by casting doubt on their orthodoxy, challenging the validity of Liberation Theology, and accusing ecclesiastical activists of operating on marxist principles.

Apparently in pursuit of his Latin American ambition, Baggio had refused the first John Paul's suggestion that he become the Archbishop of Venice and had tried to dissuade that Holy Father from making the trip to Mexico. Rumor had it that on the morning of the pontiff's death, Baggio had an argument with him over the matter. When he attempted a similar tactic with the Polish pope, he was quickly put down.

Baggio's short temper and inaccessibility at Puebla gave observers the feeling that he had lost his cool. Hence his co-president, the instinctively shy Cardinal Lorscheider had little difficulty in upstaging the Roman bureaucrat. When Lorscheider's inaugural address was recognized as an unmistakable complement to the pope's proposals, Baggio's influence faded. And it evaporated further when the local daily paper, *Uno Mas Uno,* published a letter dictated (but, by Bishop Trujillo's own admission, not sent) by the secretary general of the conference to a crony, Archbishop Luciano Duarte of Aracaju, Brazil, describing the Tammany methods Trujillo used to offset liberal influence in the preparation of the Puebla agenda – besides eliminating suggestions of agenda items and personnel made by Cardinals Landazuri Ricketts of Lima, Evaristo Arns of Sao Paulo, and Silva Henriquez of Chile, Trujillo had referred to the Argentinian curial cardinal, Edoardo Pironio, as a weakling, and called the Jesuit Superior General, Pedro Arrupe, dangerous.

Facing the 216 bishops at Puebla was the fact that the Church was headed for a showdown with the dictatorships in Latin America. The problem lay in the intransigent desire for power and the greed of an oligarchy of military leaders, businessmen and landowners, most of whom were well-educated Catholics who had teamed up with representatives of the multinational corporations from Europe and North America to enlarge their holdings of the countries' resources and wealth, depriving the peasants and laborers of a decent living by sequestering land and credit, depriving workers and farmers of the right to organize, and driving the Indians off their reservations. Caught in the bind of keeping their expensive military hardware up to date, the inflationary cost of oil for fuel and transport, and the diminishing returns on their investments, these men of the right traced their troubles to the marxist influence among university students, labor organizations, and clerics stirring up the people, rather than to the irresponsible capitalist system of which they were the beneficiaries. With little hope of a change of heart among these rightist Catholics, some bishops and clerics believed it better to suffer the current discontent rather than risk the horrors of political upheaval.

But this was not the thinking of the cardinal of Sao Paulo, Evaristo Arns, who shortly before leaving for Puebla received a study by the Brazilian Ecumenical Documentation Center on ten years of torture (1968–1978) under military rule in Brazil, complete with names and incidents (7 bishops, 115 priests, religious and seminarians, and 237 lay people had been arrested for 'subversive' pastoral activities; 34 priests subjected to torture; and 24 religious houses searched). Nor was it the mind of the fifteen foreign bishops (including four US prelates) and thirty Ecuadoreans who were taken into custody at gun-point by police during an international meeting on pastoral affairs in Riobomba, Ecuador. When the three Chilean bishops, including Carlos Gonzalez of Talca, reached the airport in Santiago they were subjected to a barrage of stones arranged, as Cardinal Silva Henriquez and the Chilean bishops conference proved later, by DINA, the Chilean secret police. Nor was it the sentiment of a group of Argentinian bishops under Cardinal Primatesta of Cordoba, who warned the government against 'officials who failed to assure the absolute exclusion of abuses which violate the dignity of man'. Nor, again, was it the mind of the majority of prelates in Bolivia, Uruguay, Nicaragua, San Salvador, Paraguay and Guatemala, in daily conflict with dictatorships intent on pursuing a pseudo 'national security' instead of human rights for their subjects.

Meanwhile John Paul spent a vigorous seven days seeing and being seen by the Mexican populace – and much of the world via the news media – and visiting a considerable area of the countryside. Conscious of Mexico's vast mixed population – ten per cent Spanish heritage, who constitute mainly the middle and upper classes; thirty per cent Indians, whose civilization flourished for centuries before the conquest but whose modern desuetude has been described as a people 'dissolved into the landscape'; and sixty per cent mestizos of Spanish and Indian blood, most of whom live a marginal existence but who are at once aloof, aggressive, volatile, almost violently religious, and devoutly Catholic.

After Oaxaca the pope went to Guadalajara, where he gave expression to the real intent of the papal visit – to bring the world's attention to the poor and needy, offering them Christ as a support in coping with the injustices all about them. The papal visit to Guadalajara proved a highly festive occurrence and as the pope took off the plane circled the city for an hour, acknowledging the millions of Guadalajarans below who were flashing sun-reflecting mirrors on the papal plane.

In Monterey, his last stop, the papal message touched on the plight of the workers who 'had to abandon their homeland in search of employment . . . frequently living in conditions unworthy of human beings'. With a final midnight stopover in Nassau in the Bahamas and a message to Fidel Castro when flying over his airspace, a tired Holy Father returned to Rome and assured some 50,000 visitors in St Peter's Square the next day that his journey had been most successful.

Back at Puebla, after a vigorous two and a half weeks' no-holds-barred discussion of the religious, economic and political plight of their people, the Latin American bishops turned out a 210-page manifesto that described the lot of the poor as 'a kind of abomination'. This was straight talking, and evidently too much for the 26 bishops who refused to sign the document and the 45 prelates who left the conference before its close. The 126 signatories set out a line of development that rejected capitalism as an anti-human materialism and marxism as oblivious of man's spiritual dignity. Insisting that the good news of man's redemption had to be lived on all levels of society, the bishops condemned oppression, torture and exploitation by governments, rich corporations, greedy landowners, and foreign financial teams, and exhorted their people to a new consciousness of their dignity as brothers and sisters of Jesus Christ.

A week after his return from Mexico, during his Wednesday audience in the Vatican, Pope John Paul praised the accomplishment of Puebla and formally accepted Liberation Theology as a legitimate expression of the Church's teaching of the Gospel. The papal message recapitulated the Puebla declaration and gave new courage to many courageous

churchmen – including Dom Heldar Camara of Recife, Brazil, feared
as the 'red archbishop' by church and governmental foes; the outspoken Nicaraguan poet, Father Juan Cardenal, then living in precarious
exile in Costa Rica; and Archbishop Oscar Romero, recommended for
the Nobel Peace Prize by a group of US congressmen after he excommunicated the El Salvador president and government for the cold-
blooded murder of a priest and four laymen a week before the Puebla
meeting. (Romero was later to suffer the same fate: while saying mass
in a convent in El Salvador he was brutally murdered by an assassin.)

But John Paul's acceptance of the Puebla declaration did not satisfy
many priests and activists who felt that the new Holy Father had missed
an opportunity of striking a blow against dictators everywhere by listing
as criminals the presidents of Argentina (Jorge Videla), Chile (Augusto
Pinochet), Nicaragua (Anastasio Somoza), El Salvador (Carlos
Romero), Peru (Hugo Banzer), and Paraguay (Alfredo Stroessner).

Nevertheless, a month later in his first encyclical, *Redemptor hominis*
(The Redeemer of Man) the pontiff confirmed his total commitment to
the pursuit of human rights and human dignity. Written by hand in
Polish with insouciant enthusiasm during the first months of his pontificate, and with an apocalyptic eye on the year 2000, John Paul's first
encyclical was a stream-of-consciousness meditation on Christian anthropology unlike any papal document within living memory. A jumble
of biblical texts applied directly to the Church's current situation, it
resembled the exegesis of an early Church father (the third-century Or-
igen commenting on Jeremiah, or the irascible Jerome in the fourth century explicating Isaiah) as it highlighted man's redemption from sinful-
ness and from the futility of human experience. Sprinkled with personal
reminiscences – his thoughts on accepting the papal office, his pastoral
experience as priest and bishop, his relations with Pope Paul VI – and
a frank admission of the weaknesses and disruptions within the Catholic
Church, the document called for a total re-ordering of today's social
and economic structures in keeping with the part that Jesus Christ
should play in modern life.

Almost imperceptibly, the pontiff was swinging Catholic doctrinal
thought from a preoccupation with essences – both divine and human
– to an existentialistic concern with man in all phases of his being.
Replete with extravagant terminology and idiosyncratic doctrinal turns,
the 18,000-word document gushed forth in vigorous waves of language

that gave the Vatican Congregation for the Doctrine of the Faith fits, as its scriveners endeavored to pull it into shape and cope with its theological content (not happy with the Polish government's censorship of Church documents, John Paul was not about to submit to censorship within his own household), and the office of Latin Letters struggled to turn the Polish pope's phrases into the renaissance Latin of a papal document.

Insisting that his rule would be collegial, in tandem with the bishops of the Church universal, John Paul asked whether the pursuit of the Council's ecumenical objectives of reunion with the Orthodox, Protestant and other religious groups, was leading the Catholic Church into dangerous compromises in doctrine and discipline – as a number of his advisers were suggesting. But thanking these pessimists for their frank observations, the pope then said it would be an act of cowardice not to pursue a movement so obviously under the guidance of the Holy Spirit.

In *Redemptor hominis,* John Paul cites his close relationship with Paul vi, whom he looked up to as a father. With this revelation, the Polish pontiff seemed to indicate that his pontificate would bring about no major deviation from the Pauline line. Nevertheless in his *Letter to Priests,* disseminated on Holy Thursday 1979, John Paul took a position almost diametrically opposed to that of Montini. Though scrupulous in his respect for the priesthood (on Holy Thursday, 1967, obviously upset by the first wave of departures from the priestly ministry, Pope Paul had referred to the defectors as 'Judases'), Paul had allowed some 30,000 priests to return to the lay state and marry within the Church. John Paul i had signed some 200 of these petitions in his short pontificate, but John Paul ii put an injunction on all such dispensations, referring to them almost cynically as 'administrative solutions' not in keeping with the delicate spiritual problem of celibacy. Insisting that the celibate state was an essential feature of the Christian priesthood – which it is not, since the oriental rites, both Catholic and Orthodox, had a married priesthood from the beginning – and that the priestly promise was the equivalent of the marriage vow (again stretching theological fact, since celibacy is imposed by ecclesiastical law while marriage is a mutual commitment), the pope pulled out all the stops in lauding the celibate priesthood's superiority over other religious states.

The result of this outburst was a fear that the pope was being over-influenced by the Polish situation where government oppression accounted for much of the strict clerical discipline and the plethora of priestly vocations; and a grave injustice to hundreds of priests who had recently applied for laicization on grounds of conscience and were now deprived of their basic right to marry which had been acknowledged, however reluctantly, by John Paul's scrupulous predecessor, Paul vi. The letter provoked a plethora of protests from clergy and laity from all over the world, many of them being forwarded directly to the Holy Father by such eminent churchmen as Cardinal Renard of Lyons and Tarancon of Madrid. They were simply ignored by the pope and the Roman curia.

Settling into the papal office on his return from Puebla, John Paul had begun a vigorous round of activities that included consultations with Vatican officials, daily meetings with cardinals and bishops visiting Rome, the reception of diplomats presenting their credentials as ambassadors to the Holy See, and audiences for youngsters in St Peter's each Wednesday. Intent on getting control of the Vatican governmental machinery, he attended some of the meetings of the cardinals dealing with Vatican policy, finances and personnel, making attendance mandatory and requiring up-to-the-minute reports.

On Sundays and holidays he ventured out to the parishes of Rome, turning his attention on the city's housing, unemployment, crime and decadence, in keeping with his promise to the communist mayor Giulio Argan, made when they met on the steps of the Capitolium, Rome's ancient city hall, shortly after his installation as pope. Taking possession of the Basilica of St John Lateran, John Paul had promised Cardinal Poletti, his vicar for the diocese of Rome, that he would spend time each month checking on the conduct of pastoral affairs in his bishopric.

During the pope's absence in Mexico, a contretemps between the bishops in the Dutch Church had boiled over, as the result of a Pastoral Consultation involving priests and laity in November 1978. Five of the seven Dutch bishops, including Cardinal Willebrands of Utrecht, had taken a realistic stand on abortion, homosexuality, and the employment of married priests, only to have their view publicly repudiated by the two archconservative prelates, Bishops Jan Gijsens of Roermond and Adriaan Simonis of Rotterdam. Called to Rome to explain matters, Cardinal Willebrands, a close friend of the new pope, was told that the Holy Father would not interfere directly in the affairs of the embattled Dutch Church whose bishops, acting collegially, should find a solution.

But John Paul did summon the prelates one by one for consultation. When these papal *pourparlers* proved ineffectual, he called for a Synod of the Dutch bishops to be held in Rome where, without direct interference, he could serve as final arbiter.

Also in November 1978, through the intervention of Cardinal Siri, John Paul had welcomed the rebel French archbishop, Marcel Lefebvre, for a half-hour private audience, and arranged for a series of discussions between Lefebvre and members of the Congregation for the Doctrine of the Faith during January. Playing his cards skilfully, the dissident prelate had not sounded off against the new Holy Father until tricked by a reporter from Rome's *Osservatore della Domenica,* to whom he confided that he still considered Vatican authorities in the wrong regarding the ritual of the mass and the theology of the Council of Trent, both of which had been changed radically at Vatican II. Despite the fact that in June 1978 Lefebvre had proceeded with the ordination of twenty-nine young priests, the Polish pontiff kept his own counsel.

There were fears that John Paul might change the Vatican's *ostpolitik* as practised by Archbishop Casaroli under Pope Paul's guidance – direct dealings between Vatican diplomats and the heads of governments in the Soviet satellite countries had led to the restoration of the hierarchies in most of these lands. These fears were seen to be unfounded with the appointment of Archbishop Casaroli as pro-secretary of state on the death of the French cardinal Jean Villot in March 1979. Villot's death forced John Paul to make his first curial appointments. Following Pope Paul's advice, he had made no major changes until in office well over three months. Instead he had merely confirmed most curial officials in office, in keeping with their five-year tenures, excepting the aging cardinals Bafile and Garrone, and the ailing John Wright. Confined to a wheelchair, Wright at seventy refused to surrender his prefectship of the Congregation for the Clergy despite his illness and the fact that he had alienated the hierarchies of Spain, France, Germany and many US bishops by his less than honest attempt to prevent conciliar reforms in pastoral and catechetical areas. Informed that his tenure was *ad nutum,* i.e. under the pope's discretion, Wright complained bitterly of the unfeeling treatment of which he thought himself a victim. In August 1979 death claimed him in a hospital in Boston, just two weeks after the death of the Council's archconservative opponent, Alfredo Ottaviani.

In his first batch of cardinals created during the secret consistory on 29 June 1979, John Paul revealed little of his intentions. Expected were the creation of Archbishop Casaroli as the new secretary of state ; the curial officials Guiseppe Caprio and Ernesto Civardi, along with the Polish Ladislaw Rubin of the papal household; his own replacement as Archbishop of Krakow, Frantiszek Marcharski; and his predecessor's replacement in Venice, Mario Ce. He created seven other residential archbishops, giving substance to the Church's international presence: Roger Etchegaray of Marseilles, Emmett Carter of Toronto, Thomas O'Fiach of Armagh, Anastasio Ballestrero of Turin, Ernesto Corripio Ahumada of Mexico City, the Vietnamese Joseph-Marie Trinh Van Can of Hanoi, and the 75-year-old Japanese Archbishop of Nagasaki, Joseph Asajiro Satowaki; while announcing one cardinal *in petto* (i.e. secretly), presumed to be the Lithuanian bishop Julijonas Stepovanicius of Vilna, where the Church is still suffering severe repression.

Strong rumors of a papal visit to the United States in late September or early October 1979 began to circulate in consequence of an urgent invitation by the Secretary General of the United Nations, Kurt Waldheim, that the new Holy Father address the General Assembly, as Paul VI had done in October 1964. But plans for such a journey, which it was hoped would include a swing through major US cities and a visit to the White House, were slow in maturing. To be weighed in the balance were the political implications of a first visit to a major world power.

A visit to Poland had first been broached immediately after John Paul's meteoric election to the papacy. In a conversation with the Polish president Henryk Jablonski, who was in Rome along with other heads of government and ambassadorial representatives on 23 October 1978 for the new pope's installation, John Paul was assured that he would be welcomed by the Polish regime as one of its most distinguished sons. But negotiations regarding the trip quickly spawned serious difficulties. The pope's intention was to commemorate the ninth centenary of the martyrdom of St Stanislaus, his eleventh-century predecessor as Bishop of Krakow, put to death by King Boleslaw the Bold in 1079. (The Church canonized Stanislaus in 1253 as a martyr who excommunicated the monarch for his unjust dealings with his people; the communist regime regards him as a dissident put to death for treason.) In simulta-neous talks between Andrei Gromyko, the Soviet foreign minister, and Pope John Paul II in the Vatican, and between the cardinal of Warsaw, Stefan Wyszynski and the Polish Party's first secretary, Edward Gierek, in Warsaw, it was agreed to postpone the papal visit by a month lest his presence in Poland on May 9th, the actual centenary, prove an occasion for political disturbance. Having agreed to the change of date, Cardinal Wyszynski declared the celebration of the saint's martyrdom a move-able feast and extended it to early June.

Arriving in Warsaw's military airport on 2 June 1979 after a two-hour flight from Rome, the Polish pontiff kissed the tarmac before ac-cepting the welcome of the Polish head of state and military honors. After an emotional embrace with the septuagenarian primate, Cardinal Wyszynski, John Paul was whisked into the middle of the nation's cap-ital standing in an open vehicle and greeted with awed reverence by well over 300,000 faithful. Crowd control was in the hands of lay ush-ers provided by the parishes of Warsaw, with the police remaining dis-creetly in the background. Despite intermittent complaints of road-blocks and the non-appearance of government-promised bus transpor-tation, there were no real confrontations between police and people throughout the nine-day visit. After stopping to pray in St John's Cathe-dral and have lunch with the Polish episcopate in the cardinal primate's palace, John Paul paid a formal televised visit to the heads of govern-ment and the Party's First Secretary in the Belvedere Palace, where the pope informed Mr Gierek: 'It is the Church's mission to make man more confident, more courageous, more conscious of his rights and du-ties, socially responsible, creative and useful. The Church does not de-sire privileges but only and exclusively what is essential for the accom-plishment of its mission.'

That afternoon during a pontifical mass celebrated in Warsaw's enor-mous Victory Square on an imposing white platform before a 38-foot-high wooden cross decorated with a single red stole (originally the papal color), the Holy Father told half a million people: 'Christ cannot be kept out of the history of man in any part of the globe, at any longitude or latitude of geography. The exclusion of Christ from the history of man is an act against man.' It was a restrained broadside, and one that set the tone for his open but benevolent confrontation of the communist regime.

In an early Sunday mass for Poland's youth, with thousands packed into the square and streets surrounding St Anne's Church, John Paul assured them of his great love for 'his children' and, blessing the thousands of crucifixes they carried, said, 'I hope you will be faithful to this sign always.' Later, flying by helicopter to Gneizno, in the heart of Catholic Poland, the Holy Father speculated on the reason for his election: 'Is it not the intention of the Holy Spirit that this Polish pope, this Slav, should, at this moment of history, manifest the spiritual unity of Christian Europe?' he asked. And referring to the fact that it was the Feast of Pentecost when in the primitive Church the Holy Spirit had descended on the apostles giving them the gift of tongues, he surveyed the centuries of missionary activity accomplished by the Church, particularly in Eastern Europe from Yugoslavia and Bulgaria to Czechoslovakia and Soviet Lithuania. That evening before joining a song-fest organized by the young people, he lectured them on their Polish Catholic culture. 'Be proud of it', he said. 'Multiply it! Hand it on to your children!'

At Czestochowa the next day, John Paul prayed fervently at the shrine of the Black Madonna in the ancient monastery of Jasna Gora (Bright Mountain), recalling the Polish belief that in 1655 the Virgin's intervention had routed the invading Swedish armies. For the pope, as for the Poles, devotion to Mary, the Mother of Jesus, was a definite political as well as a religious commitment. In this context, John Paul spent three days at Czestochowa and presided over a plenary meeting of the 77-member Polish hierarchy. In a closed-door session he told the bishops that the Christian-marxist confrontation could not be easy since it juxtaposed two diametrically opposite concepts of the world. 'Authentic dialogue,' he said, 'must respect the conviction of believers, insure all the rights of citizens and the normal conditions for the activity of the Church as a religious community.'

What he had in mind was spelled out by Cardinal Wyszynski: the freedom to build churches and name bishops without government interference; the right to publish books and periodicals, broadcast Church events and religious services; and the right of parents to educate their children in their religious beliefs and encourage their higher education; and the right to hold jobs without discrimination.

Concluding a special mass for priests at the Marian Shrine, the Holy Father confided to them that his ad-libbing was getting on the nerves of his Italian staff, particularly when people remarked that the best things the pope said were not in his prepared texts. As he moved about the country, John Paul joked with the Polish people about his difficulties : 'You are enjoying yourselves now,' he told one group, 'but I will get it for being late for my next appointment.' Later, to a group of youths serenading him at midnight with the Polish salute *Sto Lat!* (A hundred years!), he asked: 'Do you want the pope to live a hundred years?' To the crowd's 'yes', he shot back, 'Well, then, let him get some sleep.'

After a sentimental visit to his birthplace in Wadowice, where he lunched with the aged Monsignor Edward Zacher, his first religious mentor, and checked out his baptismal register, John Paul flew to Auschwitz, where he met survivors of the concentration camps including two hundred priests, and said a mass of reparation at Birkenau before 500,000 people. In the course of a moving sermon, the pope said it was impossible to visit this 'modern Golgotha' without thinking with fear 'of how far hatred can go, how far one man's destruction of his fellow man can go, how far cruelty can go . . .'

On Friday he visited the *gorale* (mountain people) of Nowy Targ, asserting that both he and the American cardinal John Krol of Philadelphia accompanying him were *gorale,* hence his enjoyment of the skiing and canoeing expeditions he had indulged in, in this rugged area, throughout his career as student counsellor, prelate and cardinal. In his talk John Paul discussed the problems of alcoholism and immorality that threatened family life, before praising the faith and constancy of this intrepid mountain people; then, introducing a political note, he complained about the vast number of pilgrims from other communist nations, particularly the Lithuanians, who had been stopped from crossing the border to greet him. Obviously tired after impromptu talks to university students, peasants, townspeople, the sick and disabled, and miners, the Holy Father spent most of Saturday in comparative rest at the Cistercian monastery in Mogila. (Prevented by the government from travelling to the heart of Silesia, the pontiff had been visited by a large delegation of determined miners, who descended on Czestochowa with their *cazka,* or plumed hats, and wives in peasant dress with brilliant-red bandanas covering their heads.)

Back in Krakow on Sunday 19 June, and surrounded by eighteen cardinals and a complement of bishops from round the globe, John Paul celebrated a pontifical mass in honor of St Stanislaw, the ostensible reason for the papal visit. While the saint had always been a symbol of Polish religious liberty, the Holy Father stressed the religious circumstances of the saint's life rather than the polemical aspects of his martyrdom. The papal omission of politics was countered by a large red flag with white eagle and crown, the symbol of royalist Poland, that fronted the altar on its enormous platform dominated by a twenty-foot white cross set up in Krakow's central square.

Before the mass, balloons were released carrying a banner with the insignia 'P.W.' in the shape of an anchor that stood for *Polska Walczaca* or 'Fighting Poland', the symbol of the anti-communist resistance in World War II. The Holy Father and the authorities ignored these provocations. Shortly before joining the motorcade that took him to the airport, the pope thanked the journalists (in Italian, English, and Polish) who had followed his circuitous pilgrimage so faithfully. Speaking from a balustrade of the archbishop's palace, he said in French, 'I hope, I hope, I hope to meet you again in this land,' apparently in reference to a possible visit in 1982 for the 600th anniversary of the discovery of the Black Madonna at Czestochowa.

After a tremendous but silently reverent send-off by the hundreds of thousands of faithful who packed the square and city streets leading to the airport, John Paul reversed the procedure of his arrival in Poland and, having kissed the ground, climbed aboard his aircraft to fly home to Rome.

In Rome he was met by a vast crowd in St Peter's Square. 'The faith of Poland,' he told them in a brief greeting, 'is a living and pulsating reality. Like all authentic expressions of faith, it projects a note of optimism.' No one appreciated that optimistic note better than the pundits of the Kremlim and the Polish party leaders, one of whom told a Western journalist that 'thirty years of indoctrination in atheistic ideals would have to be begun all over again.' The Soviet news media and most of the Warsaw Pact countries had played down the visit, and Polish television, while covering the pope's moves faithfully, omitted to record the size of the crowds that greeted him everywhere. These blackouts were more than made up for by the Voice of America, the BBC, Radio Free Europe and the Vatican Radio, provoking the Soviet television commentator to complain, 'Some circles in the Polish church are trying to use [the visit] for antistate purposes.' On several occasions, John Paul himself remarked, 'It would be sad to believe that each Pole and Slav in any part of the world is unable to hear the words of the Pope, this Slav. I hope they hear me.'

Taking stock after his return from Poland of the Church's position in the wider world, the Holy Father found himself presiding over a Church of suffering but unbowed confessors and martyrs in the newly liberated lands of Africa, from Uganda and Chad in the north to Namibia and Zimbabwe in the south, where mission stations, schools and churches were the victims of marauding guerrillas as well as volatile governments. Nevertheless, the Church in these countries was growing by the thousands and had a highly educated hierarchy, with mainly native cardinals and bishops and a heroic phalanx of catechists.

In the Middle East, the horrors of internecine war in Palestine, Lebanon, Iran and Ethiopia involved deep religious issues as well as political and economic problems, and the Pope offered to do whatever he could as a pacifier. In Asia, John Paul saw reason for both hope and despair. While Catholics in India, Sri Lanka, Indonesia and Indochina were a small minority and being hampered by anti-Christian movements and laws, there were signs of a new charisma given the Church under communist domination. This was intimated by the Archbishop of Ho-Chi-Minville (formerly Saigon), Mons. Binh, who assured the 1977 Roman Synod of Bishops that the Church would adapt itself to the new order in southeast Asia as it once adapted itself to the Roman Empire in which it had been founded.

While the ostensibly Catholic government of President Marcos of the Philippines was obviously oppressing the poor by grabbing the nation's wealth and land into the hands of their family, their activities were opposed by the heroic cardinal of Manila, Jaime Sin, and a large proportion of the priests, nuns and committed laity scattered over that widespread island empire.

Meanwhile there were encouraging signs from continental China. Native priests in exile were invited to visit their home towns and returned with the information that a vast underground Catholic and Christian Church had survived the purges of the red revolution in the mid-

1960s and Mao Tse-Tung's repression. The Jesuits were invited to re-open their medical university of the Aurora in Shanghai and, in the show-place cities, churches, mosques and temples were reopened.

The unfreezing of relations with continental China had been one of Pope Paul's greatest ambitions. Paul had gravely offended Cardinal Yu Pin of Taiwan in his political moves to appease the continental Chinese rulers. He had withdrawn the papal nuncio from Taipei in 1973, leaving only an attaché to represent the Holy See to the Chiang Kai-shek government. But as the Chinese journalist, Father Louis Wei, insisted, Vatican policy had to be concerned more with the two to three million Catholics on the mainland than with the 200,000 well-cared-for Catholics of Taiwan.

Accepting this reality, John Paul II immediately ran into an excruciating dilemma. In 1951, on the advice of the premier Chou en-Lai, a large proportion of the Chinese Catholics had formed the Patriotic Catholic Association, whose aim was to achieve the nativization of the Chinese Church in its personnel, finances and liturgy while accepting Rome's guidance in doctrine and morals. When the bishops and clergy, who had been cut off from Rome as much by the Vatican's intransigence as by communist policy, returned to the practice of the early Church and began electing their own bishops, the Holy See under Pius XII had refused to acknowledge these prelates, although they were validly consecrated by bishops in good standing with Rome. This papal refusal to acknowledge the Patriotic Catholic Association caused an internal split in the already persecuted Church and in 1958 Mao Tse-Tung closed off all relations with Rome, accusing the pope of having cold-shouldered China.

With the death of the bishop of Peking, Wang Jitin, in late 1978, the local bishops and clergy elected as his successor Mons. Fu Tieh-shan, who was duly consecrated by eight bishops before a congregation of over 700 Catholics after vainly seeking Rome's acquiescence. The dilemma facing the Holy Father was tough. Yet there were precedents for taking a benevolent attitude and recognizing a validly consecrated bishop who requested communion with the Holy See. As far back as 1973, in a talk to the German bishops at Augsburg, Archbishop Giovanni Benelli, then Pope Paul's right-hand man, had condemned the attitude of Rome in the 1650s for its incomprehensible rejection of Chinese rites and the abandonment of the acculturizing policies of the Jesuit Father

Matteo Ricci* and his learned companions, who had in the past won over the emperor and had been gradually creating a mandarin Christianity.

In 1959 Pope John had spoken of the Chinese Church in schism. He was quickly advised by both the Jesuit Father George Germain, former president of the Aurora University, and Mons. Carlo van Melkebeecke, an ex-Belgian missionary and now the bishop in charge of non-continental Chinese, that the designation was unfair, since its victims had no one to speak for them. In the question of recognizing the newly consecrated Bishop of Peking, John Paul was faced both with the intransigent curial advisors who felt such a move would be a lowering of papal authority, and the large group of local Chinese Catholics who had suffered greatly because of their unquestioning loyalty to Rome and by not accepting the native priests and bishops.

Among the countless invitations to the new Holy Father to visit various parts of the world, the anxious request of Kurt Waldheim that he address the United Nations Assembly in New York held pride of place. It was the Secretary-General's hope that the Polish pontiff's appearance before this contentious body would rally Catholic support as well as strengthen his own position. Pope Paul had accepted a similar invitation from U Thant in October 1965, interrupting the fourth session of Vatican Council II to do so.

As rumors spread about the papal visit to New York, considerable pressure was brought to bear by the Irish hierarchy to have the Holy Father stop in the Emerald Isle on his way to America. And in the United States and Canada every town and hamlet made a bid for a papal visit. John Paul's schedule was worked out by the decisive curial archbishop, Paul Marcinkus of Chicago, who had accompanied Pope Paul on his major journeys. Well acquainted with the Irish and American scenes, Marcinkus accepted the suggestion that the pope crisscross Ireland, from Dublin to Drogheda and from the Marian shrine at Knock to Limerick, in order to be seen personally by as many of the island's Catholic population as possible, and to prevent a great jamming of the roads leading to the papal venues.

---

*In the spring of 1980 the Chinese government rebuilt the tomb of Father Ricci and opened it as a national shrine.

On 28 September 1979 John Paul II left Fiumicino Airport in an Alitalia jet with a select crew of journalists and television experts bound for Dublin, and then Boston and the United States. This itinerary caused some irritation to the U N officials who had hoped the pope's visit would concentrate total attention on the United Nations Assembly. However, the pontiff felt a special affection for the Irish Catholics as being the closest to his native Poles in their Catholic consciousness. He also had hopes of strengthening the peace movement in Northern Ireland – in December 1978 he had given an hour's audience to Maired Corrigan and Margaret Williams, winners of the Nobel Peace Prize for their attempt to bring a semblance of tranquility and justice to that festering situation. But such hopes were not to be. Not only did the leaders of the Protestant north led by Ian Paisley repudiate a papal visit to Ulster, but, three weeks before the papal arrival, Lord Louis Mountbatten and members of his family were killed by an IRA bomb aboard his fishing boat in Donegal Bay and the same day some eighteen British soldiers were killed in an IRA ambush.

Despite the dark shadow of these atrocities, the papal presence was welcomed with tremendous love and affection by the Irish people, and at least two-thirds of the land's four million faithful made an attempt to see him in person. Original plans to have the pontiff visit Armagh in the north had to be cancelled for security reasons, to the chagrin of that ancient see's new cardinal, Thomas O'Fiach. Along with several emphatic appeals by the pontiff for a laying-down of arms on all sides – an approach repudiated with cynicism by the fanatical Catholic insurgents – the Holy Father seemed to have been taking the advice of several of the older Irish bishops in his warning to the people against the dangers of a consumerist society and the love of material things. These were the prelates who had learned almost nothing at the Vatican Council, and returned to their sees with minds closed to the demands by their younger priests, theologians and lay people for an updating of the Irish Church. They seemed oblivious of the turning away from the Church of thousands of youth, and the great cut-back in vocations that could be traced almost directly to their intransigent stance against a modernization of the Irish Church.

There was an infectious enthusiasm for the vital presence of the new pope everywhere he went. But John Paul's message to the nuns, to youth, and to the people, stressing the ideals of the Irish Marian spirituality, and read in the light of his warnings against the decadence of materialism, left most of his thinking audience not a little perplexed. For the first time the country was showing signs of a mild prosperity, with new homes, cars and employment opportunities in evidence almost everywhere, thanks to the Irish entry into the European Common Market in 1965; and now the pope was cautioning, instead of congratulating the people in their ability to provide the poor with a decent livelihood that would enable them to serve God with the dignity called for by John Paul's own encyclical, *The Redeemer of Man*.

The Polish Holy Father flew into Boston shortly before 3 p.m. on October 1st. It was the first and last time he would be on time during his whirlwind visit to the United States. John Paul was met at Logan Airport by Cardinal Medeiros of Boston, a group of politicians representing both the state and the church, and Mrs Rosalynn Carter on behalf of her husband; and he was assured by the First Lady that he was 'welcomed to our country with love'. That note was sustained throughout his time in Boston and New York. In New York, besides his address to the United Nations, he made an embracive tour of the city from St Patrick's Cathedral down to the Battery, and from the Yankee and Shea stadiums to Madison Square Garden. From the moment he had kissed the ground on his arrival in Boston, the Polish pope had simply mesmerized the American public, occupying the major portion of the television and radio broadcasts, taking over the youth, and receiving the homage of politicians, academics, clergy and businessmen, as well as the poor in the slum areas of Harlem and the Bronx.

His talk at the UN was a masterpiece of forensic oratory in which he insisted time and again on respect for human life and the rights of every individual to dignity and liberty, no matter what their religion, color, creed, nationality or ideology. Mentioning the delicate situation in Palestine, Lebanon, Jerusalem and the Near East, he roundly condemned the arms race and asked if this generation of world leaders were intent on handing on as a heritage to their children the horrors of world destruction now confronting mankind. The speech proved the Polish pontiff a much better political theoretician than a philosopher. And his courtesy in greeting an immense number of officials and employees of this cosmopolitan organization proved a model of Christian discretion.

It was in Philadelphia that John Paul seemed to change the tenor of his message, almost as if he were attuning himself to the obdurate policies of Cardinal John Krol, a close friend whose ancestry was of the same Tatra mountain area in Poland. In his main talks the pontiff spoke of freedom and human values, but immediately went on to caution against using liberty as a 'pretext for moral anarchy'. He condemned present-day tendencies toward 'laxity regarding the Christian view on sexuality'. To the priests gathered in the cathedral and the clerical students at the seminary he stressed the fact that they must keep their promises of celibacy to Christ, no matter what difficulties they might encounter. And in stressing the inviolability of marriage, he asserted that 'human Christian values' demand that 'every effort be made so that no child anywhere in the world face death because of a lack of food, or from a diminished intellectual and physical potential for want of sufficient nourishment, or has to bear all through life the scars of deprivation.'

That same week, almost as if prearranged, Robert McNamara of the World Bank released a statement to the effect that thirty million children* under five years of age died each year of undernourishment. But that statistic seemed to have been missed by the pontiff in his speech to the American Catholic hierarchy in Chicago two days later. There in his address to some 350 bishops the pope took a highly familiar and pastoral approach, citing his own experiences as parish priest and bishop. Then, taking the pastoral letter of the American episcopate of 1976 as a guide, he adopted a hard line in regard to the primary problems troubling American Catholics, from abortion and contraception to divorce and extramarital sex, condemning these evils as one would expect of the pope, but failing to help with suggestions of spiritual remedies in keeping with the pastoral approach of the Vatican Council.

While no one expected him to change the Church's teaching on these matters, a minority of the bishops and the American public more generally were abashed at the papal failure to say words of consolation to the millions of American Catholics who were caught in the nexus of these problems and were seeking a word of encouragement in their efforts to live as authentic Christians. While the pope praised the pastoral letters of two bishops on the condemnation of racism and a benevolent pastoral approach to homosexuals, he seemed to have forgotten in Chicago what he had admitted in Philadelphia – that no child should be brought into the world in order to starve to death. In his condemnation

---

*The actual total compiled by UNICEF was closer to ten million.

of contraception he seemed to show no compassion for the millions of women of child-bearing age who found themselves caught between the exigencies of their current family and the Church's ban on artificial contraception. Nor did he exhibit compassion for the millions of divorced people and their counsellors who were trying to remake their lives as Christians and Catholics despite the Church's official hard-hearted – almost Pelagian – policy of depriving them of the grace of the sacraments. He compounded this rigorous approach in his final sermon at a mass on the Mall in the nation's capital, to the delight of integrist and archconservative Catholics.

Meanwhile, apparently oblivious of the 'no popery' campaigns that had troubled American politics for two centuries, defeating Alfred E. Smith in his bid for the presidency in 1928 and jeopardizing John Kennedy's candidacy in 1960, John Paul was received with magnanimous courtesy in the presidential mansion by Jimmy Carter and his wife Rosalynn and family, with whom he lunched and spent two hours in private conversation. That same afternoon he met several thousand honored guests – primarily statesmen, politicians and the elite of Washington – giving short addresses from both the east- and west-wing balconies of the White House. He spent the night in the residence of the Apostolic Delegate, Mons. Jean Jadot; then motored to the grounds of the Catholic University, where he was greeted by a group of students who had spent the night in a vigil before the National Shrine on the University grounds. Ad-libbing with the students, he assured them that while they were praying, he had a good night's sleep. He then addressed a large group of nuns assembled in the basilica.

It was here that he encountered the first positive opposition when a group of sisters stood in protest against his attitude toward women in the Church, and Sister Theresa Kane, head of the Leadership Conference of Women Religious, used her welcoming address to remind the pontiff of the 'excruciating suffering of countless women, particularly sisters and nuns, who felt the Church treated them as second-class citizens of the Kingdom of God.' Sister Kane asserted that women should be included in all the ministries of the Church, a direct reference to the ordination of women as priests.

Unaware of the implications of this message, the Holy Father received her homage kindly; but in his prepared speech he seemed to have anticipated her objection by stressing the fact that Mary the Mother of God was not among the apostles at the last supper and had played no part in the hierarchical activities of the primitive Church. (In his first general audience on his return to Rome he was to tell a group of Italian Mother-Generals that they should have their sisters meditate on his message to the nuns of Ireland and the United States.)

Meanwhile John Paul had addressed the academic assembly of the Catholic University, genuinely lauding the work of theologians in the Church and seemingly reinforcing their right to academic freedom. He had a brief meeting with the members of other religions and churches before saying a public mass for some 175,000 people gathered on the Mall of the Capitol. Taking his cue from the Gospel message regarding marriage and divorce, he spoke once more as a strict disciplinarian, leaving millions of Americans befuddled between the personal magnetism of this benevolent-looking religious leader and his apparently uncomprehending attitude toward the existentialistic implications of his moralizing stance.

It was a tired but exhilarated Holy Father who boarded the plane at Andrews Air Force Base that night and headed for Rome. In his farewell greeting to the nation he had said: 'My final prayer is this: that God will bless America, so that she may increasingly become "one nation under God, indivisible, with liberty and justice for all." '

John Paul rounded out his first year as pope with a discreet visit to Turkey where his ostensible objective was to participate in the Feast of St Andrew with the Greek Orthodox patriarch Dimitrios I. Andrew, as the brother of Peter, gave this encounter a highly symbolic ecumenical significance. And for the first time in over a thousand years, pope and patriarch attended each other's liturgy – without, however, participating in the Eucharist. It was a deliberate omission that struck some observers as hardly in keeping with John Paul's reference in *The Redeemer of Man* to courage in ecumenical pursuits. The apparent explanation was that full reunion between the Catholic and the Orthodox Churches had not been formally declared, and the possibility that some of the fourteen autocephalous Orthodox leaders – Russian, Bulgarian, Coptic, Rumanian, etc – might have considered such an action premature and offensive.

Behind John Paul's Turkish visit was his desire to support the political position of the Orthodox patriarch whose right to have his headquarters in the Phanar of Istanbul was being challenged by religious and secular zealots. In view of the volatile situation in the Near East, John Paul agreed to the low-profile security-conscious precautions of the Turkish government, arriving in Istanbul without fanfare and spending the first afternoon with the civil authorities. Between the papacy and the government there had always been a cordial relationship. John Paul spent his first night in the home of the Apostolic Delegate, mindful of the fact that this modest mansion had been the scene of Pope John XXIII's labors as the papal representative to Greece and Turkey throughout World War II. The following day he indulged a Marian piety by visiting the shrine of the Blessed Virgin at Ephesus where, in the Council of 431 A D, Mary had been officially recognized as the *theotokos,* or Mother of God.

On his return from Turkey on December 1st, the Polish pontiff was confronted with a series of problems that had been festering within the Vatican since the latter part of Pope Paul's pontificate. Ever since the close of the Council, the curial cardinals and bureaucrats, whose control of the Church's doctrine and discipline had been repudiated by that ecumenical assembly, had been working feverishly to regain their dominance of Church policy.

During the 1967 Roman Synod of Bishops, Cardinals Ottaviani and Browne had been worsted in their attempt to prove that heresy was rife in the Church. In early January 1968 they and their clique of superannuated cardinals had been relieved of their positions as prefects and principal advisers in the papal offices. They were replaced by a supposedly international group of cardinals – the Yugoslav Franjo Seper, the American John Wright, the French Gabriel Garrone, the Australian James Knox, the German Benno Gut– who quickly proved more Roman than the Romans. Under their aegis, the policy of interpreting the Council's constitutions and decrees in a *preconciliar* fashion was pursued vigorously. The Council's teaching had been set forth in slightly ambiguous constitutions and decrees that first summed up the Church's traditions down to 1965 and, then, contained an opening to the future. John had called them a 'platform for a leap ahead.' Interpreted from a forward-looking perspective, the Council's teaching on the nature of the Church had opened a path to the worldwide ecumenical movement aimed at the reunion of the Catholic with the Orthodox and Protestant churches via discussions between commissioned bodies of theologians, prelates and activists that were leading to a re-evaluation of each church's original reasons for separation. The Council decrees likewise justified mutual projects of social, spiritual and moral apostolates, involving the clergy and people of these divergent religious bodies, and demanding more and more urgently a sharing of the Eucharist as the sign and consummation of the togetherness in Christ that they were achieving each day. This greater ecumenical activity of the man-in-the-street level was pursued both in the first and third worlds and on the missions.

The Council's teaching on politics, cultural and scientific progress, marriage and family life was another area where new approaches to the difficult moral problems facing contemporary men and women had been given a realistic expression. But in these and other areas of theological and ecclesial involvement, the majority of the men in the papal household were determined to return the Church to the pre-Johannine absolutism discarded by the bishops as outmoded triumphalism. Despite Pope Paul's attempt to restructure the Holy See's most sensitive congregation or bureau – that dealing with doctrine and discipline, and known in the past as the Holy Office and the Inquisition – giving it, the title of the Congregation for the Doctrine (or teaching) of the Faith and the function of promoting theological study, that body had continued its ancient repressive policies. It welcomed innumerable complaints and delations against forward-looking theologians and writers whom the curial officials attempted to intimidate or relieve of their teaching positions, ignoring the Council's guarantee of academic and intellectual freedom in the Constitution on the Church in Today's World.

Pope Paul's 1968 encyclical *Humanae Vitae* had served as a catalyst, forcing clergy and laity to face up to their obligation to give witness to the faithful's mind on the Christian way of life, over and against official decisions that did not express the authentic mind of the universal Church. In the papal document itself, no provision was made for the convictions of the other Christian churches whose faithful lived under the guidance of the Holy Spirit, a fact which had been finally if reluctantly acknowledged by Vatican Council II. The papal prohibition of artificial contraception, together with the Vatican's negative attitude toward family and population control, did not reflect the moral awareness of the majority of its responsible theologians and well-informed laity. This could be seen from the relative interpretation of the encyclical by a large number of hierarchies, from the Dutch and French to the Canadian and Italian bishops' conferences. Nevertheless, *L'Osservatore Romano* made a massive attempt to report testimony of adherence to the document by apostolic nuncios and papal diplomats, individual bishops and hierarchies seeking Vatican recognition, and a small but articulate conservative wing of the Church.

Characteristic of the curia's manipulation of the news was the relegation of the explanation made by the Italian bishops in their reaction to the encyclical to page four of the Vatican daily, instead of giving it headline attention. The author of this Italian episcopal explanation, Father Valsecchi, was eventually relieved of his teaching position at the Milan seminary of Venegono.

Another victim among many of curial vindictiveness was Father Annibal Bugnini who, as Cardinal Lercaro's right-hand man in pushing forward the updating of the liturgy, was simply levered out of his position as secretary in the Congregation of Rites when that bureau was amalgamated with the Congregation of the Sacraments. An archbishop in his own right, Mons. Bugnini was rescued by the *sostituto* in the secretariat of state, Mons. Benelli, and despatched to Iran as papal delegate. There, in November 1979 as John Paul's emissary to the Ayatollah Khomeini he pleaded for the freeing of the American hostages, and was roundly rebuffed by the Muslim leader who asked where the pope was when the Shah was committing his crimes against the Iranian people. The irony of this tirade was that while in exile in France, Khomeini's people were given hospitality by a Paris Catholic parish.

During the last ten years of Pope Paul's reign, he did not seem able to control the zealotry of the Holy Office despite the new designation and new rules he had given that body for the prosecution of a forward-looking theology rather than the persecution of conscientious theologians. Properly concerned with the revolution in sexual values that were affecting the Church's thinking as a result of the pornographic explosion and the Council's attempt to update the Church's consciousness regarding love and family life, the Congregation for Doctrine attempted to ride herd on the professors of moral theology who were confronting the civilizational changes in this area with authentic Christian answers. This became particularly noticeable after the introduction into that office of a Dominican inquisitorial influence with the appointment of the French archbishop Jerome Hamer as secretary and assessor. Archbishop Hamer had done his curial apprenticeship in Cardinal Bea's Secretariat for Christian Unity. There he enjoyed a reputation as an affable, open-minded theologian. But once he took charge under Cardinal Seper of the *old* Holy Office, he proved an archconservative who attempted to block the progressive activities of the Secretariat for Unity, and trained his inquisitional powers on the theologians and thinkers attempting to carry out the Council's Johannine injunctions.

Among the men who came under Vatican scrutiny was Mons. Ivan Illich, a maverick theologian who conducted institutes in Cuernavaca, Mexico and Petropolis, Brazil for the training of missionaries for Latin America. Denounced as an agitator who gave the new generation of priests and nuns a marxist indoctrination, he was called before the Vatican tribunal. Instead of accepting its prescription for an oath of secrecy and submitting to its inquisitional tactics, Illich demanded to see the questionnaire prepared for his interrogation.

Originally a Croatian like Cardinal Seper, Illich managed to get his hands on this jejune document and published it, after writing a respectful but indignant letter to Pope Paul in which he resigned from the priesthood over the accusations contained in this curial document. He was to be questioned on his marxist affiliations, his relations with – of all possible subversives! – Cardinal Spellman of New York, as well as Che Guevara and Father Camillo Torres, and a score of other indignities. The release of this document exposed both the anticonciliar attitudes of the congregation's leaders and the incompetence of its officials. Nevertheless, the two monsignors immediately responsible for the questionnaire's compilation were eventually promoted to archbishops within the curia.

Another victim of frequent harassment by this office was the Redemptorist moralist, Father Bernard Häring, whose three-volume work, *The Law of Christ,* had rescued the Catholic approach to moral theology from desuetude in the early 1950s. An outspoken and highly competent theologian and social thinker, Haring had earned the enmity of the Church's conservative hierarchy during Vatican Council II, where he enjoyed the confidence of both Popes John and Paul. Nevertheless he was frequently cited by the doctrinal congregation for his modern solutions to family and sexual difficulties. A world-wide traveller and lecturer as well as professor in the Rome-based Accademia Alfonsiana, Haring took an aggressive approach when questioned by the Holy Office authorities until, recognizing his inviolability and reputation for holiness, its officials finally decided they could not destroy him.

Meanwhile, the Congregation for Doctrine had attempted to intimidate a large number of professors and thinkers whose writings were being constantly denounced by their enemies and an occasional bishop, as detrimental to the faith of the ordinary people. In 1976 the Congregation issued a Declaration on Sexual Morality that contained an amazing introduction. For the first time in papal history, the Church recognized the function of sex as the determining factor in the human personality and consequently a primary element in spiritual formation. But with that premise, the document set out in absolute terms the old traditional teaching regarding abortion, birth control, extra-marital sex, masturbation, homosexuality and other problems. An attempt was then made to force the Church's moralists to comply with the document's absolutes – an impossible task, due to fundamental divergences of human experience and opinions in these matters, as well as to the diverse cultural traditions of peoples and nations.

Nevertheless Rome's zealous inquisitional office attempted to force professors such as the German Dominican Dr Stephan Pfurtner and the American Charles Curran at the Catholic University of America to conform to the Vatican absolutes. Pfurtner was relieved of his position in the Catholic University of Freiburg, Switzerland. But Curran, with a courageous history of defying both the cardinal chancellor and the board of trustees of the Catholic University of America over academic freedom in 1967, and, the following year, over a protest against *Humanae Vitae,* managed to outwit the Congregation.

Not so fortunate was the Swiss theologian Dr Hasler, whose book *How the Pope Became Infallible* so offended the curial champions of Pope Pius ix that not only was the volume censored, but the Bishop of St Gallen was ordered to strip Hasler of his priestly office – a strange punishment at a moment when the Vatican had closed off all laicizations, or reductions to the laity, of priests who had abandoned their ministry in order to marry. The bishop's reluctance to carry out the papal order was based in part upon Father Hasler's exemplary conduct as a priest, despite his disagreement with Vatican policy. His untimely death at the age of 43 in July 1980 settled the problem.

On his return from America John Paul had been hailed by a goodly portion of the secular press as the one international leader who had definitely demonstrated a charismatic optimism and revived hope for mankind. He was a powerful personality who knew how to inspire people with the confidence needed to pull them through the current global crisis. While the press and other critics inside the Church were not happy with some of the pontiff's later messages regarding specifics of the Church's moral teaching, they felt that John Paul was at least trying to restore a high ideal of family, civic and international behavior by enunciating absolutes. His witness to human rights and the liberty of the individual before the United Nations and both the communist and capitalist world had been in the form of uncompromising ideals. Hence his right to proclaim absolutes within the Church's tradition seemed justified.

But once ensconced in the Roman scene it was expected that the new Holy Father would return to at least the benevolent equanimity of Pope Paul whom he had claimed as his father-figure and mentor. His failure to adopt Paul's reluctant but merciful attitude in releasing priests from their vow of celibacy proved a shock to a large sector of the clergy and laity. The injustice of not honoring petitions presented but not yet processed under Paul VI and John Paul I came as an unbelievable jolt. And his appointment of the garrulous dandy, Cardinal Silvio Oddi, whom Paul VI had kept at arm's length, to be prefect of the Congregation for the Clergy was a downright injury. Thoughtful bishops and priests felt the clergy deserved better of the Polish pontiff than Oddi.

More ominous was the summoning in Rome in December 1979 of the world-famous theologian and Dominican professor, Edward Schillebeeckx, of Nijmegen University in Holland, for a formal questioning about the contents of his immense treatise on Christology. Called to Rome on a similar matter in 1968, Schillebeeckx's orthodoxy had been vouched for by the renowned German Jesuit Karl Rahner. Now, however, he was being attacked principally by a second-rate Jesuit scriptural popularizer, Father Jean Galot. The latter's earlier book on the nature of Christ had been severely criticized by Schillebeeckx seven years before as an incompetent compilation of undigested scriptural positions, and Galot's most recent book was being given similar treatment in the theological community.

Not only was Galot revealed as one of Schillebeeckx's inquisitors but several days before the process, the Jesuit zealot had denounced his victim-to-be on Vatican Radio as a heretic. To add insult to injury, the signature of the Dominican secretary of the doctrinal congregation, Jerome Hamer, graced the summons. Schillebeeckx and Hamer were known to have been at odds over theological positions in their earlier careers. That the pope did not order the Dominican secretary to disqualify himself from this case seemed extraordinary in the light of his proclamations on human rights and dignity.

Schillebeeckx's troubles were the result of his attempt to present the facts of the primitive development of the Church's belief in the divinity and humanity of Jesus Christ in a fashion in keeping with contemporary historical criticism. His methodology seemed to many commentators extreme, as he attempted to peel away levels of belief and explain the reaction of the apostles and earliest disciples to Christ's death and resurrection. Nevertheless, he admitted the essential fact that Christ was both divine and human, though he would not repeat the outdated formula used by the Council of Chalcedon in 451 to certify this truth as an essential part of the Church's tradition. It was on this score that John Paul apparently had Schillebeeckx among others in mind when in his encyclical *The Redeemer of Man* he cautioned against the 'fanciful theological interpretations of individual theologians'.

The situation with the Swiss professor, Hans Küng, was similar to, but more momentous than, that of Schillebeeckx. A brilliant young scholar, Küng had completed his priestly studies at the Gregorian University in Rome while living at the Germanicum or German College in the Vatican, and was ordained in 1954. Doing graduate studies in Milan, Munich, London and Madrid he obtained a doctorate in theology from the Catholic Institute in Paris with a dissertation on the idea of 'justification' in the Protestant scholar Karl Barth's works. So pleased was the latter with the Catholic scholar's grasp of his ideas that Barth wrote a preface to Küng's book when it was published. This was in the preconciliar period of 1957. From the start of his career Küng was thus favored with a dossier in the Holy Office.

With the outbreak of Pope John's council, Küng produced a monograph on the *Church, Reform and Reunion* that proved a bestseller and influenced the conciliar debate. It likewise earned him the enmity of archconservative prelates and theologians who resented his ebullient ways and indefatigable production of monographs, essays and discourses criticising Church doctrine and influencing conciliar thought. Before the Council's end he made a worldwide lecture tour and achieved notoriety as one of the four theologians prevented from speaking at the Catholic University in Washington. A series of books and symposia attempting to update the Council's theology won him a number of warnings from the Holy Office that he ignored. Then in 1970 his attack on papal infallibility, *Infallibility: A Question?*, brought him a summons to the Holy See. Questioning the competence of the curial theologians, Küng made demands to examine the dossier of accusations and be confronted with his peers as a condition for his submission to Roman scrutiny. No such compromise was granted. In 1972 Pope Paul published an encyclical, *Mysterium Ecclesiae* (The mystery of the Church), whose doctrinal precisions had Küng in mind. While Professor Karl Rahner had disagreed with the Swiss theologian in several instances, even accusing him on one occasion of adopting Protestant attitudes, Rahner witnessed to Küng's essential orthodoxy and Pope Paul apparently held the zealots on the doctrinal congregation at bay.

With the death of the Archbishop of Munich, Cardinal Doepfner, in 1976 Küng lost a friend and protector. The youthful cardinal Joseph Ratzinger, the new archbishop, had been a colleague and rival of Küng's at Tübingen University and his 1970 book, *The Church's Belief,* had been severely criticized as backward in its theological thinking. Ratzinger's avowed purpose was to imitate the service to the Church of the preconciliar apologist Karl Adam. Though unsuccessful in this endeavor, he nevertheless pleased Pope Paul and was selected as the new cardinal of Munich in 1977. Joining with the zealous cardinal Joseph Hoffner of Cologne, a sociologist rather than a theologian, Ratzinger and a group of German bishops determined to have Küng censured and removed from his professorship at Tübingen, ostensibly to offset the harm he was doing to theological students and the general public. Actually his books *Does God Exist?*, *On Being a Christian,* and *Freud and the Church* were bestsellers that were being hailed by many thoughtful Christians and critics as the most helpful supports for their faith they had ever encountered. Nevertheless, on 19 December 1979, with a carelessness for seasonal propriety characteristic of the Holy Office, Küng was informed by the Congregation for Doctrine that he was deprived of his title as a Catholic theologian and could no longer teach ecclesiastical students. His bishop, George Moser, was instructed to seek Küng's removal from the Catholic theology faculty of the state university. This move presented a complicated problem; for though the bishop's right to appoint members of the faculty had been spelt out in the Hitler-Pacelli concordat of 1933, no provision was made for removal, it being apparently inconceivable to the concordatories that a professor who had become *persona non grata* would not unquestionably bow before the Nazi desideratum.

Küng, supported by groups of theologians from the Americas, Europe and Africa who wrote indignant letters to the Holy See, protested strongly and then adopted a wait-and-see attitude. The two cardinals and Küng's bishop were called to an audience with the pope on December 28 where they were informed that the Congregation's action in depriving Küng of his title still stood, although he was recognized as a priest in good standing.

In a letter to the German bishops in the spring of 1980, John Paul went out of his way to justify the papal censure of the Swiss theologian. Calling attention to his collegial consultation with the German hierarchy before taking action, the pope nonetheless expressed the hope that an irenic solution to the problem could be forthcoming and that Küng could be reinstated as a Catholic theologian.

No such consideration was extended to the French Dominican, Jacques Pohier, whose book *Quand je dis Dieu* (When I say God) recently had been condemned by the Congregation for Doctrine. Nor was consideration given to the American Jesuit, Father Robert Drinan, who four days before the deadline for filing his candidacy for a fourth term in the US Congress was informed by Rome that John Paul wanted him out of politics. A highly competent lawyer and law-maker, and an exceptionally conscientious priest, who invariably wore clerical garb and lived with the Jesuit community at Georgetown University, Drinan accepted the prohibition with a dignified protest in which he said that in his six years in Congress he had done more priestly work than in his whole previous career. What Drinan did not mention was the injustice of the pope's interference in so local a situation, particularly since the Holy Father had been influenced by a spokesman for the fanatic Right to Life wing of the American Church. Questioned by a journalist about the Drinan case, John Paul was reported to have replied: 'A priest is a priest.'

Trepidation immediately spread through the Church, particularly in the Latin American countries such as Nicaragua where priests were actively involved in government, lest the pope's action on Drinan might be extended; but there was no Vatican follow-up. Nevertheless the pope's intransigent attitude toward priests in the political forum bothered papal critics. No one in the Church had been more involved with politics than Karol Wojtyla throughout his career as Archbishop of Krakow. And in his present position as head of the Vatican City State, dealing daily with heads of nations, ambassadors, and statesmen of every persuasion, John Paul was the essence of a political pope. His contention that Christ had not been a revolutionary figure and that priests with rare exceptions should refrain from political involvement was the source of great concern to zealous clerical apostles who throughout Latin America, the Philippines, Africa and the Far East were daily risking their lives for justice, in keeping with Christ's injunction in the beatitudes.

In late November 1979, in pursuit of his collegial concept of papal rule, the pope summoned all the cardinals of the Church to a consistory in Rome for a consultation concerned with Vatican policy and finances. The pope had in mind employing the College of Cardinals as a consultative body, similar to its function in the Middle Ages when the cardinals had wielded considerable power. He seemed determined to use them as a sort of senate or house of lords, with the Roman Synod of Bishops serving as a parliamentary sounding-board for Church policy.

A matter of great speculation and considerable criticism, the Vatican's financial situation continued to be a mystery even to the Holy Father. Shortly after his appointment as a sort of comptroller to assess the general state of the finances of the Holy See, Cardinal Egidio Vagnozzi is supposed to have said: 'It would take a combination of the KGB, the CIA and Interpol to obtain just an inkling of how much and where the monies are.' In fact, although the Holy See possesses considerable properties in Rome, in Italy, and in various parts of the world, the Vatican is kept comparatively poor by the enormous expenses of running the Vatican City state itself, the costs of the curial cardinals and its world-wide ambassadorial system, while also supporting vast missionary enterprises and bolstering enfeebled churches all over the globe. While the settlement made by the Mussolini government in 1929 of some seventy million dollars to compensate the Holy See for the Papal States had been wisely invested and had enabled Pius XI, for example, to engage in an immense construction program, World War II and an unfortunate involvement with an injudicious financier had greatly reduced the Holy See's economic status. Suggestions that the pope sell off Vatican treasures were rightly regarded as irresponsible, given the Church's role in upholding man's cultural achievements.

It was in keeping with this concern that, during the cardinalatial consistory, John Paul held a meeting of the papal Academy of Sciences, an organization started by Pius xi to demonstrate the Church's interest in man's intellectual progress and involving the world's most eminent scientists, no matter what their religious beliefs. The occasion was a celebration of the centenary of the birth of Albert Einstein and in a speech before the Academy and the cardinals, John Paul said: 'The greatness of Galileo is comparable to that of Einstein, something recognized by all. But the difference is that today, in the presence of the college of cardinals in the Apostolic Palace, we are honoring Einstein, whereas Galileo was made to suffer much by the men and the organization of the Church.' It was against the background of this remarkable admission, that the Holy Father's authorization of the harassment of Hans Küng and a host of theologians by the Congregation for Doctrine seemed so incongruous. In his talk to the academy, the Holy Father encouraged its members to continue their researches with vigour, turning their attention in particular to those involved in the so-called sciences of man.

Midway through his second year as pope, John Paul took to the skies once more. He inaugurated his new round of pilgrimages with a visit to Turin, on Whitsunday, the city of the shroud of Christ and the automobile industry whose labor strife and terrorist activities had long awaited the peaceful coming of the vicar of Christ. In his office as patriarch of the West, John Paul had taken his duty to the Italian Church seriously, attempting to create a solid, forward-looking episcopate with the cardinals of Venice (Ce), Turin (Ballestrero), Milan (Martini) and Florence (Benelli), comparatively young men intent on the pastoral formation of their people unhindered by political considerations.

Before turning his attention to the social and political problems affecting the Italian north, John Paul was given an intimate view of the Holy Shroud, widely believed to be the burial cloth in which Jesus Christ was wrapped before being placed in the tomb. The cloth has been the object of a series of rigorous scientific investigations into its age and texture and, above all, its negative image of a medium-sized man who had been scourged and crowned with thorns; and the authenticity of this relic had become a secular as well as religious obsession. Avoiding judgment on this aspect of the shroud, the Holy Father venerated the relic before turning his attention, under the guidance of Cardinal Ballestrero, to the grave pastoral problems of this busy, industrial metropolis. In talks with both industrialists and workers, John Paul sought to sketch out a peaceful means for settling their problems without entering directly into the political difficulties underlying the unrest.

In mid-May John Paul set out on a series of three major pilgrimages to Africa, France and Brazil, in a two-month trajectory that left his aides breathless. After considerable discussion with Church and secular authorities, the pope decided to begin his seven-day jaunt in Africa with Zaire and the Congo – former Belgian and French colonies – where the Church was celebrating the hundredth anniversary of its arrival. Thence he would continue to Ghana, the Ivory Coast, Kenya and Upper Volta. Immediately preceding the papal journey, a dispute broke out between the Congregation of Rites and the local bishops over the participation of the pope in the Zairean liturgy, a highly Africanized mass in the local language. The pontiff's reluctance to celebrate the Eucharist in that form was regarded as a refusal to sanction this novelty in which the priest wears a native headdress along with the regular mass vestments, spears are carried and native dancing accompanies the principal actions. The Vatican spokesman, Monsignor Panciroli, dismissed the matter, explaining that the Holy Father did not know the language and would have felt himself doing something too artificial.

In his address to the pope, Cardinal Malula of Kinshasa informed the pontiff of the bishops' disappointment at his failure to experience their liturgy; and he deplored the fact that John Paul did not have time to become better acquainted with the new African theology. This was a highly courageous act on Malula's part, hardly appreciated by the pontiff's entourage. But it emphasized at the very start of the papal voyage the fact that mere Vatican lip-service to cultural adaptation in the call for Africanization of the local churches would not be well received.

Malula's courage had to be seen against the background of the difficulties he had experienced over the course of the past decade and a half with the country's president, Mobutu Sese Seku, the product of a Catholic missionary schooling who had taken control of the government in 1965 and had gradually attempted to dominate the Church's network of organizations and schools as well as its university in Kinshasa, the Louvanianum, an offshoot of the famous Belgian university in Louvain. Mobutu had forced the people to discard their Christian names in favor of native designations, himself exchanging Joseph Desiree for Sese Seku.

In opposing the government's depredations, the cardinal had been arrested and prevented from performing his pastoral tasks, despite Rome's protests. But since 1975 a detente had been reached, returning control of the schools to the missions, primarily because of the government's inability to staff them; and, immediately before the pope's arrival, Mobutu was married by the cardinal at a nuptial mass to the lady with whom he had been living for years. It was a significant gesture, and one which was repeated by other prominent Catholic government officials, including President Houphouet Boigny of the Ivory Coast.

John Paul's pastoral visit in all six countries was accompanied by an extravagant, boisterous round of festivities, with hundreds of thousands of people coming to see and hear him everywhere he turned. He had arrived with some sixty-five speeches and addresses that he delivered in French, while displaying his ability to mesmerize crowds. While his visits were a series of local pageants, beneath the demonstrations a different drama was unfolding, as the pope attempted to deal with the realities of his predecessor's 1969 Kampala call for Africanization of the Church on this vast continent.

In the African churches the movement toward an authentic merging of the Gospel message and the native mentality called not merely for a restatement of the New Testament truths in the local languages but a reordination of the Christian values in native dress, as the Holy Father informed the Zairean bishops' conference. He spoke of wide and profound areas which had not yet been sufficiently explored in the language in which to present the Christian message, the method of catechesis, the theological reflection within the liturgy, the art and various forms of Christian community life. Insisting that the Church had come of age in these lands, the pope reminded the Catholics of Congo Brazzaville that they were in a position to consolidate the work of evangelization by carrying it to other peoples. And he assured the Catholics of Ghana that 'the evangelization of the world depends on each one of you.' During his visit with the Ghanian president, Dr Hilla Limann, John Paul spoke of the 'many values incarnate in the culture of the African

nations' that should enrich other nations. He stressed the African conception of the world in which the sacred occupies a central position;
a profound awareness of the link that exists between nature and the creator, together with a great respect for life, and a 'sense of family that
opens into hospitality and is crowned with a *joie de vivre* expressed in
the language of poetry, song and dance.' In this connection he referred
to his own Polish background as giving him a particular respect for the
effect culture has on a people.

In Kenya, addressing the diplomatic corps, John Paul drew attention
to world responsibility for the integrity of Africa where the people 'with
a few painful exceptions' were assuming full political responsibility for
their own destiny; and he mentioned the recent liberation of Zimbabwe. He said that political independence and national sovereignty
demanded that there be also economic liberty and freedom from ideological domination; and he went on to condemn restrictions of religious
freedom, racial discrimination and the stockpiling of arms.

In his homily at the mass for families that he celebrated in Kinshasa,
John Paul had said that he was making a 'pilgrimage to the sources of
marriage', thus revealing his second great preoccupation in his African
visit. Holding up the ideal of the monogamous couple, he went on to
say: 'Used judiciously African customs have their place in the upbuild-
ing of the Christian home in Africa.' He said he was thinking of the
positive values related to the sense of family so rooted in the African
soul and which should prompt reflection in more advanced societies.
Then, revealing his true concern, the pontiff said: 'Surely the most
delicate problem is to take up this family dynamism which is the legacy
of the customs of the past, while at the same time transforming it and
sublimating it within the perspectives of the society which is coming to
birth in Africa.' He reminded the bishops of their responsibility to provide adequate pastoral care for married couples and for those intending
to marry, instilling in them a sense of their identity as a couple, as well
as the ideal of an authentic Christian union.

In his final address at the Abidjan airport, the pope returned once
more to the theme of African identity. 'Be yourselves,' he told his audience. 'Guard against both Western materialism and Marxist ideological solutions to your economic and political problems.' 'For ten days,'
he added, 'I have been the astonished and thunderstruck witness of the
vitality of the young churches of Africa. I invite the whole church,

especially the ancient churches of Christendom, to look upon their sister churches in Africa with esteem and confidence and to learn from them.'

In John Paul's African message, while cultural adaptation was a principal theme, no consideration was given to the failure of the Church to come to grips with both the polygamy and clerical concubinage that were such difficult problems for the local churches. The earlier missionaries had simply condemned the former, forcing tribesmen to abandon all but one wife before allowing them to approach the sacraments, and, recognizing the impossibility of insisting on a celibate clergy, had held off from ordaining native priests down to recent times. John Paul merely insisted on the ideals of monogamy and clerical chastity, as if these institutions were universally compatible with the African mentality. This failure to come to terms with what he had recognized as an imaginative African genius was the subject of a critique in the aftermath of the pope's pilgrimage.

Where the African mentality differed radically from the Western European was in its employment of an imagination that wandered incontinently between the conscious and the unconscious, producing a poetic vision of reality that was neither false nor unrealistic. That it was not capable of scientific explanation did not mean it represented an invalid spiritual reality. It was, rather, a mythological and symbolic comprehension of mystery as true as were the sharply chiselled definitions of the Christian dogmas. This was a fact recognized by Cardinal Newman in his tract on the Grammar of Assent of faith in which he maintained that belief was an imaginative act preceding rational and articulate forms. Doctrinal development, he had asserted, came about not by argument, but by an imaginative response to the symbols on which the forms were based.

African theologians were now calling for re-creation of the local mythologies in direct relation to the Gospels and not filtered through a Western European metaphysical system. If the African imagination were to be liberated from the artificial limitations of hellenistic doctrinal definitions and allowed a free response to God's truth, mediated through the good news of the scripture, an authentic response would be given to the questions constantly posed by the African mentality confronted with the wonders of nature and the vagaries of his human experience. It was precisely because the static formulas of Christian instruction and the rigid liturgical formulas of Catholic and Protestant worship did not meet the needs of the vivid imagination of the African mind, that so many breakaway churches dotted the countryside, in a crude attempt to achieve a soul-satisfying synthesis of Christian beliefs and African traditions. By failing to address this fundamental need for an existentialist acculturization, despite the tremendous joy with which he was greeted and the respect paid to his messages, the Holy Father's African pilgrimage proved less than effective. In the immediate aftermath a mood of confusion and perplexity seemed to prevail.

This mood was captured in a report unconnected with the papal visit but, by an ironic twist of circumstances, not unconnected with the pope's message. In his address to the bishops of Kenya, the Holy Father had gone out of his way to praise the Pastoral Institute of the East African Episcopate (AMECEA) at Eldoret, only to discover on his return to Rome that the April issue of *Afer* (the *African Ecclesial Review*) carried a strongly worded response to the curial agenda on 'The role of the Family' prepared for the October 1980 Roman Synod of Bishops.

Describing the Vatican paper as flawed in a number of important ways, the pastoral council of the diocese of Arusha in Tanzania complained that it spent too much time justifying the curial right to speak on marriage and the family, rather than honestly addressing the issues involved. Getting to the heart of the matter, the critique stated that no husbands or wives could have been involved with the preparation of the curial document, and accused the Holy See of addressing itself only to the nuclear family whereas the extended family, which 'may be lost to much of the affluent west,' was still very much a reality in other parts of the world. Hence it should not be presumed that the entire world would follow the pattern of the urbanized, industrialized and highly mobile societies of the rich and developed countries where marriage was so obviously suffering shipwreck.

Dealing with the curial description of conjugal relationships, the authors insisted that while the sacrament of marriage was not achieved by contract or ritual but by the loving relationship of the partners, the Western style of romantic marriage after courtship was not the direction that the rest of the world would or should take. Presuming that Catholic monogamous marriage was not the only ideal or the only form of matrimony, polygamy must be considered as part of the cultural diversity to which John Paul had made such frequent reference. Likewise, the Synod should give some consideration to 'natural' marriages, and in so doing it should produce not one but several documents 'each tailored to the particular needs of the various segments of the Church'.

No sooner had the Holy See absorbed this broadside than the bishops of Vietnam reported on the recent congress of the Vietnamese hierarchy held in Hanoi to determine what the Church could do for the nation in its present state of socialist construction. A ten-member committee, with Cardinal Trinh Van Can as chairman and Archbishop Nguyen van Binh of Ho Chi Minh City and Archbishop Nguyen Kim Diem of Hué, were received on April 30 by Premier Pham Van Dong who praised the bishops for their acceptance of the communist system as a viable way of life in conformity with Christian values of unity and defense of the nation.

Sandwiched in between his African and Brazilian tours, John Paul spent seventy-five hectic hours in a visit to France. Geared to an official appearance before the United Nations Educational, Scientific and Cultural Organization (UNESCO), John Paul's pilgrimage aimed at settling a deep problem within the French Church as well as indulging a devotional sentiment at the shrine of St Thérèse of Lisieux, known as the Little Flower, a 26-year-old Carmelite nun whom Pius xi had canonized as the patron saint of the Church's vast missionary enterprises.

On the pope's mind, as he revealed in a television broadcast before the trip, was what he termed a 'crisis of growth' in the 'eldest daughter of the Church' – a designation going back to the conversion of King Clovis and the Franks in the fifth century.

Touching down at Orly airport on Friday afternoon, 30 May 1980, the pope was whisked by helicopter to the Champs-Elysées where he was officially welcomed by the French president, Valéry Giscard d'Estaing, and the cardinal of Paris, François Marty. His itinerary included four principal masses: on the esplanade before the cathedral of Notre-Dame, in the Basilica of St Denis in the communist workers' quarter on Saturday, at Le Bourget airfield with over a thousand prelates and priests on Sunday, and at Lisieux on Monday. Meanwhile he addressed groups of bishops, priests, nuns, university student, workers, government officials, young people and the Polish community of Paris, before delivering his major speech to UNESCO.

In his colloquy with the French hierarchy, John Paul confronted a major problem of the postconciliar period. Maintaining that in the aftermath of the Council certain interpretations of its teaching had arisen, at times very violently, that did not correspond to its authentic doctrine, the pontiff signalled 'progressivism' and 'integralism' as equally at fault. The former, he said, was impatient to adapt the contents of the faith, Christian ethics, liturgy and the organization of the Church to the demands of the world and to current changes in thought, without taking sufficient notice of the common sense of the faithful who were troubled by these actions. On the other hand he accused the integrists of shutting themselves rigidly in a given period of history and absolutizing theological formulations and liturgical expressions, while fearfully rejecting legitimate development and thus denying the presence of the Holy Spirit working today with the pastors and people united round the successor of St Peter.

Speaking to the clergy outside Notre-Dame, he recalled the great tradition of saintly but sensible French priests, from Francis de Sales to the Curé d'Ars, before eulogizing Cardinal Suhard, the Archbishop of Paris who had suffered so greatly during World War II and was the founder of the Mission of France and a great champion of the worker-priests movement. To the amazement of many in his audience, John Paul gave unequivocal approval to this apostolate, despite the long history of Roman opposition and the loss to the priesthood of many of its earlier members.

In his address to the French bishops, the pope took up the problems of the 'crisis of growth' and insisted that the Church was no longer in a position to continue the internal controversies that had sapped its energies in the past. He described the bishops' function as interpreters of the Council's teaching and encouraged them to take the lead in building unity with an eye to both the deep issues troubling their faithful and the psychological problems preventing the French Church from going forward in truth and charity. Of France's population some seventy-five percent are presumed to have been baptised Catholics, whereas only fifteen percent practice their religion; and whereas France supplied a large proportion of priests, missionaries and teachers for the universal Church in the past, ordinations to the priesthood were down from some 550 in 1968 to 120 in 1979.

In his address to the university students at the Catholic Institute of Paris, the pope was both familiar and provocative, recalling his own long university experience as a professor and challenging his audience to continue the traditional French respect for theological actuality, science and culture that had characterized the Sorbonne and the ancient University of Paris down the ages. But it was in his talk to the workers at St Denis that he gave a long explanation of the Christian vision of the nature and dignity of the human person. Insisting that work is instinctive to the nature of man, leading to but not constituting his dignity, the pope asserted that man's hunger for bread was complemented by his need for truth and freedom as well as his right to education, religious and political liberty. Designating the condemnation of the arms race a 'categorical imperative', the Holy Father said the workers should ask themselves why man's creative talents should be transformed into destructive powers geared to greed, hatred and the possibility of a monstrous self-destruction.

In his final, formal address to UNESCO, the pontiff asserted the Church's support for this institution from its beginnings (without referring to the struggle of his predecessor John when nuncio in Paris to force participation on the Vatican despite the secularist aims of UNESCO's founders). John Paul insisted that there was an inviolable link between Christianity, culture and the spiritual nature of man. Turning to the remarkable achievements of modern science and scholarship, he spoke of contemporary man's noble intentions, before deploring the exploitation of current research and discovery for ignoble ends, not the least of which was destruction, death and the possible annihilation of mankind. He wound up his speech by calling for a new mobilization of human resources to achieve a priority of the ethical over the technical, and of the spiritual over the material nature of human endeavor.

During the return voyage to Rome John Paul saw fit to justify his travels as undertaken in the service of the Church and of man whose horizon 'expands continually and requires the pope to make himself present everywhere the needs of the faith and the affirmation of the various human needs call him. It is to confirm the Christian faith and promote these values that the pope travels on the pathways of the world.'

While the pope was taking a well-deserved respite from his French pilgrimage the German Church was engaged in one of its biennial Catholic congresses known as a *Katholikentag*, held in Berlin from 4–8 June. Under the vigorous leadership of Berlin's newly appointed bishop, Joachim Meisner, some hundred thousand enthusiastic Catholics, a majority of them younger people from both West and East Germany, demonstrated their belief that 'The Love of Christ is Stronger!'

Government officials from both Federal Germany and the Democratic Republic were on hand, as was Mother Theresa of Calcutta whose presence seemed to electrify the gathering under the direction of a mixed commission of prelates, priests and laity.

Side by side with the official gathering, a '*Katholikentag* from below' had been organized by several Catholic groups in disagreement with official Church policies. On their roster were two of the world's leading theologians, Hans Küng, who had not been invited to the official congress, and John Baptist Metz, who had declined the official invitation despite the fact that he had delivered the principal address at the 1978 *Katholikentag*. Küng spoke of the future of the Church in Germany, warning of the threat to the development of the Christian religion from the establishment – the attempt to stifle progress and muzzle consciences in favor of a false uniformity. In the 'church from below', he said, there was no threat of revolt nor of dissidence, as the ecclesial establishment claimed. Rather the priest and faithful sought to pursue Pope John's *aggiornamento* and looked for the spirit of Christ's compassion in the application of the Church's laws. In particular he called upon the hierarchy to exercise Christ-like mercy in allowing remarried divorcees to return to a participation in the Church's sacramental life and to welcome a married priesthood, in keeping with the status of the apostles and almost all the early churchmen.

Professor Metz deepened this critique by pointing to the faithful as the essential body of Christ to which the hierarchy was a service not a domination. If the Church were to change – and it must, he charged – it would only do so when the *sensus fidelium* under the guidance of the Spirit accepted the truly universal and therefore diverse character of the Church's teaching. It was the hierarchy's task to find and define this development, a service that the pope and the German episcopate were shirking by their efforts to support the 'euro-centric' post-conciliar establishment. This Western outlook was a bourgeois mentality no longer acceptable to the Church in Latin America fighting for the rights of the exploited, nor in the newer churches of Africa and Asia confronted with the post-colonial world.

It was these pastoral convictions that had prompted the cardinal of

Munich, Joseph Ratzinger, to reject Metz's appointment to the chair of Catholic theology at the University of Munich in 1979, an action considered punitive by even so balanced a theologian as Karl Rahner.

Criticism of the heirarchy and Pope John Paul's continued intransigence on the question of a married priesthood and remarried divorcees was echoed in the official *Katholikentag,* where a call for the forgiving love of Christ was extended to an existentialist exercise of true freedom in both the Church and secular society. Emphasizing the commitment of the participants to the Church's presence among the poor and the exploited, there were two collections of well over 450,000 Deutchmarks for Mother Theresa's far-flung missions. Despite the critical spirit that characterized much of the congress, it closed with an enthusiastic testimony of loyalty to the Church and the Holy Father.

John Paul had hardly recuperated from his lightning-like visit to France when he was involved in preparations for his Brazilian journey, which was to be a protracted twelve-day 17,500-mile *tour de force* and whose announcement to the media had provoked a series of controversies involving local prelates, curial officials and the Brazilian government. At stake was a tug of war between the conservative elements in the Brazilian episcopate who supported the government's anti-communist policies and a majority of the nation's priests and prelates determined to make the Holy Father's visit a meaningful experience that would bolster their efforts to bring justice and peace to the nation. Well aware of the difficulties troubling the country, John Paul insisted that all the bishops visit him individually in the Vatican for their five-year *ad limina* report to Rome before he ventured on this mission to the country with the largest Catholic population in the world (some 98 out of 112 million people), a majority of whom lived below subsistence level and were being absorbed into innumerable revivals of African cultist religions.

Characteristic of the split in the Brazilian church's hierarchy were the accusations made in the decade following the Council by two intransigent bishops, Dom de Proença Sigaud of Diamantina and Dom Castro Mayer of Campos, that many of the priests and bishops were tainted with Marxism and were unwittingly serving the communist cause. They had in mind specifically the Archbishop of Recife, Dom Heldar Camara, known popularly as the red archbishop, and his large following of priests, nuns, bishops and committed laity among whom were victims of the brutalities of the government's repressive tactics; and the rightist paramilitary squads organized clandestinely by the movement for Tradition, Family and Property.

In his conversations with the bishops, John Paul was given a broad view of the innumerable movements devoted to the revitalization of Christian life in all parts of Brazil. Speaking for the attempt to uplift the exploited masses through a type of *communidades de base* were the prelates of the nine states of the northeast, one of whose leaders, Dom José Pires, Archbishop of João Pessõa, said that when he took spiritual charge of the state of Paraiba in 1966, he found 'penury, poverty and repression' prevalent among that state's two and a half million inhabitants. He quickly decided that the Church would have meaning for these people only if it was engaged in discovering social and political remedies for these evils. For his pains he was frequently taunted for being engaged in communist games.

Taking the government's side in the church-state contretemps, Cardinal Vicente Sherer of Porto Alegre in the industrialized south reacted strongly to a Letter to the Pope from a group of priests describing living conditions in impoverished sectors of the land. Labelling this missive 'impertinent, irregular and improper', the cardinal said that Pope John Paul did not need any kind of ideological advice from priests telling him where to go and what to say in Brazil.

This broadside brought into the open the struggle within the Vatican over the papal itinerary that had to be changed four times before the conservative party succeeded in having the papal visit begin in Brasilia, the nation's capital, making his arrival an official state occasion and giving the administration of General Joao Figueirdo a key role in the welcome. In opposition were the prelates who wanted the pope to emphasize the pilgrimage-to-the-poor aspects of his voyage by downgrading the government's involvement and starting with Fortaleza in the impoverished north, where a Eucharistic Congress was to be held under the auspices of Cardinal Aloisio Lorscheider. With his cousin, Bishop Ivo Lorscheiter of San Angelo, and Cardinal Evaristo Arns of Sao Paulo, Lorscheider was a chief proponent of Brazil's progressive Catholicism.

In the end a complicated itinerary was worked out, exposing the Holy

Father to all the elements of the Brazilian scene in thirteen major stop-overs that included a (protested) visit to an Army headquarters in Sao Paulo, two *favelas* or extensive slum areas outside Salvador and Rio, a leper colony and the exploited Indian territory of the Amazon region. There was an ironic thrust in each of these visits that included protestations by victims of the military's repression and the refusal of the Indians of the north to engage in a festive dance for the Holy Father. Instead the latter came to him in great sorrow, manifesting their fears that their posterity would soon be exterminated by the genocidal policy of the Brazilian oligarchy.

Several weeks before the papal visit the Brazilian government's Institute for Colonization and Agrarian Reform published a document alleging that the Catholic Church was one of the largest rural landholders in the country and engaged in the exploitation of the poor farmers, squatters and shareholders. The document listed 441,000 acres of agricultural land held by the Church and said that in several cases prominent clergymen had sold property to rich entrepreneurs in the knowledge that squatters would be expelled. The government exposure pointed to Cardinal Aloisio Lorscheider who had sold five thousand acres in 1975 to a business group that threatened the expulsion of some 345 families. The Institute maintained that it had to interfere to prevent the squatters' removal, a particularly irritating contention for Church leaders who had themselves criticized the government for failing to act when small farmers were being evicted. While denying any intent to provoke animosity against the Church, the Institute's document was an answer to the Bishops Conference that, several months earlier, had condemned capitalist exploitation of the rural poor and called for a new economic model for the country.

A particular target of the government was the gentle but indomitable cardinal of Sao Paulo, Evaristo Arns, whose activity on behalf of the exploited had provoked a 1974 report from the Attorney General's office that had claimed: 'The clergy today constitute the most active enemy of national security, promoting through purely subversive methods the substitution of the existing political, social and economic order with a new model in every aspect of life consonant with the Marxist philosophy.'

In preparation for the Brazilian trip, Pope John Paul saw Cardinal

Arns in Rome on four separate occasions. There is some evidence that John Paul was persuaded to clear up the uncertainty beclouding his approach to the clergy's involvement in the social, political and economic issues. The ambiguity resulted from his Puebla speech in which he declared that Christ had not been a revolutionary and that priests should stay out of politics, a statement used by General Pinochet of Chile, for one, as he turned his police loose on priests, nuns and bishops opposed to repressive, national policies.

The papal progress through Brazil was accompanied with wild festivity on all sides. As he had done in his other nation-wide jaunts, the pope delivered a plethora of speeches, sermons and addresses to every conceivable group of people, hypnotizing one and all by his histrionic talent and command of languages. His speeches were singularly geared to his total commitment to the battle for human and political rights. While he reiterated his warnings against Marxism, and the involvement of clergy and committed laity in ideological movements, his message to both the government and the Church was clear and unmistakable, placing Catholicism irrevocably in support of the impoverished. John Paul's twelve days' pilgrimage began with a thinly veiled attack on the Brazilian military regime's national security policies. It reached a crescendo during his tour of the slum areas: 'A society,' he said, 'that is not socially just and does not intend to be puts its own future in danger.'

Observers could hear an echo of Cardinal Arns' declaration: 'My greatest worry is that Brazil is going to adopt reform rather than basic change.' And when John Paul said that the Church must serve the cause of justice by using its voice to summon consciences and guard people and their liberties, the voice of Dom Heldar Camara claiming that Christian indifference to the poor in the past had justified Karl Marx was also being echoed.

After visiting thirteen cities in a huge criss-crossing of the vast country, John Paul departed from Manaus in the Amazon for Rome. It had been an exhilarating but exhausting experience for him and his aides, not to mention the media and other agencies. As he admitted to the people awaiting his arrival in the Vatican, he was dead tired but elated. Justifying these voyages once more, and the endless detail work they put on his assistants, he said his function as pope was to manifest Christ to people everywhere, imitating the Apostle Paul. With that remark he headed down to Castelgondolfo for a much-needed rest, assuring his aides and the media that he had completed his pilgrimaging for the second year of his pontificate.

John Paul was proving to be a tireless pontiff in the thousand and one items to which he gave his attention each day. He selected a comparatively youthful Jesuit Professor of Scripture, Father Martina, as the new archbishop of Milan, a great surprise to the curia; and he kept a finger on the renewal of the hierarchies all over the world. He was indefatigable in his public audiences to youth in St Peter's each Wednesday, and afterwards to the general public. He likewise received ambassadors and officials of nations friendly or hostile to the Church; and he dealt almost daily with innumerable religious and secular societies holding conventions or merely making a visit to the Eternal City. On sudden impulse, he frequently helicoptered down to Castelgondolfo to enjoy the salubrious air of the Alban foothills and the beauty of the *castelli romani*. Though two recent popes had died there, John Paul seemed impervious to Italian superstitions. On installing an olympic-sized swimming pool in 1979, which he allowed the families of the papal employees to use in his absence, he quipped: 'It's cheaper than another conclave.'

In his rearrangement of the papal household, John Paul was obviously influenced by Cardinal Agostino Casaroli, the man who replaced the French cardinal Villot as secretary of state. An old hand at papal diplomacy, and a trusted friend of Wojtyla's since his first visits to Poland and the iron curtain countries as Pope John's emissary in the early 1960s, Casaroli is the essence of a Vatican statesman. Known to colleagues as an 'artist of concordats', the secretary of state is an affable conversationalist, astute and witty, whose knowledge of the Church's structure and its relations with the outside world is unequalled in the present generation. Unobtrusively Pope Paul's most trusted advisor – in 1968, he was called on to manage the final stages of the encyclical *Humanae vitae* and was Pope Paul's other self in dealing with the communist countries – he had become John Paul's ecclesiastical mentor as well as political adviser. His conciliatory abilities were used to heal the breach in the Italian cardinalate between the Siri and the Benelli factions after the election of the Polish pontiff. Casaroli's unobtrusive administrative abilities were exhibited in his assumption of full control over

Vatican affairs in contrast to the limited powers exercised by his predecessor, Cardinal Villot, whose supremacy was blunted by the effi-
cient but brusque execution of Pope Paul's wishes by Archbishop Benelli, the substitute secretary of state. In the reshuffling of the top curial
offices, Casaroli brought in a Spaniard, Monsignor Martinez Somalo,
as the *sostituto,* Monsignor Achille Silvestrini as secretary in the office
of the public affairs of the Church, and Monsignor Juozas Backis Au-
drys, the son of the ambassador-in-exile of Lithuania to the United
States, as sub-secretary in charge of relations with the communist
world. Critics spoke of the new regime as the mafia of Piacenza, Casaroli's home town.

Rumors that the pontiff had delivered a dressing-down to the Jesuits
in the fall of 1979 were partially true. The pope's call for a closer observance of the Jesuit rule, a return to clerical garb and an avoidance of
questionable secular interests were embodied in the Superior General,
Father Arrupe's pre-Christmas letter to the Society. But these admoni-
tions were a regular practice in keeping with traditions going back to St
Ignatius and were also a feature of other religious institutes and orders.
John Paul was conscious of the heroic work being done by Jesuit missionaries, suffering persecution and incarceration with their people in
various parts of the Church; and as he told a vast audience on his visit
to the Gregorian University in the fall of 1979, he was proud of their
intellectual and theological accomplishments.

In his hope to make peace with the People's Republic of continental
China, the pope dispatched Cardinal Etchegaray of Marseilles on a three-
week visit at the Chinese government's invitation. The French prelate
made contact with the newly consecrated Bishop of Peking despite the
lack of Rome's approval for his election. Ironically, Hans Küng in the
early fall of 1979 had been the first representative of religion to lecture
before a Chinese cultural association since the communist takeover. His
achievement was followed by a similar invitation to Cardinal Franz
Koenig of Vienna, head of the Vatican Secretariat for contact with
non-believers. With the obvious thaw in religious relations for Buddh-
ists, Muslims, and Christians, it seemed certain that the Holy See was
edging toward a recognition of the Chinese Catholic Church, and the
re-establishment of the Jesuit University of the Aurora in Shanghai.

Of the Polish problems troubling the pope, the attempt of the government to run a super-highway through the town of Jasna Gora, thus sep-

In calling Vatican Council II into being, Pope John hoped to produce a revolution in the Church – a return to the basic principles of the Christian way of life that would teach people to love their neighbor as themselves for the love of God. To achieve that end, he instructed the conciliar fathers to concern themselves with the consciousness of modern men and women. He hoped thus to have the Church reshape its thinking so as to penetrate the consciences of contemporary mankind. Without interfering too directly in the workings of the Council, John gave it certain clear directives, namely that its discussions were to be conducted with total freedom; that there were to be no condemnations of individuals or curtailing of free speech; and that a change in the ideological explanation of Christian teaching was not only possible but profoundly necessary. Then, on the sidelines, he produced two great encyclicals, *Mater et Magistra* and *Pacem in Terris*.

These two documents set the stage for a fundamental revision of Catholic teaching regarding the human person, insisting on the basic right of every individual man, woman and child to have his or her dignity as a human being upheld no matter what the circumstances. Discarding completely the ancient adage 'Error has no rights,' Pope John said that in effect this axiom was a nonsensical statement. Only a person has rights; and a person in error retains those rights – hence governments and the Church should be the first to uphold the sacredness of the human person, endowed by the Creator with intelligence and a freedom of choice to be used in achieving a mature and responsible individuality.

Fundamentally it is this concept that is at issue as the Church strives to adapt Christ's basic injunction – the love of God and the love of neighbor – to the exigencies of contemporary society. To achieve this goal, it has been necessary to literally turn the Church upside down in its concept of itself and its relation to the world. Instead of the modern juridical concept that saw the Church as an inverted pyramid balanced on the papacy as the foundation rock, Vatican Council II returned to the traditional notion of the Church as the aggregation of believers whose contours could only be described in the symbols used by Jesus Christ in the New Testament. In the third chapter of the Dogmatic Constitution, the hierarchical character of the Church's organizational structure was outlined, and both the supremacy and the infallibility of the pope in dealing with matters of faith and morals were reaffirmed. But this governmental system was immediately designated as a *service*, rather than

arating the famous Marian shrine of Czestochowa from easy access to the people, was defeated by direct papal intervention. John Paul's interference in the affairs of the Pauline monks running the monastery of Czestochowa by giving Cardinal Wyszynsky plenipotentiary powers over the Pauline order seemed to have re-established peace, at least in that order's European foundations. He had also quashed the Vatican-authorized investigation made by Bishop Guilfoyle of Camden, New Jersey and Father Paul Boyle, the General of the Passionists, of the scandals connected with the Doylestown, Pennsylvania, shrine of Czestochowa. This five-year-long inquiry involved financial schemes and improprieties, a possible criminal case against the former superior of the Polish-oriented monastery and shrine, and the involvement of the cardinal of Philadelphia, John Krol, and Bishop Guilfoyle in what appeared to be a cover-up of the Polish monk's financial dealings. The story had broken just before the pope's visit to the United States, but was not picked up by the major units of the American press, apparently out of courtesy to the papal presence in the country.

There is no question but that John Paul desired to introduce a heroic, spiritual element into the Church's life and consciousness at this stage of world development. He saw the need for spiritual absolutes to offset the degradations to which contemporary society has let itself be reduced by the mad seeking after wealth, material possessions and experiences of the bizarrest kind. He was likewise conscious of the armageddon of destructive forces facing mankind in the frenzied pursuit of armaments for global annihilation, as well as the trampling on the rights of the individual in the name of 'national security' or 'socio-political liberation'.

But while it was his duty to place clearly before the world the highest ideals of the love of Christ, accompanied by sacrifices of every kind in pursuit of the love of one's neighbor – the ideal that was behind his recall of priests to the permanence of their vocational commitment to Christ, and of married people to the finality of their covenanted unity – still, his experience as a seasoned and thoughtful world traveller should have come into play here. As seen from outside the Vatican, his role as the Church's supreme teacher should be to have 'compassion on the multitude' in comforting the sinner and leading the Church with infinite charity to the aid of the priest, the nun, the married and single laity who were trying to reintegrate their lives within the context of the Christian way of life. For this, they needed grace, the sacraments, and the therapeutic solace of the liturgy. To cut off individuals from these supernatural aids because they were living in a so-called 'state of sin' no longer seemed tolerable. It represented the pelagian notion that they could achieve salvation by pulling themselves up by their own spiritual bootstraps. Only by taking a ruthlessly realistic view of the salvation function of its sacramental and eucharistic graces would the Church, under a pope truly solicitous for individuals rather than ideas and social structures, prove adequate to its modern obligations.

Only in so doing could this pope regain the momentum achieved by his original witness to the Christian involvements in the world, a momentum that his apparent indulgence in the severity outlawed by Pope John at the start of the Vatican Council II lost him during the second year of his pontificate. And it is only by imitating the magnanimous patience amid turmoil and conflict that characterized Pope Paul VI's pontificate – a sufferance admittedly not well appreciated during his lifetime – that the Polish pontiff could put himself in a position to regain the leadership of the whole Christian community that he seemed to have had within his grasp during the first stages of his experience as Bishop of Rome. This trust on the part of his Catholic faithful as well as the Orthodox and Protestant churches would not be forthcoming if he seemed to have returned to the omniscient, triumphalist attitudes of the Pacellian church. He had to exhibit the common sense of John XXIII and the forbearance of Paul VI to merit true recognition as John Paul II.

9

... *Plus C'est la Même Chose*

In the course of the century and a half separating the death of Pius VI from the election of John XXIII, the Catholic Church under the aegis of the papacy fought a rearguard action against the evolutionary forces of contemporary Western civilization. In a series of retrograde pronouncements the popes rejected the fundamental drives for liberty, equality and fraternity that had been the objectives of the French Revolution, despite the fact that all three of these objectives could be squared with the teaching of Jesus Christ in the New Testament. And instead of rejoicing in its liberation from the burdens of political rule – first with the usurpation of the Papal States by the Napoleonic forces at the turn of the nineteenth century, then by their abolishment under the *Risorgimento* in 1870 – the popes had reacted by asserting the Church's right to exercise political sovereignty despite Christ's denial of worldly kingship before Pilate, while rejecting a fundamental evangelical counsel — Christ's frequent exhortation to his disciples that they pay attention to the 'signs of the times'.

In a series of condemnations that reached a critical stage with the encyclical *Mirari vos* of Gregory XVI in 1832 and climaxed with Pius X's rejection of Modernism with the papal decree *Lamentabili* of 1907, the Church had rejected the ideals of democracy, liberty of conscience, political and social equality, and the involvement of the Church in the struggle for justice in the economic and social structures of the contemporary world. Behind these rejections were grave fears lest by accommodating its teachings to the ambiguous achievements of eighteenth-century Enlightenment, the Church would compromise its other-worldly objectives and allow itself to be engulfed in a whirlpool of secular interests.

a dominative power. And in the overall governance of the Church, the residential bishops were acknowledged as forming a college, with and under the Bishop of Rome. Concrete form was given to this concept in the establishment of a Roman Synod of Bishops – a triennial gathering of the elected representatives of the local hierarchies from round the globe, to discuss with the supreme pontiff the Church's more immediate needs.

Despite the turmoil that attended his fifteen-year pontificate, Pope Paul had worked consistently to disengage the Church from its preconciliar thinking and give it a new self-consciousness. Then, with the arrival of John Paul I in August 1978, the whole world felt that at last the Catholic Church had shaken itself loose from the shackles of a fear-inspired curial rule.

It was against this background that John Paul II set out on his impressive jet visitations of Mexico, Poland, Ireland and the United States, mesmerizing the immense crowds who gathered to see and hear this authentic man of God. And while, after each journey, he left behind a certain perplexity over the rigidity of his moral enunciations, his personal magnanimity impressed the most critical observers both in and outside the Church. The first year of his pontificate gave the clear impression that a world leader had suddenly arisen, calling for an end to the insane armaments race and the internecine warfare gradually destroying modern civilization. On each of these visits John Paul was received as a religious leader, the representative of Jesus Christ, with warmth and great joy. In comparison with other world leaders – President Carter or Mr Brezhnev, Mrs Thatcher or President Sadat – there was simply no ground for appraisal; nor was there any religious figure who could come near his stature. He thus seemed to have restored the papacy to a position that it had occupied on occasion during the Middle Ages when the pope as suzerain Lord of the Mediterranean littoral had exercised a leadership that affected both the Christian and the Muslim world, dictating the 'Peace of God,' and interfering effectively in the political arena. In a remarkable sense John Paul seemed about to vindicate the papal prerogative of serving as the conscience of mankind, when, suddenly, the mesmerism of his personality and the charisma of his office seemed lost by his return of the papacy to an organ of authoritarian rule.

By entangling himself in the petty concerns of anticonciliar bishops and the Roman curia in their persecutory drive against some of the Church's more responsible theologians (there were indications that not merely the Congregation for Doctrine, but those concerned with Education, the Sacraments and Rites, were also in the process of tracking down nonconformists in the seminaries and universities), John Paul lost the momentum of global leadership. His protest that, in the curial determination to control the intellectual freedom of Catholic thinkers, their human dignity was not being abused, was met with incredulity.

To the outside world – and there was respectful criticism of his handling of the anti-heresy campaign from Protestant and other religious leaders fearful that he was destroying confidence in Rome's ecumenical trustworthiness – it was simply inconceivable that a man from behind the Iron Curtain subject to a process of thought-control from his youth and exposed to ideological absolutisms on the part of a government organization, would in any way encourage the procedures followed by the curia in their attempt to control the Church's thinking.

The only possible explanation for the new pope's growing intransigence was his desire that the papacy provide a heroic barrier of law and order at this apparently disintegrating phase of world history. But the line between a triumphalistic, totalitarian Church, repudiated by Vatican Council II, and the 'People of God' being led to heroic virtue in confronting today's world, is exceedingly thin. Thus far, critics maintained, the Polish pontiff's position appeared to be motivated more by ideological intransigence than by charismatic inspiration.

Justification for this judgment was furnished by an address that Carol Wojtyla delivered, as cardinal of Krakow, in 1971. In it he defined the task of the theologian as being to 'defend the sacred deposit of revelation' in close association with the bishops but subordinate to them. Theology, he granted, must reinterpret the Catholic tradition in forms closer to contemporary culture. This demanded, at times, a critical spirit ; but it did not include the right to call into question the essential content of revealed Church doctrine. Nevertheless, he agreed that Vatican II had marked a distinct change in doctrinal approach. Its anthropology had turned from a cosmological orientation to a personalist foundation for human behavior. Thus he admitted a great difference in seeing people as contingent beings *vis-à-vis* seeing them as participants in dialogue with a personal God. It was the latter vision that the Council accomplished.

Earlier, in his book on the *Acting Person,* John Paul had made an attempt to validate the Aristotelian-Thomistic anthropology by way of an analysis of deliberate human action. After discussing the 'human' in its fundamental elements, the cardinal pursued more of a philosophical than a theological exercise. Nevertheless in the end he distinguished between 'solidarity' and 'opposition' in the function of the Christian thinker confronted by the demands of faith and the needs of the community. In this monograph, Wojtyla again justified the critical spirit as a function of the 'righteous conscience', giving the impression that, for him, uncritical loyalty was no virtue, nor was loyal criticism a vice. Against this background, the Polish pope's current tolerance of the curial attack on his theologians is quite extraordinary. A partial explanation of that papal intransigence is the supposed need to protect the 'right of the faithful not to be disturbed in their traditional beliefs'. Ironically, without the curial interference, the ordinary faithful would hardly be aware of the nonconformist theologians. What is disturbing, however, is the presumption that the ordinary Catholic is to be treated like a child and not credited with a mind of his or her own. It is likewise a slur on the theological community round the world, as if it were not capable of policing its own discipline and much more effectively dealing with heretical tendencies by using the tools of tradition and scholarship.

Part of the contemporary tragedy affecting the Roman Church is the metaphysical training to which most of its current leaders were subjected. The vision of the universe stamped on their youthful consciousness gave them a structured concept of God overseeing all of creation from on high. In turn, the universe, with the earth as at least its epicenter, seemed organized in a hierarchical fashion that in some way was imitated by the order of Roman imperial rule, and the political concept of power and authority that characterized the Greco-Roman world into which the Church was introduced. It is this cosmological concept of the Church in its interior organization that is now being challenged not merely on a political plane, but from within.

For centuries, Christ's phrase 'All authority has been given to me' was interpreted as the *potestas* or power not merely to preach the good news but to exercise the political authority of ruling, backed, when necessary, by the use of force, either spiritual – excommunication, interdict, censure – or coercive persuasion and judicial violence.

In returning the concept of the Church to that of the *demos theou* – the people of God – the Council introduced the notion of democracy, the part the people are to play in governing the ecclesial institution, starting from the ground up with parish councils, diocesan involvement and, eventually, through the *sensus fidelium* influencing the Church's consciousness. This means an acceptance on the part of Rome of a realistic pluralism of theologies based on the cultural and moral *mores* of different peoples. It requires the recognition of the prerogative of the other rites and churches to their organizational independence while preserving a communion in faith and charity with Rome. The pursuit of this ideal will require a total redimensioning of the papal structure – a task that the 'man from afar' could accomplish.

There was, however, a strange dichotomy between the declarations of the Polish pontiff during the first months of his reign – when with youthful enthusiasm he projected a papacy dedicated to revitalizing the Church in keeping with the positive accomplishments of Vatican Council II – and his more recent actions. Admitting that the Church committed to his care was not free of internal difficulties and division, the new pope seemed to feel it was nevertheless more united in belief and service to the apostolate than ever before. This judgment was based on the collegial accomplishments of the Conferences of Bishops that was given expression in the Roman Synods, where the testimony of the residential prelates from literally round the world was gradually reflecting the status of the Church in confronting the problems of mankind.

It was only when this consultative body was subjected to unwarranted restrictions and pressured by the Roman curia, as happened during the 1971 Synodal debates on celibacy and contraception, that the Church suffered the consequences – the subsequent rejection of Rome's dictates in these matters.

Rynne's Law seemed to supply an explanation for this phenomenon. During the preparatory stages of the Council, the documents to be discussed had been structured by the curial prelates in charge so as to reject out of hand the progressive views called for in John's summoning of that body. In each instance the preparatory document by its very recalcitrance to change became a witness to the fact that the Church was already well on its way to a far-reaching mutation in the explanation of its discipline and teachings.

The Pastoral Constitution, for example, not only accepted John's call for an updating but set out to describe the status of the contemporary world in its culture, family life, politics, economic and social reality, in such fashion that the secular world could recognize itself as accurately depicted. With the background of this conciliar achievement, the prelates and theologians were able to provide new insights combining traditional Catholic teaching with new solutions obviously inspired by the Spirit.

At stake in the conciliar re-orientation were a series of problems in the disciplinary order whose solution in a realistic fashion seemed to be opposed by the present pontiff in the name of tradition and a high spiritual ideal.

Of the difficulties confronting the pontiff that of the Church's credibility was the most serious. As a result of the innovations achieved by the Council, a considerable disruption of Church structures and a downgrading of ecclesiastical authority ensued. Paradoxically, with the conciliar unleashing of many doctrinal absolutes and the undoing of disciplinary bonds there was an exodus from the Church of both the died-in-the-wool conservatives who felt betrayed by changes in an institution that boasted of its intransigent laws and traditions, and among the progressives who felt the changes were not radical enough or too slow in implementation. Together with large numbers of the faithful, particularly the youth for whom the Church had become either the locus of their guilt complexes or a meaningless experience unrelated to their everyday lives, a considerable phalanx of priests and religious, nuns and brothers abandoned their calling, most of them desirous of marriage and anxious to serve the Church in other capacities.

In dealing with the priesthood, Vatican Council II had given but a cursory glance at the status and needs of the twentieth century. While an attempt had been made during the 1971 Synod to confront the difficulties of clerical celibacy with honesty, the debate had been quashed by Cardinal Wright and officials of the Congregation for the Clergy who informed a group of African bishops that if they insisted on discussing the issue they would brand their priests as second-class citizens in the Catholic clergy. Meanwhile the great exodus from the ministerial priesthood had begun, mainly in the developed world, and then spread to the missions where vast numbers of the clergy found themselves suffering from an identity crisis and in almost complete disagreement with the Roman curial endeavors to retard the implementation of the Council's achievements on the local, pastoral level. Angered at first by these sudden desertions of their sacerdotal calling, Paul VI referred to these priests as 'modern Judases'. But, regaining his composure and despite his sensitivity regarding sex, the Holy Father gradually displayed a true compassion, granting some thirty thousand dispensations to marry. While there were several hurdles in the process of returning to the lay state, from vindictive delays to humiliating procedures, Paul acknowledged the basic right of every mature individual to marry despite vows or promises not to exercise that right. By way of precedent, he had the example of Pius XII who had given permission for the ordination of a number of married clergymen coming into the Catholic Church as converts; and of Pope John XXIII who gave oral instructions to nuncios and apostolic delegates to permit priests who had left the ministry and were living in stable matrimonial situations to receive the sacraments.

On becoming pope, John Paul II suspended the process of granting laicizations and said he would study the matter. Then in a long, sentimental letter to priests on Holy Thursday, 1979, he attempted to justify his action by claiming that celibacy was an essential feature of the Catholic priesthood. He declared that, as a consequence, an 'administrative' solution to the abandonment of a sacerdotal vocation was not in order. This papal ordinance caused immense scandal and suffering to thousands of former priests and their families who in good conscience had applied for dispensations from the vows under Paul VI and John Paul I.

In his attempt to hold the line on this ideal, John Paul was confronted with formidable opposition. The fact of the matter was that celibacy had not been a factor of the priesthood in the primitive Church. The current curial ideal of a celebate clergy is not built upon solid theological foundations. There is no conclusive scriptural basis for this disciplinary structure that Christ referred to as a special charisma or gift vouchsafed to the few, and that St Paul lauded as a *desideratum* in view of the apocalyptic vision of Christ's second coming within Paul's own lifetime. The primitive Church attests to a married clergy, as does the tradition of the Oriental churches down the centuries. Nor is it an irreverence to admit that in the Western Church neither among the lower clergy nor among the prelates and hierarchs has the rule of celibacy, generally speaking, really worked. Both the repeated synodal, papal and conciliar legislation and the testimony of medieval folklore (captured, for example, in Chaucer's *Canterbury Tales*) give unrejectable testimony to this contention.

Within the context of pastoral necessity, the current lack of priests and sacerdotal vocations has reached a critical stage in most areas, where Catholics seem to be multiplying and the lack of priests is depriving them of the Eucharistic celebration without which there cannot be an authentic Christian church or community.

This latter consideration has forced such stalwart churchmen as Cardinal Renard of Lyons, Tarancón of Madrid, Koenig of Vienna, Darmojuwono of Indonesia, and hundreds of bishops from Latin America, Africa, the Philippines, Canada and the United States, to place before the Holy See petitions and pleas from groups of priests begging the pope to change the rule and permit an optional celibacy alongside a married clergy in the Latin rite. The Holy Father would thus provide for the pastoral care of his immediate flock and prepare to bring the western patriarchate in line with both the Oriental and the Protestant churches. At the same time he would be readying the Church for an eventual Vatican recognition of the ministers of the various Christian churches as true priests, and encouraging some of the more fundamentalist Church bodies to consider a return to an episcopal structure in their governance. Thus far, beyond a trickle of laicizations granted on his own recognizance, John Paul has given little indication of a willingness to consider this request in whose universality observers see an indication of the intervention of the Holy Spirit. Theologians of a cynical bent see the solution as coming from the lower echelons of Church consciousness when bishops, forced by the lack of celibate priests, take the law into their own hands and recall already married priests to the active ministry and ordain married men – an application of what might be termed a Rynne syndrome, the working of an ancient rule stipulating that custom eventually changes statutory law and will thus force the hand of Rome on this issue.

In this respect, an area of grave concern was the restructuring of the religious orders and congregations – Franciscans, Dominicans, Benedictines, Oblates, Redemptorists, Vincentians, Passionists, etc. – that in the decade and a half since the close of the Council have been in turmoil. Among them the failure of the Church's most prestigious order, the Society of Jesus, to have properly prepared its members for the revolution in moral attitudes has been the most striking. For their spiritual preparation was the most rigorous of all the orders. It consisted of a two-year novitiate or training period, devoted to spiritual exercises of self-examination in total seclusion. After a three-year scholasticate in which they served primarily as teachers in Jesuit high schools and colleges, again under strict spiritual guidance, the candidate for the priesthood took a four-year course in theology. Great stress was placed on the individual's spiritual maturity which was to be capable of seeing him through all trials and difficulties. While most secular and religious-order seminarians were advanced to the priesthood between the ages of twenty-four and twenty-six, Jesuits were not ordained until they reached their thirties. Nevertheless the Society lost some 10,000 of its members within a decade and a half, while the other orders lost proportionate numbers. Most left to get married.

What is hopeful, however, in the crisis occasioned by this exodus is that the vast majority of these men, together with the laicized members of the diocesan clergy, have remained within the Church, many of them obtaining substantial positions in government and the business community, and using their influence for the benefit of the Church. Frequently, besides, they serve as catechists and counsellors in their local parishes, thus acting as a new leaven in the Christian community's spiritual awareness. It is this fact that thus far seems not to have sunk into the present pontiff's consciousness.

With the Council's end and the decree on religious life, a revolution likewise swept through convents and religious orders of women. When opposition developed between the immobile generation of older sisters and the newly orientated nuns, there were mass departures from the monasteries and convents. The older generation were threatened in the stability of their lifestyle that they had been taught was for all practical purposes a revelation from the Blessed Virgin, while the younger members felt oppressed by the physical and spiritual demands, and a lifestyle that forced them into teaching or nursing professions without, in good part, the proper training or a true adaptability to that function.

Many of these young and middle-aged women remained within their religious congregations but obtained positions in the outside world of business and social service, living together in small communities of three or four, while continuing to contribute to the well-being of the older nuns. Others left to marry.

The turmoil experienced by these dedicated religious women was increased by the policies of the Congregation for Religious in the Vatican under the intransigent control of Cardinal Antoniutti, who tried to prevent the conciliar-authorized updating of the nuns' rules. Among other things, he busied himself with dictating the length of the sisters' skirts and other such trivialities. He also encouraged the French rebel archbishop, Marcel Lefebvre, in an attempt to stem the tide of change among all the religious orders, instead of facing up to the excruciating problems confronting the great mass of dedicated women whose presence and work had helped form the backbone of the Church. John Paul's insistence in his addresses to nuns that they return to convent life and follow traditional rules for garb and activities showed little sympathy for the women whose dedication to Jesus Christ was every bit as deep and absolute as any conformist curial male. At the same time for the forseeable future a solution of the problem of the ordination of women to the ministerial priesthood seemed unlikely, both because of the traditional Roman opposition and the intransigence of most Oriental churches.

With the Council's about-face in its consideration of marriage the problem of birth control became a major issue. The conciliar fathers recognized the right and obligation of parents to limit the size of their families in keeping with their material and spiritual well-being. But great confusion was injected into the controversy following the Council by the refusal of the Holy See to take a realistic view of the population problem. Wedded to a pronatalist philosophy, possibly stemming from the biblical injunction 'increase and multiply' and a sentimental attitude toward the presumed generosity of parents taking upon themselves large families, curial prelates together with Pope Paul VI proposed an idealistic reorientation of the political and economic structure of the world in order to allow for an apparently limitless population increase. As Paul VI indicated in his speech before the General Assembly of the United Nations in 1965, 'irrational means should not be employed to prevent new mouths from approaching the Lord's table' – a statement that struck demographically oriented statesmen as one of the most insensitive remarks ever to emanate from the papacy. This papal statement seemed all the more incredible in face of the inconscionable fact that at least a third of the world's population were suffering from hunger and half of that number were actually dying of starvation.

While Pope Paul was conscious of this horrible situation, he did not seem to be able to take a realistic approach to its solution by encouraging married couples to cut back drastically on the size of their families as an act of social virtue. Instead Pope Paul spoke of a 'contraceptive mentality' as if it were an evil, and discouraged governments and private agencies from helping the indigent not to conceive children whom they could not feed, clothe, educate and give the possibility of achieving a responsible way of life – and this, in the face of the at least ten million infants dying of starvation each year and the millions of abandoned children roaming the streets of the great metropolises of the third world in total degradation. A similar lack of sensitivity seemed apparent on the part of the present pontiff *vis-à-vis* the human equation of which he declared himself so forthright a proponent in his philosophical and poetical writings. Speaking invariably of the 'human' in a vocabulary that reflected Kant and Marx as much as Jesus Christ or Thomas Aquinas, he seemed oblivious of the deep depletion of the individual person caught in the maelstrom of vital problems concerned with self, family, friends and civic as well as religious relationships. And while in speeches and sermons he pounded home an ideology of human rights, his objective seemed to be increasingly to obtain or assert the freedom of the individual in the secular or governmental sphere only to insist on conformity by that individual to the curial, man-made interpretations of the divine will in the specifically Catholic milieu.

John Paul thus seemed to offer no compassionate resolution for the current battle over the Catholic concept of Christian marriage. The conciliar determination to eliminate the traditional teaching that procreation was the primary end of marriage was violently opposed by members of the curia down to the very end. Its opponents realized that by making love and mutual assistance the fundamental consideration behind the marital bond, the whole structure of the juridical considerations on which the traditional solutions to conjugal failures were based would be eliminated. In this prophetic vision, these men were perfectly correct. To this day, the curial rearguard are fighting to prevent the millions of

Catholics who have suffered shipwreck in their marital adventures from enjoying the merciful attitude of the Council.

As the Church turned its attention to the wider aspects of the world's problems, John Paul was faced with the fact that in its decree on religious liberty, the Council had reversed the thinking of well over a thousand years in which the Church's leadership felt it had the obligation to safeguard God's law by forcing its faithful to give 'both internal and external assent' to scholastic definitions of religious truths, no matter how much such concepts offended the consciences of the individual. Just how solidly inbred this notion was in the Italian theological tradition was illustrated by Pope John Paul I. As cardinal of Venice, he confessed that the conciliar decree on religious liberty had for him been the most difficult to accept of all the Council's mutations in Catholic thinking.

A similar difficulty was experienced by a large number of primarily European prelates in the Council's teaching on the individual's right to 'conscientious objection'. This notion flatly contradicted all they had been taught about the well-being of society, and seemed to dismiss the virtue of partiotism with its idea *'bonum est pro patria mori'* ('it is a good thing to die for one's country') – now looked upon as one of the most dangerous notions ever accepted by mankind.

While in his numerous speeches in various parts of the world, and particularly before the United Nations in New York, and UNESCO in Paris, John Paul had demanded absolute respect for the religious integrity of the individual on the part of governments, and condemned war and the arms race in absolute terms, he had not addressed the specific issues of freedom of conscience within the Church, nor made his position totally clear on the right of the individual to reject military service for conscience reasons. Here he represented the ambiguity of the Council's teaching in its final failure to condemn war as intrinsically evil since it directly contradicts Christ's command to love one's enemy. He thus missed the opportunity to follow up his fulminations against the idiocy of the arms race with an absolute indivisible ideal of world peace. There seemed to be an enigma here between his hesitation to demand absolute virtue in regard to what Christ called the 'second great commandment', and his intransigent demands regarding the terribly personal problems involved in the Church's preoccupation with sex and marriage.

In the area of ecumenism Pope John Paul II appeared to have slowed down the dynamism that characterized Pope Paul's Secretariat for Christian Unity. The pope's desire to have every 'i' dotted and 't' crossed in the doctrinal area seems to ignore charismatic signals from the Spirit being experienced by various churches at ground level. He refused to accept the fact that the Eucharist is the sacrament of communion between Christians whose commitment has been described by St Paul as 'one faith, one Lord, one baptism, one God and father of all'; to a large portion of his committed flock, this is an incomprehensible position. It suggests that the final union of Christians depends more on intellectual co-ordination than on spiritual experience. In essence this means that agreement of hierarchies and theologians is of much greater significance than the inspired experience of the ordinary Christians who, in their efforts to carry out Christ's beatitudinal injunctions in mutual co-operation, are deprived of the main source of the togetherness that Christ prayed for.

In its internal battles down the ages over the modalities of its mysteries and the rigors of its moral pronouncements, the Church has wasted time, talent, and not infrequently blood. The plagiaristic outpourings of a majority of its Rome-oriented scholars have lined the shelves of libraries in ecclesiastical schools and monasteries without the slightest effect on the Church's main task of teaching mankind to love God and love one's neighbor. The acrimony indulged between Catholic theologians, not to mention in their controversies with Protestants, heretics, schismatics and other opponents, has been a poor example of the good news of Christianity. This was a fact alluded to in the first encounter between the newly elected Archbishop of Canterbury, Dr Runcie, and the pope during the papal visit to Ghana. In a two-hour meeting the Polish pontiff and the Anglican primate prayed together and then exchanged mutual confidences, without attempting to solve the obstacles still preventing mutual communion between what Pope John had referred to as sister churches.

One area of concern for ecumenists was the recent reception into the Catholic Church of a thousand or so traditionalist Episcopalians including some seventy-three married clergymen who left their Church in protest against the ordination of women within their communion. Rome accepted their submission, allowed the married ministers to function as Catholic priests after re-ordination and granted certain privileges with regard to the use of the Book of Common Prayer in their liturgical function. This was labelled by critics as a typical Roman disregard of the mutual trust between the theologians and representatives of the two Churches attempting to work towards an agreed recognition of their individual traditions and ministries. On the part of the pope and curia it was all a very logical procedure, since the Catholic Church considered itself the principal depository of divine revelation and had the obligation to welcome into its bosom sincere seekers of absolute truth.

Nevertheless, the result of recent discussions between Catholic theological commissions and the representatives of the other churches points to a gradual agreement on the nature of authority in the Church. They envisage the possibility and need for the pope to be accepted as the *primus inter pares* of the patriarchs and presiding elders or prelates in the other communions. Agreement is likewise on the horizon between the main church bodies regarding the priestly ministry, the Eucharist, and an acceptance of each others' diverse traditions regarding their sacramental and disciplinary regimens. The end-result of these *pourparlers* and liturgical assemblies seems to be approaching a critical point. What seems required now is that the present Holy Father seize the moment – before the Holy Spirit intervenes drastically with, possibly, a catastrophe as the catalyst of unity.

In a pragmatic preparation for his apocalyptic vision of world unity for the year 2000 John Paul could begin with a radical reduction of the Roman curia by restoring to the residential bishops and Episcopal Conferences within the Catholic communion most of the curial supervisory powers now exercised in Rome, from the dissolution of marriages to the laicization of clerics, as well as the election of bishops and the supervision of catechetical structures.

Here of course is a principal obstacle to Christian reunion. For in the projection of a united Christian Church the organs of the current Roman curia would no longer prove adequate or acceptable to the *oikumene* or truly universal Church. Severely criticized during Vatican Council II for exercising power and making policy rather than serving as administrative organs for the Church and the Holy Father, the congregations or bureaus of papal rule were reconstituted under Paul VI in 1967 only to have the reformation result in a change of nomenclature rather than a mutation of policy or personnel.

In this regard, an interesting if minor problem surfaces with the institution of the cardinalate – an eleventh-century creation of the papacy to safeguard the inviolability of papal elections. Based on the tradition giving the parish priests of Rome the right to elect their bishop, this office gradually achieved a singular power in the overall governance of the Church. During the Middle Ages and the Renaissance the college of cardinals functioned as the principal counsellors of the pope, frequently bringing great pressure on the successors to Peter in settling Church policy. Given a catholic complexion early on by the inclusion of archbishops of the major sees of Christendom, the Sacred College is today a truly universal body representing the world-wide Catholic communion. Just how this body of papal electors will be absorbed into a newly constituted synodal control of the Church cannot be foreseen. It would seem incongruous that the Orthodox patriarchs and heads of the Protestant churches should be subsumed into this hypothetical body of Roman parish priests, although several of the patriarchs of the Catholic Oriental churches have been created cardinals. At the same time not to return to the fifth-century rule enunciated by Pope Leo I: 'He by whom all are to be governed should be elected by all,' seems equally out of place.

Meanwhile in seeking a model for an organization adequate to a communion in faith and charity between the Christian churches, thought must be given to the experiences of the Oriental, the many Protestant and the early Roman churches. Their synodal governance was under the presidency of a patriarch or senior elder in what was referred to as a *synodos endemousa,* or permanent synod of patriarchs, bishops, clergy and lay theologians intent upon reaching a consensus of opinion under the guidance of the Spirit before attempting to settle doctrinal and disciplinary matters. At Vatican II, as in the recent series of Roman synods of bishops, it was the *parrhesia* or dauntless courage, referred to by St Paul and given to the bishops in council, that overcame the obstacles and fears of the Church's obstinate traditionalists and that prepared the way for the current drive for reunion. Only in concerted action does the Spirit lend aid and inspiration to the Church's deliberations. Curiously, this is a fact recently observed by John Paul himself in a statement to the effect that the Church, and not any individual has the gift of infallibility.

In saying this the pontiff seemed to be pointing to the ideal solution for the ecumenical problem when the Bishop of Rome will be recognized in his scriptural and traditional function of providing a 'solicitude for all the churches'. He will do this, of course, only after interpellating all the churches in regard to their witness to the Gospel on the primary problems confronting mankind before shepherding them to a consensus in keeping with the prodding of the Spirit. Meanwhile John Paul will continue the service inaugurated by Pope Paul VI and so vigorously pursued by himself in giving personal on-the-spot witness to the faith and charity that is the presence of Jesus Christ in the world. Only thus will the Holy Father have a fundamental effect in bringing peace on earth by reordering the spiritual awareness of mankind.

A master of the human gesture, as befits a pastoral prelate with both philosophical and poetic leanings, John Paul II knows instinctively how to capture the immediate sympathy of an audience – not only by admiring infants, blessing babies, and absorbing the old and young, and feeble and the infirm in his bearlike embrace, but also in more meaningful gestures from hearing confessions as a simple priest in St Peter's before Easter, to marrying the daughter of a Roman street-cleaner and baptizing the infant of a Polish diplomat. Likewise in his Wednesday audiences both to youth and the general faithful he has developed a series of catechetical instructions on marriages, morality and modern problems, thus exercising the prerogative of his pastoral office. In his visitations of the parishes of Rome and environs as well as in his mingling with the inhabitants of Castelgondolfo, his summer residence, and in his fearless approach to the immense crowds who greet him on his jet journeys, he demonstrates an affectionate friendliness. Nor is he lacking in the grace of hospitality, inviting guests of every station to breakfast, lunch or dinner. Nevertheless he possesses a formidable presence not unlike the imperious stance of Pius XI, making it all but impossible for prelates to cross him or even call his attention to matters of pastoral importance on which they know he has strong contrary convictions. This trait has proven particularly forbidding in the question of the laicization of priests in which his first concessions were granted more to rid the priesthood of ne'er-do-wells, than from compassion for the conscientious applicants whose return to the celibate state is rendered impossible by the families they have engendered. Nor is there evidence that he has taken a truly realistic look at the horrors of the hopeless indigents in the slum areas he visited in Africa and Latin America. While reacting with indignant fulmination against the greed of the rich and the injustice of dictatorial governments, John Paul has done nothing to alleviate the conscience problems of the faithful who are gradually realizing they have no right to bring more children into the absolute misery in which they live. By reiterating Paul vi's deploration of a 'contraceptive mentality' and outlawing the use of artificial contraceptives, he seems oblivious of the connection between the failure of the so-called natural birth control and the appalling abortion rates that differ little between Catholics and secularist milieus.

What is obvious, however, is the fact that John Paul is a man of deep prayer and constant meditation whose genius for organization and whose penchant for travel is giving the papacy a new relevance to the problems of contemporary mankind. It is probable that as the cardinals and prelates of the Catholic communion, as well as the representatives of other churches, religious and civic societies, begin to find the courage required of their positions in speaking frankly to the Polish Holy Father, he will begin to exercise the benevolent solicitude for all mankind that Christ entrusted to Peter when he told him to 'feed my lambs and feed my sheep'.

It is impossible to foresee in which direction the Polish pontiff will lead tomorrow's Church. But in view of the extraordinary fashion in which he came to the papacy, and mindful of the incredible opportunity the Church has today to reach all of mankind with the message of peace and brotherhood that is the essence of the Christian faith, it seems impossible that he will simply carry on in the fashion of his predecessors.

It is clear that John Paul wants to give the Church a highly spiritual *élan* and an ethereal self-consciousness that all but ignores worldly considerations in the pursuit of other-worldly ideals. In this attitude he reflects the enigmatic nature of the Church that from its inception considered itself 'in', but not 'of', this world. The paradoxical feature of that conception is reflected in the pope's acceptance of the Roman nature of the Church's structure – a very materialistically organized institution.

Essentially the Roman mind sees the Church as an organization held together not merely by a communion of faith and charity, but by a body of laws demanding both intellectual assent and physical compliance with decisions laid down by the pope as the Vicar of Christ. The offices surrounding the papacy are continually pouring out documents and decisions dealing with aspects of the Christian life whose main purpose seems to be placing obstacles in the path of the Holy Spirit and an obstruction to grace. In the pursuit of uniformity instead of communion, the curial organs of the Holy See are constantly cautioning against the adaptation of the gospel message to local conditions while giving loyalty to the notion of pluralism and decentralization.

In recognizing the process involved in a final reorientation of the Christian Church, Rynne's Law will play an important role. For the Roman Catholic dispensation in the person of the pope and curia will be seen to have strenuously opposed a majority of the conciliar reforms in doctrine and discipline, only to discover that their opposition revealed an ecclesial consensus about the communion in faith and charity demanded by Christ in his prayer: 'Father, that they may all be one . . .'

The final agreement that will reconstitute an ecumenical Christianity will be anchored on the acceptance of a dogmatic pluralism in the explanation of Christian faith and a mutual respect for traditional beliefs in regard to the sacramental system, the cult of the Blessed Virgin Mary and of the saints, episcopal rule, a renewed priesthood, and a sensitive approach to Christian marriage, the problems that have surfaced in connection with the sexual revolution and the volatile population problem, and an intransigent pursuit of peace and justice in the political order, including an uncompromising condemnation of the arms race and the proliferation of nuclear weapons.

What is becoming clear in the race between a total disorder in the political arena of contemporary society and the possible restoration of global sanity through a realistic revival of spiritual values, is the fact that no political leader is capable of bringing about the revolution in justice and peace necessary to prevent a world conflagration. But this irenic miracle is within the reach of the Churches, given the type of compelling leadership of which the Polish pontiff had shown himself capable during the first year of his reign. Stripped of his ideological worries and liberated from the structural exigencies of the Vatican, the Holy Father could exercise the solicitude for all mankind entrusted to Simon, son of

Jonah, by Christ, when he was designated as Cephas the Rock, and instructed to 'confirm his brethren'. In this perspective, elevated to a truly catholic prominence in faith and charity, under the guidance of the Slavic pontiff, tomorrow's papacy will supply invincible evidence that the more it changes, *plus c' est la même chose.*

Bibliographical Note

It is impossible to give an exhaustive list of the books and articles pouring from the press concerned with the papacy. Instead I list below the books that have entered more immediately into the composition of this essay.

François Charles-Roux, *Huit ans au Vatican: 1932–1940* (Paris, 1946)

Anthony Rhodes, *The Vatican in the Age of the Dictators, 1922–1945* (New York, 1973)

Karol Wojtyla, *The Acting Person* (The Netherlands, 1979)
   Segno di contradizione (Milan, 1977)
   Easter Vigil and Other Poems (New York, London, 1979)

Carlo Falconi, *The Popes of the Twentieth Century* (London, 1967)
   Il Pentagono Vaticano (Bari, 1958)

Patrick Granfield, *The Papacy in Transition* (New York, 1980)

Peter Hebblethwaite, *The Year of Three Popes* (London, 1979).
   The Runaway Church (rev. ed., London, 1978)

Giacomo Martina, *La Chiesa in Italia negli ultimi trent'anni* (Rome, 1977)

Rene Laurentin, *Enjeu du II Synode* (Paris, 1969)
   Reorientation de l'Eglise (Paris, 1972)

Francis X. Murphy, *John XXIII* (New York, London, 1959)
   Politics and the Early Christian (New York, 1968)
   'Constitutio Pastoralis: An Introduction', in *Studia Moralia,* 4 (Rome, 1966), 19–41.
   Moral Teaching in the Primitive Church (New York, 1968)

'Vatican Politics', in *World Politics,* 26 (1974), 542– 59

Catholic Perspectives on Population Issues (Washington, 1977)

(with G. MacEoin) *Synod '67: A New Sound in Rome* (Milwaukee, 1968)

Peter Nichols, *The Politics of the Vatican* (London, 1968)

Xavier Rynne, *Letters from Vatican City* (New York, 1963)

The Second Session (New York, 1964)

The Third Session (New York, 1965)

The Fourth Session, (New York, 1966)

Giancarlo Zizola, *Quale Papa?* (Rome, 1977)

Index